LEARNER CENTERED TEACHING

A Humanistic View

Gerald J. Pine
Angelo V. Boy
University of New Hampshire

LOVE PUBLISHING COMPANY
Denver, Colorado 80222

EDUCATION SERIES

Copyright © 1977 Love Publishing Company
Printed in the U.S.A.
ISBN 0-89108-063-5
Library of Congress Catalog Card Number 76-62661
10 9 8 7 6 5 4 3 2 1

TO OUR STUDENTS
who have enriched and expanded our learner-centered
approach to teaching

CONTENTS

i

CONTENTS

Preface

Effective teachers create learning atmospheres which are cognitively and affectively expanding; learning atmospheres which enable the learner to become a more adequate and knowledgeable person. Such teachers have deeply affected both the intellect and attitudes of learners in settings ranging from early childhood learning centers to post doctoral research institutes.

Teaching is a noble profession, but far too many teachers are frustrated and discouraged by the experience. They engage in teaching as a perfunctory procedure and are never personally fulfilled by what occurs. They view themselves and learners as powerless and anonymous elements in an educational hierarchy and seek expedient and superficial answers in order to survive.

We empathize with such teachers and hope that the humanistic concepts of teaching and learning presented in this book will provide some insights which will make teaching more exciting and personally rewarding; but learner-centered teaching is not an easy accomplishment. It depends upon the teacher being able to make a crucial transition; to evolve from being a controller and dispenser of information to being a fully expanded person who possesses the personal freedom and courage to create learning atmospheres which stimulate learners to be intellectually and psychologically involved.

Learner-centered teaching is implementable in proportion to the attitudinal commitment of the teacher. It can occur if the teacher has a genuine desire to be humanistic. This demands an evolvement toward being more respectful of others and their rights; more movement toward being psychologically secure; more involvement in values which enrich others; more trust of human behavior; more openness to experience; and more of an inclination to be initiatory, spontaneous, vibrant, and responsive.

We desire that this book serve as a realistic contribution to humanizing the teaching and learning process. Our experience and research indicate that humanistic concepts are implementable and will enrich the behavior of both the teacher and learner as they engage each other in the process of education.

In the process of writing this book we have learned much about ourselves. First, as we reviewed the manuscript we became painfully aware of our frequent use of male pronouns in referring to the teacher. We had not escaped the subtle and pervasive effects of sexism. We attempted to change the manuscript by using plural forms such as "they" and "them" and "teachers" in place of "the teacher." But this did not help matters. Our writing became more awkward and less precise. We tested the use of "he/she" and "she/he" with several readers who found this approach to be cumbersome and distracting. In consultation with our editors we decided to retain the original use of the male pronoun as a generic word referring to both males and females — a policy which has been adopted by many publishing houses. We hope this decision will not offend our readers who have become sensitive to and conscious of the sexism which is inherent in language. Secondly, we have become much more aware of our strengths and shortcomings as teachers. Most of our faults as teachers are reflections of our personal and very human frailties and insecurities which are small but important enough to affect our teaching more often than we wish. In the continual struggle to confront ourselves and become better teachers we also have grown in writing this book and sharing our ideas. We hope *Learner-Centered Teaching* will help other teachers in their struggle to become more effective and more humane in the classroom.

Gerald J. Pine

Angelo V. Boy

Part One

The Teacher

In one sense all good teachers are learner-centered because they all focus upon learners and their needs. What is distinctive about learner-centered teaching is that the *process* as well as the objective is learner-centered; learner centeredness is an *attitude* rather than a technique. It is an attitude toward oneself, colleagues, administrators, and parents, as well as toward the learner. The essence of this attitude, we believe, is existential humanism, which asks that teachers become more sensitive to themselves as persons. They need the courage to take a view from within in order to change themselves and become facilitating individuals.

1

1

The Learner-Centered Teacher

To develop people with positive selves, the school needs teachers who are in the process of becoming, teachers who can enter into meaningful and growth-facilitating relationships with students. This calls for teachers who are, first and foremost, persons. It is in response to relationships with a person that the student's personal growth occurs.

Although much has been said about the personal development of the individual within the context of formal education, there is a wide gap between what we want to do and what we are doing to enhance the development of young people. We believe the critical factor in narrowing this gap is the teacher-pupil relationship. "It is the relationship that teaches rather than the text" (Goldhammer, 1969:365). Pupils feel the personal emotional structure of a teacher long before they feel the impact of the intellectual content offered by that teacher. Students discover who they are, and what they are, as a result of daily interactions with each other and with the teacher. It is the teacher who determines to a great degree the positive or negative effect of his teaching. Goldhammer (1969:365) states that a teacher's values, emotional capacities, cognitive styling, views of life and of the world, his methods of dealing with anxiety, and his relationship to his inner self represent his teaching essence. In other words, teaching is a personal expression of the self.

TEACHING: A PERSONAL EXPRESSION OF THE SELF

Effective teaching is more than just doing something with learners; it is being a fully functioning person, the most adequate person. The teacher who is a whole person will make the most significant contribution to the development of learners as self-actualizing persons. We believe that the teacher's role as an educator is transcended by his existence as a human being. A teacher must be comfortable with himself as a person before he can be comfortable with others. The teacher who does not accept and respect himself will find it difficult to accept and respect others; the teacher who is threatened by his own feelings may not be able to handle the feelings of those around him. A warm and secure teacher continually reflects that warmth and security, and the teacher who values others cannot help but communicate this basic humanism. Being a teacher requires an existential honesty with self and others.

The humanness of the teacher inevitably shows through in his teaching. Therefore, it is essential for the teacher to be aware of his own strengths and shortcomings. He should involve himself in the process of introspection so that he can become more aware of his own personality and how it affects his teaching function. The teacher must be what he *is;* therefore, it is important that he know himself.

This does not mean that the teacher should completely do away with his personal mode of existence. As a human being, he has a unique identity which is expressed in concrete behavior. But he can free himself from identifying all human existence in terms of his personal-cultural frame of reference. Developing an awareness of his own biases and stereotypes will enable the teacher to sense the unique potentialities in those who differ from him in expression and perception. "The teacher's understanding and acceptance of himself is the most important requirement in any effort he makes to gain healthy attitudes of self-acceptance" (Jersild, 1955:3).

However, self-awareness is not enough in the development of the self-actualized teacher. Just as pupils need positive experiences to develop fully as persons, so do teachers. The teacher is no less valuable than the pupil, no less "end" than he is, no less alive, and, in many respects, no less needful. (Goldhammer, 1969:365). Teachers need to be treated as likeable, wanted, accepted, and knowing persons. They need opportunities for emotional enrichment. Expansion of the self comes from continuous involvement in therapeutic, facilitative, and enhancing experiences. These experiences should be provided as integral elements in teacher preparation and continuing education programs. Through self-expansion, the teacher can become more at ease with himself and more fully realized as a person. As a result, he will be more facilitative in fostering the growth and development of the pupil as a unique person.

People have to *become* fully functioning and emotionally expanded; they are not born that way (*Perceiving, Behaving, Becoming,* 1962). The self-actualizing personality is an achievement realized through growth-producing experiences. We are concerned about teachers as persons because we do not believe that, in themselves, good lesson plans, teaching approaches, curriculum, media, or materials produce happy, fully functioning people. Although these things can help, it is the teacher's personality that makes the difference in the development of productive and positive human beings. Fully functioning people are the crowning achievement of psychologically mature teaching, which emanates from psychologically whole persons.

CHARACTERISTICS OF THE LEARNER-CENTERED TEACHER

What is the learner-centered teacher like? From our own observations and the work of others (Coombs and Snygg, 1959;

Kelley, 1947; Maslow, 1954; and Rogers, 1961) we would describe the learner-centered teacher in terms of the following behaviors:

1. *He thinks well of himself.* He has a positive self-concept — he likes himself.
2. *He is unified and integrated.* The dichotomies between real self and role self, between the selfish and the unselfish, between the conscious and the unconscious, between the inner and the outer self, between the affective and the cognitive, become resolved in the psychologically whole teacher. The expanded person is congruent and genuine. He is honest with himself and with others.
3. *He thinks well of others.* Liking and accepting himself, he likes and accepts others. While he can and does act independently, he realizes his development and personhood are interdependent with the development and personhood of others. He engages in and likes cooperative relationships, and functions harmoniously in such relationships.
4. *He develops, holds, and lives by human values.* His values are related to the welfare and enhancement of people. He tends to develop and to live by values which enhance the self, enhance others, and enhance the human community.
5. *He sees himself in the process of becoming.* He sees life as a continuous process of becoming rather than a static state of being. He knows that dealing with problems is a characteristic of living. He not only accepts change, but he also makes changes.
6. *He sees the value of mistakes.* He is adventurous, and is not afraid to move forward, to test the unknown, and to tread new paths. He knows he cannot always be right. He makes experience an asset and profits from his mistakes. He continually refines, modifies, and redefines himself as a person.
7. *He trusts himself.* He trusts his feelings and his intuition. He trusts his experiencing and the evidence of his senses. His inner reactions and experiences serve as a rich resource for behaving and for problem solving.

8. *He is open to experience.* He is open to his feelings and to the data of his experiencing because he is not defensive. He is open to the data and points of view expressed by others. He is open to the stimuli of his environment, to what is going on now, internally and externally.

9. *He is initiatory.* He is more creative than reactive. Although he can flow smoothly with his environment, he just doesn't react to it. He is an initiator who exercises control over his life and his environment. The self-actualizing teacher does not wait for others to do something, he moves ahead and is often on the edge of change in his work, in his community, or in his group.

10. *He is spontaneous, vibrant, and responsive.* His spontaneity and vitality are expressed in positive and enhancing ways. This does not mean that the psychologically whole teacher is a "hail fellow, well met" individual; rather, he enjoys life, is sensitive to the needs of others, and lives optimistically and energetically.

Of course, the learner-centered teacher is not perfect. He experiences conflict, anxiety, guilt, and hurt. However, for the self-actualizing teacher, there is movement from expending energy on neurotic, pseudo problems to dealing with the real, unavoidable problems inherent in the human nature (Maslow, 1954). He feels troubled when the situation indicates that he should feel troubled. He does not ordinarily create his own problems, but when reality creates problems for him, he responds in a very human way.

The learner-centered teacher trusts himself and is genuine; he is continually in touch with his feelings. At times he may be confrontive in his relationships with others and express anger. However, anger is expressed in caring and facilitative ways which call for involvement and response. His honesty is not destructive because he cares, and because there is followup to any expression of honest anger. He acts to preserve the relationship and to make sure that anger serves as a constructive tool.

7

LEARNER-CENTERED TEACHING

The learner-centered teacher works to develop a positive, humanizing, and psychologically nourishing classroom climate. His teaching style reflects wholeness and is characterized by deep respect for the learner; effective communication; acceptance of students; concentration on the needs, problems, and feelings of students; and permissiveness.

Respect for Students

Effective teaching derives from a philosophy in which respect for the learner is uppermost. This means respecting the learner's individuality, his complexity, his uniqueness, his capacity for making choices, his right to govern his own life and select his own values and his idiosyncratic potential. Respect for the learner is based upon the teacher's recognition of the dignity of the learner. Dignity as defined in most dictionaries means "intrinsic value." When we say we act in recognition of the dignity of the individual, we are saying that each person has value. That value is not determined by what the person has done, what he has said, what clothes he wears, where he lives, how he looks, how he speaks, what his occupation is, what grades he has achieved, or how he relates to other people. The value of each student is *not* a product of externals.

It is easier for the teacher who has respect for his own intrinsic value to deeply respect students. The teacher who lacks self-esteem cannot view others as having esteem. To the degree that a person believes in his own dignity, he will believe in the dignity of another. Erich Fromm puts it beautifully:

> The logical fallacy in the notion that love for others and love for oneself are mutually exclusive should be stressed. If it is a virtue to love my neighbor as a human being, it must be a virtue — and not a vice — to love myself, since I am a human being too. There is no concept of man in which I myself am not included. A doctrine which proclaims such an exclusion proves itself to be intrinsically contradictory. The idea expressed in the Biblical "Love thy neighbor as thyself!" implies that respect for one's own integrity and uniqueness, love for and understanding of one's own self, cannot be separated from respect and love and understanding for another individual. The love for my own self is inseparably connected with the love for any other being (1956:49).

8

Because of the reciprocity of the teacher-student relationship, if the teacher values the student, a deeper appreciation of intrinsic self-worth evolves in the student. The more the student sees himself as an individual of worth and a person of dignity, the more he begins to respect himself and, consequently, the teacher. Respect for the student engenders respect for the teacher.

Acceptance of Students

Accepting a person means allowing him to *be* so that he may *become*. When a person is not required to defend himself, when he can be what he is, he is free to change. The student who is free to be unique, to be different, to hold his values, is free to look at himself and his life without fear. Accepting the student gives him the opportunity to express his meanings without ridicule, attack, or moralization. It allows him the right to see things the way he does.

Humanistic teaching provides the necessary atmosphere of safety. Unless the classroom atmosphere is safe, the individual will not allow internal perceptions to be expressed. When the student experiences acceptance of himself as he is, he feels safe to explore his thoughts. The teacher who does not accept his students makes it difficult for them to accept themselves. Students feel comfortable only when they experience acceptance. If a student does not feel that "it's all right to be myself here," if he does not feel that his difference is valued, he will become defensive. He will be compelled to protect his existing perceptual structure and will concentrate on dealing with the threat represented by moralization, condemnation, or belittlement. A constricted view of the self results in the constriction of communication and a closing of the self to the teacher. The student who is accepted, who feels, "it's all right to be me, I can say what I like, I can be negative, I can be positive, I can be confused, I can talk, I can be silent, no one is going to judge me or preach to me, I can be what I feel," will freely and openly relate to the teacher and to his classmates, and will express his internal perceptions.

Accepting the student is offering unconditional positive regard for him. The teacher neither approves nor disapproves of feelings that are expressed. There are no reservations, conditions, evaluations, or judgments placed on the student's feelings. He is valued

9

regardless of what he expresses, whether it is joy, anger, envy, or self-depreciation. True acceptance is unaffected by any peculiarities of the student; it is not acceptance up to this or that point and no further. It does not depend upon the student's acting or talking a certain way, upon his socio-economic background, upon his religion, or upon his I.Q. It is not dependent upon the student's meeting certain moral or ethical criteria. It is total positive regard for the student as a person of value.

Effective Communication in the Classroom

Effective communication occurs when the teacher receives what his students want to communicate and the students receive what the teacher wants to communicate. Communication between teacher and students is expressed through affective, cognitive, verbal, and nonverbal means. Effective teaching requires open communication, and this is encouraged by a non-threatening atmosphere that fosters teacher and student resonance to each other's existence.

To be resonant to another, a teacher must be reasonably free from the influence of his own needs and anxieties, which distort perception. He needs to develop "emotional antennae" that are keenly sensitive to the subtle cues that constitute the subliminal language of communication — *tone* of voice, posture, bodily movements, physical mannerisms, and facial expressions. Sensitivity to the verbal and nonverbal cognitive and affective codifications opens up possibilities of communication which otherwise would be closed. Such awareness enables the teacher to *directly experience* his students and to receive and transmit intuitively. Perhaps the notion of directly experiencing is best captured in the words of Emerson, "What you are speaks so loudly that I can't hear what you say." Although productive communication demands that the teacher be sensitive to what the student says and how he says it, it also asks the teacher to fully experience himself.

In order to tune in to the wavelength of the learner, the teacher must be free of interferences residing in himself. The secure teacher is maximally open to experience. His perceptual field is capable of change and adjustment; there is no need to distort perceptions to fit a preformed structure or an existing pattern. Openness to experience is contingent upon the teacher's freedom from threat, which is an expression of positive feelings about self and an identification with other people.

An especially important component of effective communication is the ability of the teacher to *listen*. The kind of listening we refer to here is non-evaluative. To listen, the teacher immerses himself in the learner's flow of experience. Listening to the learner is not like listening to a news broadcast or a lecture, where we listen with one ear, as it were, while thinking about something else or structuring our opinion about what is being said. It is not "polite" or "social" listening, in which the teacher waits for the learner to finish talking and then leap in to get a point across. It is not the kind of listening where the teacher merely tolerates the learner's verbalizations, nor is it an analytical process in which the content of the learner's communication is broken down into small parts to be examined for their significance. Listening means being in complete cognitive and emotional contact with the individual. It is a process requiring the teacher to be selfless, so that his own biases and problems will not inhibit the other's learning. Hermann Hesse, in his beautiful story, *Siddhartha,* eloquently describes this kind of listening in one of the lessons Siddhartha learns from the river:

> But he learned from it continually. Above all, he learned from it how to listen, to listen with a still heart, with a waiting open soul, without passion, without desire, without judgment, without opinions. (1951:109)

And Siddhartha experiences genuine listening as he speaks with his friend Vasudeva:

> As he went on speaking and Vasudeva listened to him with a serene face, Siddhartha was more keenly aware than ever of Vasudeva's attentiveness. He felt his troubles, his anxieties, and his secret hopes flow across to him and then return again. Disclosing his wound to his listener was the same as bathing it in the river until it became cool and one with the river. (1951:109)

The learner needs the attention of the teacher. When he experiences deep listening, he recognizes that the teacher is attentive, that he cares, that he is interested. Deep listening encourages self-discovery and facilitates the development of *empathy,* another important element in effective communication. Empathy is the placing of one human spirit within another so that there is emotional congruence between teacher and learner. The teacher empathizes when he tries to assume the internal frame of reference of the learner — perceiving the world as the learner perceives it and seeing the learner as he sees himself — and communicates his understanding to the learner. The fully functioning teacher is able to empathize because he shares with his fellow beings common meanings and objects of experience.

Empathy is experiencing the learner's reality even though that reality may not be congruent with "objective" reality. This is difficult to do, because most of us have learned to look at others according to external and objective criteria. But looking at another person in terms of an external frame of reference is one of the biggest roadblocks to effective communication. Productive communication cannot occur unless the teacher understands the learner. Viewing the learner from an external frame of reference may help the teacher to *know about* that individual, but it will not help him *know* the learner. To know and understand, one must be able to empathize.

The Needs, Problems, and Feelings of Students

The more the teacher focuses on the needs, problems, and feelings of the student, the more he emphasizes the existential character of learning. He communicates to students that it is their needs and their concerns which are important, that their feelings and their experiences are of value and relevance. He gives students the feeling that they can trust in their own beings and discover new meanings from within to guide their behavior. Focusing on the individual frame of reference enables students to become more aware of their internal resources and helps them gain an understanding of the reality of "self" in the school, in the home, and in the world. The teacher who centers himself on his students says, in effect, "It is you who are important, it is your experiences that count and not someone else's, it is your being that is significant, it is your internal 'advice' that is relevant." In this kind of classroom atmosphere the student begins to feel that some of the most meaningful learning is the learning that comes from within. Out of *his* perceptions, and *his* visceral and internal state emerges the best possible answers and behavior for *him*. When the student experiences the full and free commitment of the teacher as a resource person who has faith and trust in him, he begins to realize that his inner sources of information and open communications with others can and do lead to a more satisfying life.

Permissiveness

Perhaps one of the most distinctive characteristics of self-actualizing teaching is permissiveness. Unfortunately, "permissiveness" has been endowed with many negative connotations in our society. It is often interpreted to mean freedom to destroy property, to injure others, to create physical chaos, or to do what one likes without regard for others. Permissiveness, as used here, means "the freedom to have ideas, beliefs, values — permission to be oneself and to pursue interests and curiosity in search for meaning in life" (*Perceiving, Behaving, Becoming,* 1962). Permissiveness is an atmosphere created by a relationship that reflects acceptance, empathy, respect, and understanding for the client. The teacher cannot create an atmosphere of permissiveness by merely telling students they are free to express themselves. Students feel free to explore their capacity for self-directive growth when they experience permissiveness, not from being told that they are in a permissive situation.

A permissive atmosphere requires emotional security and self-acceptance on the part of the teacher. The teacher's beliefs and values will be constantly tested by students who hold different views. The fully functioning teacher does not feel compelled to defend his beliefs whenever they come under attack. To do so would be to destroy the teacher-student relationship. If the student is to grow and understand the meanings of his experiences, he must feel free enough to reveal his internal self without fear of contradiction or interference from the teacher. The emergence of the authentic self, the evolvement of self-understanding, and the exploration of the internal world of the student come about when the student knows he can remove the protective layers that cover his inner feelings.

THE EFFECTS OF LEARNER-CENTERED TEACHING

The teacher who creates a meaningful teaching relationship with youngsters will find that growth occurs among students as a result of their positive reaction to the communicating atmosphere in which they exist. Involvement with a skilled, competent, psychologically whole teacher affects the learner in a number of ways:

1. *He assumes responsibility.* In the classroom he becomes involved in the pursuit of knowledge and assumes the responsibility for his intellectual growth because of the teacher's attitude toward the relationship. Since the teacher has freed him to learn, he learns.
2. *He is accepted.* In the classroom he feels that he is respected as a person who has a worthy contribution for both today and tomorrow. The positiveness of the teacher's attitude enables the student to feel an acceptance that encourages him to relate comfortably to the teacher. The sense of comfort in the relationship facilitates his emotional development.
3. *He is motivated.* As a result of his experience with a teacher's enthusiasm for his work, the student develops a desire to probe more deeply. He senses a value in knowledge and acquires a desire to learn those things which are pertinent.
4. *He is actively involved in the process of growth.* Intellectual maturity occurs because the teacher's educational process is focused upon the student and his needs. In such a relationship the teacher is not the dominant figure; classroom procedures are designed to produce an active, participatory involvement on the part of the student.
5. *He interacts on a human level.* Because of his association with a communicating teacher, the student does not assume a pseudo role but reacts to learning at an emotional or human level. Anyone who has thoroughly learned anything has learned it because there was an accompanying emotionality to the process. What was being learned was

deeply significant; the learner felt its importance in a visceral manner.

6. *He exists in a safe atmosphere.* The student must feel free from threat if he is to be secure enough to respond to teaching. No one has ever been coerced into learning or into changing his behavior. Changes occurred when the student feels safe enough to inquire into knowledge or into himself.

7. *He is understood.* The professionally skilled and psychologically integrated teacher is vitally concerned with the student's frame of reference. His awareness of the student finds its expression in an understanding attitude that allows the student to be hesitant or confident, aware or insensitive, courageous or fearful. When the student feels understood, he is able to move in an unfaltering manner in the teaching relationship.

8. *He is self-disciplined.* He finds the resources within himself to be his own master because he has experienced teaching relationships that helped him see the importance of managing his own life. Teachers bring about this awareness by providing an atmosphere in which the student has to rely upon himself for control rather than upon an external source. The student learns to look to himself rather than to authority figures for answers to his functioning.

9. *He verbalizes with ease.* When the student associates with an effective teacher, he is able to communicate comfortably and honestly. He feels no need to be defensive in a relationship when he knows that he can be himself. Such comfort enables him to respond to learning with much more accuracy, because his verbalizations are not couched in language designed to protect rather than to reveal. He is able to discuss issues of relevance rather than what he feels the teacher wants to hear.

10. *He achieves insight.* As a result of his association with a skilled teacher, the student discovers the fundamentals of learning and gains insight into himself. He is able to bring meaning into his experiences because the relationship has provided him with an opportunity to weigh and sift

different ideas. He achieves a spiritual awareness of his existence that gradually enables him to shed more light upon things to be learned and assimilated. The teacher provides an atmosphere in which the student's insight is relevant and significant, rather than merely handing down his own concept of appropriate insight.

11. *He is more aware of appropriate attitudes.* Because of the qualitative nature of his association with a teacher, the student does not have to be told what attitudes are appropriate or inappropriate. As a human being he is aware of which attitudes help or hinder his functioning as a person, and the teacher-student relationship has helped him discover those attitudes which either enhance him or cause him turmoil. He is not only aware of personally appropriate attitudes, but he also sees himself in relationship to others and shapes his attitudes so that he is able to function effectively within the context of society. He looks beyond himself. The feelings of others in response to his attitudes are more openly sensed and internalized.

12. *He is valuing.* That is, he becomes involved in the development, processing, and synthesizing of values, ordering them in a hierarchy that is beneficial to his functioning. Because of his association with an effective teacher, he rejects the values which hamper his existence and moves toward those which enable him to find more meaning from learning and life. This sifting and processing of values occurs because the student exists in an open relationship in which he confronts these values and is, in turn, confronted by them. It is only when a student rejects certain values that he moves toward values of a higher order that have more personal significance.

13. *He responds to genuineness.* He senses the genuine quality of the teacher and reacts by expressing his own genuineness. Students can easily sense whether or not the teacher has an unconditional, positive regard for youngsters. When the student internalizes the genuine quality of the teacher, he involves himself as a reaction to that quality. He trusts the relationship and finds that he can accelerate

his progress. The teacher who only pretends to be genuine will be met with little more than a feigned smile from his students.

14. *He evaluates the interaction with the teacher.* Evaluations are generally transmitted to the peer group and result in the development of a positive, mediocre, or negative image of the teacher among the students. A feeling of mutual respect can greatly enhance the effectiveness of the teacher. When the peer group has found significance and meaning in the student-teacher association, rapport is easily established.

In summary, we believe that students respond primarily to the teacher as a person. Optimal learning and personal development in the classroom occur through the relationship of the student with the psychologically whole teacher. The challenge for teachers is two-fold: to seek and create the opportunities which will stretch and expand themselves as persons; and to create conditions whereby students also can grow and become more fully functioning persons. The latter task can be more easily and effectively accomplished if the teacher moves toward becoming a psychologically whole person.

REFERENCES

Coombs, Arthur W., and Snygg, Donald. *Individual Behavior: A Perceptual Approach to Behavior* (Rev. ed.). New York: Harper and Row, 1959.

Fromm, Erich. *The Art of Loving.* New York: Harper and Row, 1956.

Goldhammer, Robert. *Clinical Supervision.* New York: Holt, Rinehart, and Winston, 1969.

Hesse, Hermann. *Siddhartha.* Translated by Hilda Rosner. New York: Vintage Books, imprint of Random House, 1951.

Jersild, Arthur T. *In Search of Self.* New York: Teachers College Press, Teachers College, Columbia University, 1952.

Kelley, Earl C. *Education for What Is Real.* New York: Harper and Brothers, 1947.

Maslow, Abraham H. *Motivation and Personality.* New York: Harper and Row, 1954.

Perceiving, Behaving, and Becoming. Washington, D.C.: Association for Supervision and Curriculum Development, 1962.

Rogers, Carl. *On Becoming a Person.* Boston: Houghton Mifflin Co., 1961.

2

Humanizing Teaching

Much has been written about the important role of the teacher in the formation of human behavior. One does not have to look far to uncover testimony supporting the strategic and influential role teaching plays in the development of civilizations and societies. What has been said for hundreds of years by numerous writers is true today — *teaching is important, it is valuable, it matters, and it is needed.* The teacher provides the life space for learners in the classroom. If he is creative, imaginative, and invests himself in nurturing a community of learners, he will derive countless enhancing experiences from his work.

Teachers have considerable autonomy in the classroom. Freedom to create, to change, and to foster growth is more a function of the teacher's personal attitude than a matter of external controls. It is easy to project the blame for a lack of creativity and resourcefulness onto an external agent. Teachers can blame the conditions under which they work, or they can criticize administrators for not giving them what they want, but most teachers actually spend ninety-nine and forty-four one hundredths percent of their teaching time with little or no interference from other adults. Freedom and autonomy in the classroom are sacred values in teaching, but, it is what is done with that freedom and autonomy that counts.

Everything a teacher does or says has, or could have, a significant impact on the personal growth and development of pupils. The teacher offers learners opportunities to discover their resources and limitations. He can help the learner to realize and accept himself or he can interact in ways that may bring the learner humiliation, shame, rejection, or self-disparagement (Jersild, 1952). The imaginative, fully-committed teacher can promote the personal growth of his pupils and his own growth at the same time. While it may sound like a "motherhood statement," there is perhaps no more rewarding, satisfying, and fulfilling experience than the awareness that what one has done as a teacher has significantly contributed to the inner development of students. There is a personal joy, which is difficult to articulate, that comes from observing their growth and development as highly functioning positive human beings.

TEACHING AND THE SELF: A SYMBIOSIS

In every act of teaching the teacher defines himself as a person. A person's view of teaching mirrors his view of himself, and his teaching behavior reflects his essence as a person. The individual who is deeply attuned to himself and to the significance of the teaching process knows that by translating his awareness into action he humanizes himself as well as his students.

There is a symbiotic relationship between a person's self and his work (Stefflre, 1968). A person enters this symbiotic union by changing his concept of self to fit the work role, by changing the work role to fit the self, or by changing a little of both. If this relationship is to be enriching and self-enhancing, the work must be molded so that it becomes a personal expression of the self. There are few vocations which offer so much opportunity for self-expression. Through teaching a person can move beyond what he is, actualize his potential in the most optimal ways, and realize a creative positive self. Yet there are certain "occupational diseases" that can be associated with teaching. These diseases can inhibit and stunt personal growth. The greater our awareness of these hazards, the greater are our chances of controlling them and not letting them get in the way of personal development and fulfillment.

Occupational Diseases of Teaching

Some psychoanalysts have described teachers as sublimated dictators who carve out an empire for themselves in the classroom. They argue that teachers who work in an elementary school setting are drawn there by the unconscious desire to manipulate others, realizing that small children can offer little or no resistance. It is also argued that many teachers in our secondary schools have a need to manipulate others and wish to relive their adolescence through their students. Friedenberg's critical analysis of the teaching role offers another provocative point of view:

> In American society, the role of the schoolteacher is the least costly and most readily available role commonly accepted as of professional status. The educational requirements for the job are high enough to be consistent with a measure of professional status, but they are very easily fulfilled. The necessary courses are offered in every local college; should a Master's degree be sought for the sake of further advancement, it may be obtained in three summers at the state university or even in night classes by those who live and teach in a town where a college or a university offering graduate work is located. This is far less taxing than what a physician, attorney, engineer, scientist, or university professor must go through in the course of acquiring his license; each must maintain at least a year and usually much more of residence and full-time work in his specialty at a university-grade institution.
>
> For a young man or woman without such backing or special abilities, a schoolteaching career provides the most status in proportion to risk; he can be ninety-nine percent certain that nobody and nothing will really get in his way so long as he is ambulatory and not an obvious grotesque.
>
> They (teachers) are more preoccupied with acquiring and maintaining small increments of status for a small investment and without much risk than with disciplined self-expression through the medium of professional competence. (1962:126-127)

While the validity of such indictments can be debated, they seem to point up the importance of teacher self-evaluation in assessing professional motivation and behavior. Self-examination leads to self-discovery and greater sensitivity to the occupational diseases of teaching.

Yauch (1966) catalogued the following as the hazards or diseases of teaching:

1. *The telling technique.* It is easier to "instruct" than to devote the greater amount of time and effort to help learners find their own answers. It is much easier to "tell" than to teach; if teachers are not careful, they find themselves acting as constituted authority for all human knowledge, relating to all others as the "teller."

2. *The "god" complex.* The step from assuming a position of unquestioned authority to believing in one's infallibility is logical and almost inevitable. Teachers wield a great deal of power by virtue of their position. Their authority is only a little less than that of the parent. It is easy and quite comfortable for teachers to retire to the sanctity of their position as authority when they are challenged.

3. *Perfectionism.* Perfectionism can be an uncritically accepted faith that the typical teacher follows, both personally and in his relations to his pupils. He holds his ideals high and demands that his ideals control everyone's conduct. In the classroom, this is best illustrated by our concept of academic success. We grade on the basis of 100 percent, with the clear indication that anything less· is unacceptable. Although we grudgingly accept the fact that all children cannot achieve this goal, it remains one toward which we stubbornly strive. Someone has observed that a successful scientist is one who fails every time but the last, but in school we are expected to succeed every time.

4. *Ververbalization.* So much of the school day is spent in verbal interaction that teachers are often convinced that it is the *only* effective means of instruction. We are linguistically naive in the sense that we tend to identify the word and the reality for which it stands as the same thing. Language is a tool for learning; it can never be learning itself.

5. *Narrow perspectives:* Living closely within the school with too little contact with what goes on outside it, can only result in constricted perspectives which limit the teacher's contribution to the learner's true education. Dealing rather exclusively with whatever segmented parcel of human knowledge we choose to use can easily lead to the assumption that it represents all. But a moment's reflection can remind us that much of what we teach in school is only remotely related to what a student needs to know in order to be truly educated. Some of the most important lessons can only be learned through direct experience.

The teacher who is aware of the hazards can take measures to prevent their occurring. It is essential to develop relationships with people in other occupations where the teacher's kind of language is not pertinent, to engage in adult activities entirely unrelated to teaching, to seek the companionship of others who are authentic and courageous enough to confront and challenge the teacher's authority, to develop a sense of humor and the ability to laugh at oneself, to see a play, or take a trip. Such experiences make it possible for teachers to develop a nonexploitive commitment to the work of teaching, and to avoid the potentially dehumanizing diseases that would prevent them from becoming fully functioning as teachers.

THE NEED FOR HUMANIZING EXPERIENCES

Facilitative teaching requires empathic understanding, realness, deep respect for the worth of the individual, concreteness, and psychological investment. In order for teachers to optimally develop these qualities, they need humanizing experiences. *People become what they experience and teachers are no exception.* Unfortunately, as Silberman (1970) points out, there are aspects of the teaching environment, which are psychologically debilitating; the lack of trust, and the stereotyped expectations placed upon teachers tends to diminish them as persons and move them into a role which is dehumanizing. Too often the real self of the teacher becomes hidden by the role self, which is characterized by a

23

professional facade of rationalism and stoicism. The teacher role is influenced by this stereotyped, unflattering image created by the public, and perpetuated by mass media. It is imperative for personal growth that the teacher discard the professional mask and become more real. Herbert Kohl suggests one approach for doing this:

> For ten minutes (a day) cease to be a teacher and be an adult with young people, a resource available if needed and possibly a friend, but not a director, a judge or executioner. Also, try to make it possible for the ten minutes to grow to fifteen, twenty, so long as it makes sense to you and your pupil. It is not unlikely that those ten minutes may become the most important of the day, and after a while, they may even become the school day. (1970:70)

This suggests that teachers can do more than react to experiences; they can *create* experiences which will nourish them as persons. Teachers need to find ways to reveal themselves as persons. This is not easy to do, because most of us have been inculcated since childhood with the importance of keeping a reserve. Many of us have learned to hide our feelings and thoughts because we fear being rejected or hurt. Self-disclosure does involve risks, but those risks are the source of personal growth. Being who we are and finding out who we are can be a scary experience. For the teacher who is willing to make the psychological investment necessary to close the gap between the role self and the real self, the risk of sacrificing the depersonalized professional mask is more than compensated for by the richness and fulfillment that comes with the liberation of the "essential" self. Disclosing one's self to others provides a therapeutic release, enables one to develop strong affiliations with others, and affirms the uniqueness and separateness of our existence.

The Importance of Close Friendships

Authenticity, genuineness, and self-revelation are necessary qualities for facilitative teaching. If the real self of the teacher is visible only outside the school, then the chances of human therapeutic experiences developing in the classroom are nil. Despite the continuous contact with children, teaching can be a lonely profession (Silberman, 1970). Teachers need a chance to discuss their problems with each other, they need opportunities to share their successes, and they need time to blow off steam. Friendships offer one of the most rewarding contexts for self-discovery Friendships require give and take; they are reciprocally therapeutic relationships which provide opportunities "for exploration and mutual learning about self and others which can be the basis for thoughtful revisions in self-organization and consequent modifications of behavior and methods" (*Perceiving, Behaving, & Becoming* 1962). Derek Wright (1970) reports in Britain's *New Society* magazine that in defining close relationships people put an emphasis on self-disclosure. He interprets this to mean that each person carefully nominates a few companions in the more intimate role of unofficial therapists. Teachers need "unofficial therapy" that enables them to search for a deeper understanding of themselves and provides emotional investments for their own lives. If teachers are to humanize the classroom and have a profound influence on the lives of the children and adolescents with whom they work, then they must experience close and honest friendships that allow them to be real and genuine. If they cannot find the means of expressing their real selves, then they will be unable to free their students to become authentic optimally functioning persons.

Everyday Relationships

Through his relationship with colleagues and students the teacher can learn more deeply about himself as a person. Jersild believes that the significance of relationships with others provides a simple but profoundly important aid to self-examination:

> If one would know what he thinks about himself and how he feels about himself, let his glance turn to others, for the kinds of thoughts and feelings he has with regard to others are likely in one way or another to reflect his attitudes toward himself. (1952:46)

Through their relationships with each other, teachers can explore their own capacities for self-directive growth and can develop positive repanded selves.

Rather than competing with each other, teachers need to engage in cooperative relationships. This calls for giving, sharing, and receiving. Kildahl (1970) indicates that there is little alienation among people who join and work together for a common and concrete human goal. He feels that one of the ways in which people derive a sense of meaning — a sense that their life counts for something — is to give direct, physical help to others. The implication for teachers seems to be quite clear. Mere verbalizations about teamwork are not enough. Teachers, beginning and experienced, young and old, need not only to exchange their ideas but also to share materials and help each other out in concrete ways.

Teachers can learn to be more real as they interact with each other in a *non-exploitive* manner. A non-exploitive "veteran" teacher offers assistance to a newcomer not to win him over or induct him into an existing "teaching" value system, but because he genuinely cares to help the newcomer in whatever way he can. A non-exploitive young teacher does not attempt to convert a more experienced teacher to a new approach, but shares whatever skills, techniques, and ideas he has when they are requested. Helping relationships have to be built on mutual trust, concern, empathy, listening, compassion, and honesty. If teachers cannot create humanizing experiences among themselves, if they cannot be open with each other, then surely it will be difficult for them to be real in the classroom.

All that has been said about teachers can be said of school administrators and teacher educators. Administrators who trust, like, accept, understand, and empathize with their teachers help them to *experience* being trusted, liked, accepted and understood. Teachers, like any other group of people, need to experience these attitudes and not just be told about them. Perhaps the most significant contribution an administrator can make to effective learning processes and personal growth among pupils is to develop a non-threatening emotional climate for teachers.

Teacher educators need to pay more attention to the dimension of personal growth. Students tend to model their teaching behaviors and attitudes on their interactions with and observations of professors and supervisors. The professor or supervisor who is growing and learning, who trusts his students and is real with them, who listens to students and confronts them in facilitative ways "teaches" humanism.

Again, it is not enough to talk about personal growth. Students need to *experience* individualization, acceptance, understanding, trust, authenticity, and being liked. In order for learners to enhance the self they need humanizing experiences whether in an elementary school, high school, or university setting. The more teachers provide these neded experiences for their pupils, the more they in turn become humanized.

Tape Recordings as a Tool for Self-Discovery

One of the ways a teacher can determine the degree to which he is real and authentic in the classroom is to record his class sessions with students. Video and audio tape recordings provide one of the most useful means for evaluating the quality of the teacher-pupil relationship. Recordings of class sessions offer the teacher a richness of data unequaled through any other procedure. Through video and audio tapes teachers can capture the "real thing," of that interaction between pupil and teacher — the dynamism and the fluidity of personality and behavior, the emotional as well as intellectual communications, and the varied other dimensions of human behavior. With tapes the teacher can begin to explore such questions as: Is that me in the classroom? Am I real with my students? Do I listen? Do I allow students to be real? Do I create an emotional atmosphere free from anxiety? The teacher can determine the quality of the pupils' response to him as a person and can gain valuable insights which will help him in his personal growth. By asking his colleagues to critique recordings of his interactions with pupils, the teacher can learn not only how he affects his students, but also how he is perceived by his peers. This kind of information fosters self-discovery and personal confrontation within the teacher, enabling him to become more sensitive and more attuned to his pupils and peers as people.

Recreation as a Humanizing Experience

In 1892, in *Talks to Teachers,* William James said of the "Gospel of Relaxation," "Just as a bicycle chain may be too tight so may one's carefulness and conscientiousness be so tense as to hinder the running of one's mind" (1958:132). James' ideas on relaxation are as appropriate for teachers today as they were over seventy years ago. While the work of teaching should be taken seriously, there is always the danger that the teacher will take himself too seriously. A balance needs to be struck so that the teacher can integrate play with work. The teacher who knows how to play will seldom become discouraged or bored with teaching or with life. Recreational experiences offer change, a chance to look at life at one's self from a different perspective. Rest and relaxation are necessary elements for self-renewal and an enriched life for the teacher.

The fully functioning teacher *lives* life — he participates in or creates experiences "just for fun." He realizes that even though recreation is a necessary element in the evolving process of humanization, it cannot compensate for the drudgery of work that a person has no real interest in or commitment to. Because of his deep involvement in teaching, the humanizing teacher does not find it necessary to think of recreational experiences and activities merely as something to counterbalance the displeasure he finds in the vocation of teaching. Effective teaching represents an integration of work and play.

The humanizing teacher loves his work, but because he is maximally open to experience, he knows that the fully lived life cannot be achieved solely through teaching. He looks forward to diversions that present him with opportunities for unpredictable and fresh experiences of his potentialities for sensing, wondering, loving, and laughing. Whether painting, boating, watching a ball game, dancing, singing, or hiking, he lets himself go to drink in the beauty and vitality of the moment.

There is no list of magical recreational experiences that enhance the teacher. What is one person's pleasure may be another's poison. Teaching with commitment can be demanding as well as rewarding, but the rewards will diminish if commitment is not balanced by experiences that recreate and renew the self. Teachers who engage in few or no hobbies, do little traveling, and restrict leisure, social, and community activities are not as likely to realize their potential as are teachers who zestfully participate in activities beyond the requirements of teaching. A life that is confined to teaching begets narrowness in perceptions, feelings, and perspectives. Recreational experiences can require commitment and a large expenditure of time and effort, but what makes any experience refreshing rather than fatiguing is the attitude with which the activity is approached.

Recreation offers an additional dimension to living; for the humanized teacher, there is a reciprocal interplay between his teaching and his play. To an objective observer, teaching might not seem to be work at all, and the teacher may well appear to work very hard at his recreational pursuits. There is no contradiction. The humanized person's teaching is most often characterized by joy as well as commitment, and his recreation by commitment as well as joy. Work and play complement each other and serve as wellsprings for a creative and vital existence.

Recreational experiences offer the teacher an interlude — a break in the pattern of his professional life — that often reveals to him the secure comfortable web he has woven around himself. The position of the teacher tends to evolve into a secure social and academic role, and if he is not careful he will come to overestimate the wisdom of his own words. One of the occupational hazards mentioned before was the development of the "god" complex. Recreational activities that bring the teacher into contact with a variety of people and experiences "scratch and nick" his thinking and help generate a balanced view of teaching and its relationship to life.

It is particularly important to cultivate a sense of humor. Laughing at himself and the absurdities of life helps the teacher avoid making mountains out of molehills and creating his own problems. The laughter and joy experienced at a party offers a therapeutic release, and acknowledging our own pretensions through well-intentioned humor helps us free ourselves to be better people.

The serenity, strength, vigor, and perspective the teacher derives from his play are resources to be utilized for his own growth and for the growth of his students. We cannot give that which we do not have. Without the opportunity to re-create ourselves as persons, our teaching loses its vitality and freshness, and our reservoir of psychologically-nourishing experiences becomes depleted. Recreation replenishes the teacher's psychological storehouse and adds new dimensions to his teaching. The ultimate beneficiary is the student.

PROVIDING HUMANIZING EXPERIENCES IN THE CLASSROOM

The more the teacher seeks, creates, and is offered experiences that build his concept of self, the more he develops a deep respect for and understanding of his pupils as persons. Operating from a base of personal security, realness, and awareness, he humanizes the classroom by providing a growth-facilitating emotional environment and by developing approaches for releasing and nourishing pupil potential through a learner-centered teaching approach. Some of the more promising ways of helping pupils to expand the self have been identified by the American Association for Supervision and Curriculum Development (*Individualizing Instruction,* 1964:161-162) and include the following:

1. Observing and listening to learners with care and concern.
2. Achieving openness in pupil-teacher relationships, to permit improved response and interaction.
3. Helping learners toward the objective of personal relevance.
4. Recognizing and accepting different ways of responding, according to learners' individualized styles and needs.
5. Stimulating creation and recreation of self-image that encourages further development.
6. Questioning, probing, and responding in ways that lead learners to assume responsibility.
7. Standing aside judiciously to let the learner discover and exercise his own resources.
8. Making development of the learner the chief goal in teaching subject matter.
9. Achieving free affective responses and seeing its relevance to intellectual development.
10. Achieving free and constructive communication with learners.

11. Helping learners sense the living dynamics of man's creations, as revealed by history and the current scene.
12. Clearing the way, by whatever means, for stretching learners' minds and abilities in creative, self-fulfilling endeavor.

The more the teacher invests himself in this kind of teaching, the more teaching enhances the self. The more creativity and compassion the teacher puts into teaching, the more teaching defines him as a creative and compassionate person. The more the teacher humanizes his teaching, the more teaching humanizes him. The more the teacher cares for his students, the more they will care for him. The more the teacher frees his students to grow, the more he frees himself to grow.

REFERENCES

Friedenberg, Edgar. *The Vanishing Adolescent.* New York: Dell Publishing Company, 1962.
Individualizing Instruction. Washington, D.C.: Association for Supervision and Curriculum Development, 1964.
James, William. *Talks to Teachers.* New York: W. W. Norton Company, 1958.
Jersild, Arthur T. *In Search of Self.* New York: Teachers College Press, Teachers College, Columbia University, 1952.
Kildahl, John P. "Twelve Ways to Survive the Rat Race," *Boston Globe Magazine,* June 14, 1970, pp. 28-34.
Kohl, Herbert R. *Open Classroom.* New York: Vintage Books, imprint of Random House, 1970.
Perceiving, Behaving, and Becoming. Washington, D.C.: Association for Supervision and Curriculum Development, 1962.
Silberman, Charles E. "Murder in the Schoolroom," *The Atlantic Monthly,* Vol. 225, June, 1970, pp. 82-97.
Stefflre, Buford. "Vocational Development: Ten Propositions in Search of a Theory," *Personnel and Guidance Journal,* Vol. 44, 1968, p. 611. Washington, D.C.: A.P.G.A.
Wright, Derek. "The Price of Friendship," *Time,* June 8, 1970, p. 54.
Yauch, Wilbur A. "Keys to Understanding in School Relations," *The Teachers Encyclopedia,* Englewood Cliffs, N.J.: Prentice Hall, 1966, Chapter 35.

3

Teaching
and
Valuing

The test of any belief is its translation into action; it might be said that a belief which is not put into action is not a belief at all. It is one matter to verbalize a belief; it is another to implement it. The valuing life is characterized by actions based on values and standards that have evolved from inquiry, meditation, and contemplation. The examined life is "the life that is marked by the endless search for touchstones by which to judge the choices that a man must daily make" (Shoben, 1963). Out of the choices we make and the actions we take, we shape our lives, our work, and the world we live in. Choices and actions emanate from the quest for personal values. It is a personal search for an answer to the most human of all questions: what is the meaning of life?

THE VALUING LIFE:
EXPLORATION AND FORMULATION

The valuing life is one of exploration and formulation, in which the depths of human existence are plumbed in order to discover personal meaning. Shoben (1967) speaks of the critically informed life in the sense that the person "proclaims himself as responsible for his own actions, i.e., he acknowledges himself as a selective choosing being; inquires critically into the nature and implications of the alternatives open to him and the motives and incentives entailed in his discarding some to accept others; and evolves as a part of the process of criticism a set of standards for himself by which he evaluates his own behavior." Thus defined, the valuing life can be characterized as the responsible use of freedom to discover and create moral values for living through critical thought.

To be human is to be valuing, in that the person who lives his nature acts as the valuing center of his life. The search for values, requires reflection, honesty, courage, and discipline. The valuing life is a creative life that penetrates through conventional and superficial thought as declared by Nietzsche in *Thus Spake Zara Thustra:*

> No people could live without first valuing; if a people will maintain itself, however, it must not value as its neighbor valueth... Valuing is creating; hear it yet creating ones! . . . Through valuation only is there value; and without valuation the nut of existence would be hollow. Hear it, ye creative ones! (Kaufman, 1956: 102)

In creating our values we create ourselves. "As a man thinketh in his heart so he is." What we believe is what we are. It is difficult for an individual to function or behave out of context with what he is. The individual who lives his thoughtfully nourished values lives fully and fearlessly; the one whose life contradicts his values lives anxiously.

Valuing is not an isolated event in the life of an individual. It is an ongoing process of continual examination of criteria and values. All thought and action are evaluated and made part of a person's beliefs; the valuing life is an evolving experience. It changes, but from it comes a greater degree of self-knowledge, an expanded sense of self-determination, and more facilitating behavior.

The work of Mowrer (1967), Jourard (1964), and Glasser (1965) suggests that the person whose behavior is congruent with his values and who is morally responsible is a healthy person. The morally responsible person has created moral values for living that are reflected in his behavior, but he is not a "moralistic" person. Morality is the relation of behavior to one's values. The norm of morality is the totality of our human nature. If the nature of humanity is seen as a loving and cooperative nature, then moral values proceeding from this nature will guide behavior that facilitates and enhances human development.

Moral values that have emerged from an examination of the self provide a coherent framework for interpreting experiences and trying out new behavior. Our senses are bombarded daily by a barrage of data, experiences, events, and situations that require interpretation for personal integration and meaning. The guiding principles for interpretation and action are found in our personal values and beliefs.

THE TEACHER AND HUMAN VALUES

It is probably correct to say that every aspect of teaching presupposes some implicit moral and human value. Teaching is an expression of values and attitudes, a process in which the teacher transmits a fairly clear picture of his own personal concept of man, his nature, and his function on earth. The fully functioning teacher's identity expresses unfolding attitudes and values that mirror his continual examination of self and the unique relationships in which he participates. Developing a sensitivity to the existence of values and how they influence behavior is important if a teacher desires to bring greater meaning and awareness to the dimensions of teaching. Not only will such sensitivity enable the teacher to develop a greater understanding of students, but it will also enable him to develop a keener understanding of how his own personal values can either help or hinder the personal growth of his students.

If the teacher is to promote the personal growth of youngsters, he must value their integral worth because of the mere fact of their existence. When a person values personal power, personal recognition, fortune, or his own superiority over other people, he has difficulty valuing anything beyond himself and his edification. But a humanistic individual must value beyond himself; he must value humanity as well as his own existence. He must value those qualities

35

which comprise the human personality and serve as the basis for human functioning. He must value an awareness of humanity's basic goodness and understand the factors that often hamper movement toward the good. He must sense the enabling attributes and tendencies that make human life the highest form of existence.

If the individual values humankind, he will move toward an awareness of the burdens that permeate existence, and will develop an empathic quality in his associations with others because he cares for mutual self-development and movement toward a meaningful existence. Because he cares, he places himself in relationships that will enhance others as he attempts to perfect his own existence. He does not block the expressiveness of others; he helps them to become more aware of themselves by providing relationships in which they can explore the essence of their own existences. Because the teacher values humankind, he shapes his work so that he is relating to people, rather than being involved in the mechanics of teaching. He doesn't retreat behind the defensiveness of paperwork; he shapes his teaching so that he is in a communicating relationship with students.

Unless the teacher has a deep-seated respect for the dignity, worth, and integrity of the individual, he can never hope to communicate at a deeply empathic level. Lip service tributes to humanity are not enough for the fully functioning teacher; he welcomes opportunities to aid others in their quest for self. He provides them with the significance of a truly warm and caring attitude. The valuing teacher moves from an attention to things and products to a caring for others.

TEACHING AS VALUING

Within each student there exists an array of values that influence the way he acts and reacts in any given situation. The verbalizations of students are often expressions of values emanating from their self-structures. Therefore, as the teacher responds to his students, he is responding to an interwoven pattern of self and values. Because a person's values are a reflection of how he views himself, they provide a useful key to understanding the student's self-structure. The teacher who is growing and learning must become aware of the differences between his own values and beliefs and those of his students, how his values and beliefs affect each of them, and how values and beliefs interact as students and teacher become involved in the learning process.

Teaching provides the opportunity to live values, to implement self — to be a loving caring human being. The valuing teacher possesses a caring attitude that is so deeply a part of him that it is sensed and responded to by students. It is this caring attitude which is often the difference between effective and ineffective teaching. Students react to a teacher's caring by responding freely and deeply in the learning process. Because of the valuing teacher's genuine concern the student is able to learn with greater ease; he is able to delve into the various aspects of his functioning because he feels that the teacher is authentic in his caring for him as a person.

Goldhammer has stated that "we are much more strongly inclined to *cure* lonely people than we are to *love* them (1969:365). Unfortunately too often in teaching we are more inclined to try and cure students than we are to care for them. Too many teachers view teaching as a mechanistic procedure in which the student is cajoled, convinced, and manipulated into learning. They proceed in a manner that is insensitive to the student as a person with a unique array of values and behavior patterns. They retard the personal growth of students by encouraging verbalization in areas of teacher interest instead of creating a learning relationship that offers students an atmosphere in which they are free to discover who *they* are, and what *their* values will be.

The degree of teacher caring is in proportion to the degree to which he exists for the well-being and development of the student. Facilitative teaching requires a deep commitment to examined values and to the belief that given freedom an individual has the ability to perfect his existence. Translating this commitment into behavior characterized by love, compassion, and a genuine caring attitude makes teaching a valuing experience.

No field of endeavor which touches human lives can afford to leave its philosophical presuppositions unexamined. The psychologically whole teacher not only lives his values, he reflects upon

37

them. What distinguishes the fully functioning teacher from the classroom technician is an examined philosophical rationale that enables him to handle the what and how of teaching without resorting to a "cookbook" approach. His procedure is not a compilation of different recipes for different situations and people. Out of his rationale emerges a consistent identity and strength to move ahead. Nietzsche has said, "He who has a *why* to live can bear with almost any *how*" (Kaufman, 1956: 201). The teacher who has a "why" for teaching can take care of "whats" and "hows." He does not have to search for just the right method to handle unusual situations, new experiences, or different people. His "why" for teaching enables him to react and respond and create out of a deep sense of commitment. One cannot honestly engage in the overt practice of a religion unless there is a substantive inner belief which is the core of that religion. By the same token a teacher must have a rationale, a *why*, if his teaching functions are to have meaning for his students and for himself.

REFERENCES

Glasser, W. *Reality Therapy.* New York: Harper and Row, 1965.

Goldhammer, Robert. *Clinical Supervision.* New York: Holt, Rinehart, and Winston, 1969.

Jourard, Sidney M. *The Transparent Self.* Princeton, New Jersey: D. Van Nostrand Co., 1964.

Kaufman, W. A., ed. *Nietzsche.* New York: Meridan Books, 1956.

Mowrer, O. H. *Morality and Mental Health.* Skokie, Illinois: Rand McNally Company, 1967.

Shoben, Edward J. "The Examined Life and Mental Health," in *Morality and Mental Health.* Edited by O. H. Mowrer. Skokie, Illinois: Rand McNally Company, 1967.

Part Two

The Learner

By definition learner-centered teaching is focused on the learner. We assume that all learners have self-actualizing tendencies and basic psychological needs, and that the teaching relationship is the primary means for nourishing self-actualization and meeting those fundamental human needs. In any consideration of teaching, curriculum, and the various instructional approaches we must begin with an understanding of children and adolescents. Learner-centered teaching is a process which accommodates the values, attitudes, feelings, and personal concerns of the learner and integrates these personal elements with intellectual and academic development. In the next two chapters we develop our perspective on the human dimensions of children and adolescents, which determines the characteristics of learner-centered teaching.

4

A Humanistic
View of
Children

We believe that the two most important needs of children are the development of a positive self-concept and a feeling of competence. For most children only two places exist where these needs can be met: the home and the school. When children enter school, they come with different levels of maturity, with individual strengths and weaknesses, with differing abilities to learn, with unique physical and emotional factors, with special blends of fantasy and reality, and with differing expectations of what school life will be. They come eagerly and reluctantly, with positive anticipation and with fear, with a richness of background and with intellectual deprivations, with curiosity and with apathy, with skills and without skills. Some are economically deprived, some are wealthy; some are emotionally starved, others are self-confident.

As the major social institution to which children are exposed during the crucial developmental years, the elementary school "provides not only the stage on which much of the drama of a student's formative years is played but also houses the most critical audience in the world — peers and teachers" (Hamachek, 1969:19). It is through their relationships with each other and their teachers that children develop their self-concepts and build their mastery of basic skills. If they are to grow and develop fully they must feel worthwhile and experience success. They need a school environment that encourages exploration and investigation; one that recognizes and applauds a child's initial steps and accomplishments. Schools should establish feasible individual and group goals; create opportunities for communication and for the expression of feeling among children, and value their creativity and uniqueness. The school must maintain the challenge of personally meaningful standards and value idiosyncratic learning. "Very few children come to school failures, none come labeled failures. It is school and school alone which pins the label of failure on children" (Glasser, 1969:26).

CHILDREN'S CONCERNS

There is a tendency to think of the child's world as being filled with lollipops, games, tree houses, lovely family portraits, and first walking shoes bronzed into bookends. In the American culture we have fictionalized childhood as a time of joy and merriment in which children skip and play in a perpetual rose garden. The fantasy of childhood has been conceived and promulgated by an adult world which writes the story books, takes the pictures, showers the gifts, constructs the commercial playlands, and designs the clothes. The attempt to idolize childhood is often well-intended, and will certainly continue as long as there are adults who aesthetically or commercially feed themselves at the table of the child's world.

But the inner world of children is not all milk and honey. They have basic human needs that are often overlooked by adults who persist in manufacturing a child's world that is thing-centered rather than relationship-centered. Whether children live in the inner city or in affluent suburbs, they must face the normal problems of living; finding some meaning in this process called existence, attempting to gain understanding, acceptance, and empathy from their parents, and trying to gain acceptance from their peers and brothers and sisters. They desire to understand themselves, and how they relate to others. How they act on this self-knowledge is far more relevant to the security of children than the artifacts of adult civilization which surround them.

Because adults are emotionally far removed from the experiences of childhood, they tend to forget the painful aspects of being a child in an adult world. They don rose colored glasses when they look back, recalling only the pleasant experiences. They repress thoughts of experiences that caused them pain and shaped their current behavior as adults.

Many adults have a "he'll grow out of it" attitude toward the typical concerns and personality traits of the child. Some children do outgrow the lesser problems which confront them. But for most children, negative aspects of personality that go untreated or unnoticed carry over into the adolescent and adult years. The troubled child is likely to display delinquent behavior, under-achievement, self-centeredness, destructive tendencies, rebelliousness. Later in life they tend to experience bizarre attitudes towards sex, personal irresponsibility, strained relations with spouses, personality clashes with supervisors, lack of personal commitment, and an inability to love or to find meaning in life. For some adults the problems are so extreme and their behavior so unacceptable, they end up imprisoned or admitted to mental institutions.

Anyone who reads a daily newspaper realizes that many troubled adolescents and adults exist within American society. Spectacular stories concerning people's inhumanity towards others make the reader wonder where our civilization is headed. Can we ever really make a contribution to world peace when we have so much difficulty in overcoming problems within our communities, within our homes, and within ourselves? No large-scale research project is needed to tell us that we are individually and collectively a troubled people who need to find an existential meaning and value in our lives.

The personal and emotional problems of adulthood are not easily overcome because the problems are solidified by the passage of time from childhood to adulthood. Anyone who has tried to assist a troubled adult realizes how much time, energy, and professional skill is needed to help him move toward more appropriate and self-enhancing behavior. The problems of the troubled adult are far more difficult to resolve than those of a child; there is so much time between the problem and its source. Today's behaviors are but a manifestation of self-destructive experiences that are rooted in the formative years of a person's life. Because children are just beginning and life seems relatively uncomplicated, they internalize every experience in its full totality. Childhood is a period in which experiences find easy entry into children's self-concepts because they are psychologically open and welcome each opportunity to learn more about life and themselves. Experiences can have either a positive or a negative impact. Adults who are generally able to deal with life are people who were exposed as children to more self-enhancing experiences than self-destructive experiences. During or after self-destructive experiences they encountered the warmth and understanding of significant persons who were able to help them work through the troublesome experiences of growing up.

A concentrated effort is needed to help children deal with those normal and developmental problems that hamper their effective functioning, and which, if not resolved, will later affect their behavior during the adolescent and adult years. The egocentric woman who is fifty years old may overcome her problem if she has the good fortune to be in contact with a person who possesses the skill to help her unravel the nuances of her personality which affect her behavior. However, her egocentrism might never have existed if as a child she had had the opportunity to be in contact with a mature adult who offered her an opportunity to talk about her emerging egocentric personality.

We've often heard that an ounce of prevention is worth a pound of cure. It is a simple statement that has been with us for centuries, and it is still loaded with meaning. If we as a civilization wish to develop an adult population which acts and reacts with a higher degree of sensitivity, then we must use our energies to help our children develop positive self-concepts, relationship skills, and a sense of competence. We have invested in schools which are expected to improve the intellectual competence of the future citizens. But human intelligence and rationality are housed in a body that possesses feelings and emotions, and this affective component of our humanity often clouds and hampers the effective use of our intellect. Adults who have problems may intellectually know right from wrong and know which behavior will bring them pain or pleasure and still behave irrationally. When people behave irrationally, it is often the result of ignorance about how the attitudinal and emotional self controls overt behavior.

Schools committed to training the intellect are only training a portion of the person who will take a place in society making decisions which will affect others. They are training the intellect and forgetting that a person also possesses emotions which can sidetrack and hamper the effective use of that intellect. Schools that only take pride in the number of volumes contained in their libraries, the academic credentials of their faculty members, the number of students who belong to the National Honor Society, or the percentage of their graduates who are admitted into prestige colleges, value a hollow concept of education. Certainly knowledge is important, but it alone is not enough if children are to develop into secure adults capable of dealing with the problems that surround the daily routine of living. If schools are to educate the total person, then a serious attempt has to be made to help children become sensitive to their emotional beings. They need to learn how to keep emotional problems from interfering with the pursuit of knowledge and the use of the intellect.

Human existence is filled with situations in which people "know" what they should do, but because of a certain affective components within themselves, their behavior goes against the grain of rationality and logical sequence. A parent may know that a child needs an abundance of love during the formative years, but emotionally he may be unable to provide this love. We may know the kind of person we would like to marry, but when the moment of decision comes, we are ruled by emotion. Intellectually, people can determine right from wrong, but lives are often shattered because someone did not *feel* like doing something that they knew to be correct.

45

Children are engaged in the same struggle between intellect and emotions. They may sit in a schoolroom because they know it is important to learn how to read, but become nonreaders because they are not emotionally involved in the process. They may intellectually know that it is wrong to look at another child's paper during an exam, but emotionally they feel compelled to do so. Children may know that the teacher is in the business of helping them, but may still possess the *feeling* that they do not want any help from anyone. They may know that having friends would provide inner comfort, but emotionally they prefer to be alone.

Many teachers present neatly packed lessons that they believe will increase the storehouse of knowledge for each child in the classroom. There is the assumption that if a teacher follows a particular well-ordered procedure in presenting knowledge, then that knowledge will be absorbed. Perhaps the knowledge would be absorbed if each child were emotionally ready to learn whatever is being presented; but for the typical child in the typical classroom, the degree of learning will be proportionate to the degree to which the child is emotionally free to learn. That is, if a child is emotionally involved with parental conflicts, teacher autocracy, peer aggressiveness, sexual identification, or other strong feelings, whatever knowledge is being dispensed by the teacher will be blocked by the child and not allowed to enter his intellectual structure. Because of this emotional involvement, some children learn only a small portion of what is presented to them. Children absorb information when they have been able to resolve their emotional problems and set their intellects free.

Youngsters become more productive learners and are better able to deal with adolescence if they are given an opportunity to work through those problems which interfere with their learning and hamper their effective functioning as persons. This does not mean that schools should give up the goal of training the intellect. It means that schools need to develop a sensitivity to the emotional needs of students that matches their concern for the intellectual development of their charges. Most schools have been inattentive to the normal problems of children because of a lack of time and the scarcity of adequately educated personnel to provide noninstructional, emotionally centered relationships with learners.

Berk has inquired about the normal developmental problems of fourth graders in Public School 171 in East Harlem, New York. Here are some of the concerns those youngsters identified:

"Why don't I have any friends?"
"My problem is — my sister she break my things all the time."
"Why don't I read good?"
"My problem is — everybody start up with me all the time."
"Why the teacher don't like me?"
"My problem is — I don't like to fight."
"Why my mother make me sweep and not my brother?"
"My problem is — I have no place to do my homework."
"Why some children call names all the time?"
"Some people tattle and like to get others in trouble."
"You can't have friends if you fight all the time."
"Some children call other children bad names."
"Sometimes, someone wants the teacher's attention all the time and can't give anybody else a chance."
"You can't be first all the time."
"My little sister is a pest — she bother me all the time."
"My little brother break my paper and books."
"She bother me when I do my homework."
"I hit him when he bother me."
"My sister, she gets away with everything."
(1967:174-175)

Problems will exist as long as there are human interactions. Children should receive assistance in dealing with their concerns not only because resolving the conflicts will make students more receptive learners, but also because the help they receive today is an investment in being more adequate adults for tomorrow.

THE INDIVIDUAL AND THE FUTURE

Our best preparation for an evolving society is helping children face the future with confidence in their own abilities and with a faith that they are worthwhile and important members of whatever culture they might find themselves in. Thinking about the needs of children in today's schools, we ought to look at what the individual will need in order to function effectively by the time our children will be adults.

1. *A positive self-concept.* A positive self-concept provides tremendous advantage in dealing with life. It is like having money in the bank. It provides an inner security: with a positive view of self, one can risk taking chances; one does not have to be afraid of what is new and different. But the present positive self-concept is not sufficient for motivation and performance. It is the image of the future self—the future-focused role image—that strongly affects educational, personal, and social competence. Such an image delineates what one can become, and provides a wholesome, achievable goal that helps the individual cope with a diverse, rapidly changing world. A positive self-concept featuring a strong future-focused role image can be consciously cultivated. People *become* fully functioning and future focused —they are not born that way. The self-actualizing, future-focused personality is an achievement accomplished through humanistic education.

2. *Multiple existence.* The traditional notion of stability, one job, and one place has already begun to give way to the notion of transition, many jobs, and many places. Many of the tasks of the future will exceed individual capacity and require interdependence and collaboration, as well as independence, and self-reliance. The egocentricity of the individual will need to be modified to allow full development of the cooperative self as well. Life in the future calls for individuals with the ability to participate in cooperative processes, to sustain many allegiances without contradiction, and to tolerate incompletion.

3. *A sense of competence* is a crucial aspect of the self-concept. In the future, individuals who do not know what they are good *at* will not be sure what they are good *for*. Competence is an achievement, not a gift. Adequacy, autonomy, and control over some aspect of one's life emanate from the knowledge that one is good at something. The human spirit does not thrive on failure and individuals will need the nourishment of success. Experiences of success and failure are important to development. Solving problems —

experiencing failure and turning it into success — is critical. The crucial elements in the balance between success and failure are competency and the perceived experience of self-enhancement that results from success.

4. *Relationship skills.* The demographic pressures of life will create a paradoxical situational press — the collective imperative and the need for intimacy. Individuals will be required to work and live more and more within group contexts. This calls for the ability to relate with many people who have different values, perspectives, and life styles. At the same time, the need for relating to a few people on an intimate basis will become even more intense: compassion, empathy, honesty, genuineness, and caring will be much sought after. The ability to communicate with others and the capacity to nourish values relating to the welfare and enhancement of others will be essential for a self-fulfilling life in the future.

5. *A new view of work and play.* Occupations (employed work) and leisure (non-employed work) will need to be considered, not as a polarity, but as a fusion. The key to the concept of work as a self-fulfilling experience is that work should not be restricted to employed activities. Work exists in and out of an occupation. Work — strenuous, demanding, satisfying because it is self-fulfilling — will be the common element of both occupation and non-occupation. The blending of employed and non-employed work into a whole will lead to the ultimate of a committed or responsible whole in which one works both for self-fulfillment and for the fulfillment of others. This will become a vocation — a calling, a mission — in which one can find personal purpose and meaning.

How do we help children now so that they can become effective individuals in the future? First we must teach children to love themselves. "If we don't teach children to love themselves God help their neighbors. Modern studies of human development are forcing us to realize how correct Jesus was when he said, 'Love your neighbor as yourself'" (Lachapelle, 1970). Children learn who they are and what they are in the mirror of other people.

> The self is learned. What is learned can be taught. What can be taught is fair game for the public school. The question is not one of whether we approve of teaching for a positive self in the public schools. We could not avoid affecting the self if we wanted to. We may ignore the self in our teaching. We cannot, however, escape the fact of our influence upon the self or our ultimate responsibility with respect to whether the effects of schooling are positive or negative (*Perceiving, Behaving, and Becoming,* 1962:101).

THE SELF AND COMPETENCY

The discovery, exploration, and enhancement of the self are not the traditional curriculum of the schools. Indeed, many critics of education believe that such matters are inappropriate concerns for the public schools. These critics are deeply concerned at what seems to them to be a growing preoccupation with values, personal growth, and human relations. Often they ask the either-or question: Shall our schools teach for adjustment, or shall our schools teach for knowledge? "The plain fact of the matter is we need *both* well adjusted people and people who know something. As Arthur Combs once said in a speech, 'Clearly we do not want from our public schools either smart crooks on the one hand or well adjusted dopes on the other!'" (*Perceiving, Behaving, and Becoming,* 1962:102). We are painfully aware that intelligence, knowledge, and an excellent college education do not guarantee incorruptibility. Schools must become much *more* concerned with the unique experiences and feelings of the children they educate. We need to create classroom climates that encourage the development of the self as a legitimate part of the learning process.

Our second major concern in preparing children to function effectively in the future is to help them develop a sense of competence. Children need to know they are good for something, that they can develop some measure of control and autonomy in dealing with their environment. One of the principal ways children develop a sense of competence is through mastery of reading, language, and mathematics. Experiences of competency cannot be provided in situations where all children are treated alike. The necessary success experiences cannot occur in classrooms that are organized in lock-step fashion. Children are by their nature unique and individual, and the learning experiences must "fit" the people they are (*Perceiving, Behaving, and Becoming,* 1962:107). This calls for individualized instruction and ways of pacing instruction so that learning can be increasingly rewarding and self-directive. It requires establishing realistic goals for children that are within their capacities; goals that will offer the kind of success experiences they need to develop a sense of competency. In short, the development of competency in children calls for learner-centered teaching that allows each child to feel important, able, worthy, and successful. Competent learners are more apt to perceive themselves as capable and worthwhile. They will be more productive and effective individuals, and enhance the world they live in.

Bessell (1970), in his discussion of the general principles of mastery, sums up the nature of responsible competence in a series of statements that we have adapted to illuminate our discussion:

1. Competent children have acquired and continue to acquire knowledge and skills that are personally meaningful and satisfying to them in terms of their survival or enhancement.
2. Competent children have received sufficient recognition and approval for what they have accomplished to make them have confidence in what they are capable of doing. They have been challenged with tasks at such a level that success was certain. They have a measure of self-confidence that is equal to their capabilities — no more, no less.
3. Competent children are tolerant, and have a positive attitude toward their mistakes, which they perceive as an integral part of the opportunity to learn, not as proof of inadequacy.
4. Competent children have a positive identification with the capabilities and accomplishments of others, whom they perceive as fellow members of the human race. They enjoy helping others to become more effective, and are not arrogant or condescending.

51

The conditions that support the emergence of positive self-concepts and competency among children are created in classrooms by teachers who center on the learner. These attributes will not develop in classrooms characterized by a preoccupation with order, an over-emphasis on authority, or a strict adherence to mechanical cookbook or lock-step approaches. The teacher who believes that mistakes are sinful, that children are not to be trusted, cannot be a positive influence. The assumptions and characteristics that do facilitate the development of positive self-concepts and competency have been well articulated by the Elementary Project Board of the Chittendon School District in Shelburne, Vermont (1972):

1. Children have an innate drive toward growth and it is assumed that they can take initiative in their own learning.
   a. To a large extent they know their own needs.
   b. They are capable of making intelligent decisions about their learning.
2. Children grow in competency through experiencing real situations, which they create and manipulate themselves. They learn by exploring possibilities and using trial and error as a learning device.
3. The child's own way of learning, that of discovering and experimenting, is recognized and used, so that emphasis is placed on learning by the child, rather than on teaching by the teacher.
4. The ability to solve problems, whether social, mathematical or economic, is given precedence over rote learning. Children equipped to function adequately are able to relate new knowledge to a new situation in order to solve problems. They are able to conceive problems as well as solve them. They can use judgment and forethought, and are able to reason and to imagine.
5. Emphasis is placed on the individuality and originality of the child, rather than having each child conform to a set pattern of thinking. Children have ample opportunities to construct and invent, unhampered by comparison.
6. An educated person knows the tools with which to express thought and feeling. Children learn the vocabulary of expression and cultivate an individual language of expression through all art forms.
7. Children learn better when internally motivated. Work absorbs their interest because they know something of its purpose. Because they are involved in the planning of the learning activities, their interest is vitalized and their motivation increased.
8. Each child experiences a measure of success every day. Only children who feel good about themselves are able to learn effectively.
9. Cooperation among children is emphasized. Competition not only inhibits but minimizes the satisfaction of learning for its own sake.
10. The classroom offers an environment in which the attitudes, interests, and capabilities of each child are seen as part of the richness and variety of that environment.

If these kinds of facilitative conditions can be established in the classroom, children will begin to see themselves as planning, purposive, responsible, and competent individuals. They will like themselves, and consequently will like other people. This is what learner-centered teaching is all about.

REFERENCES

Berk, P. "A Group Guidance Club in the Elementary School," *The School Counselor,* 1967, p. 14.

Bessell, Harold. *Methods in Human Development — Theory Manual.* El Cajon, Calif.: Human Development Training Institute, 1970.

Elementary Project Board, Chittendon School District, Shelburne, Vermont. Mimeographed report, 1972.

Glasser, William. *Schools without Failure.* New York: Harper and Row, 1969.

Hamachek, Don E. "Self-Concept Implications for Teaching and Learning," *School and Community,* May 1969.

Lachapelle, Dolores. "Teach Children to Love Themselves — or God Help Their Neighbors," *The Catechist,* 1970.

Perceiving, Behaving, and Becoming. Yearbook of the Association for Supervision and Curriculum Development, 1701 K Street, N.W., Washington, D.C., 1962.

5

A Humanistic View of Adolescence

Humanistic teaching has a significant role to play in enabling young people to meet the challenge of change and *becoming*. Part of the rationale for humanistic education includes a consideration and understanding of the psychological essence of adolescence and the cultural milieux which affects it.

ON BECOMING

An adolescent is a young person who is *becoming* an adult, who is changing rapidly, who is no longer a child but still not yet a man or a woman. There are no clearly defined chronological boundaries which separate adolescence from other periods of growth and development. In fact, adolescence seems to be culturally defined. In more primitive cultures, adolescence begins and ends with puberty rites, which may last for a few days, a week, or a month. Adolescence as we know it is relatively unknown in many societies. It would appear that the more highly sophisticated and technical the society, the longer the period of adolescence is. Generally speaking, in the American culture adolescence occures somewhere between the ages of twelve and twenty. Puberty, the onset of sexual maturity, marks the beginning of the process. The changes that accompany puberty make adolescents act, look, and feel different from the selves they were before. Their attitudes towards others, towards life, and towards themselves change. While they struggle to adjust they may amuse, amaze, bewilder, or confuse those around them. They are perplexing not only to others, but also to themselves.

The central developmental task of adolescence is self-definition (Friedenberg, 1962). Adolescents are seeking an answer to the question, "Who am I?" They are in the process of becoming individuals with unique personalities that differentiate them from other people. The sense of identity — the need for being aware of who one is and what one's relationship to others is — becomes most pressing during adolescence (Erickson, 1950). T. S. Eliot has summed up the primary goal of adolescence in a phrase:

> finding out
> What you really are — What you really feel.
> What you really are among other people. (*The Cocktail Party,* Act I, Scene i)

Adolescents are precariously balanced between childhood and adulthood, vacillating between one role and the other. Their feelings are all mixed up. They want to be treated as adults, but they are apprehensive about their ability to take on this role. They are not sure they are ready to accept all the responsibilities of adulthood — but they sure would like to have the pleasures! One day they will be cooperative and considerate; the next they may appear to be thoughtless and unkind. They may go with startling speed from one extreme to another in friendships, beliefs, plans, and dreams. For some, life has more crises than an old-fashioned movie serial. In *The Tale of Two Cities,* Charles Dickens gives a capsule description of the ups and downs of normal adolescence:

> It was the best of times, it was the worst of times; it was the epoch of belief . . . it was the season of Light, it was the season of Darkness; it was the spring of hope; it was the winter of despair.

What makes the adolescent such a vacillating person? We know that adolescence is characterized by a number of complex developmental tasks arising from the head for a sense of identity and the urge to relate with others. These tasks are the adolescent's special problems, and they involve a great deal of ambivalence. Adolescents must shed childhood patterns of dependency, work out new patterns of living, and prepare for the adjustments of adulthood. The problems of adjustment does not imply maladjustment, but rather refer to a variety of modifications that most people must make in order to grow, mature, and develop. *It is normal for adolescents to have problems.* Indeed, one might say to live is to have problems. Bennet brings this point out very well when she says:

> Having problems is simply a characteristic of living, which is a continuous process of *becoming* rather than a static state of being. It has been said aptly that living involves not so much a matter of the adjustment to problems as the *adjustment to having problems.* Learning self-direction involves learning to face problems and to deal with them as effectively as possible (1955:46).

It is unfortunate that the word, problem, has been used to imply "sickness." Too many teachers have been threatened by the word and have tended to view the developmental concerns and the growth needs of "normal" adolescents as pathological. In doing so, they have narrowed the concept of normality to a degree that any divergent or unexpected behavior is regarded as abnormal and outside the sphere of school counseling. It is worth pointing out that one (Renaud and Estess, 1961) study found that the case histories of 100 normal, but superior, American adult males did not differ from those of psychiatric patients with respect to childhood experiences traditionally considered prognostic of maladjustment.

The problems of adolescents as described here are typical problems, which often overlap each other. They are concerns common to most of us as we progressed through adolescence. They are obstacles to be dealt with, and the process of solution and adaptation presents more of a problem to some individuals than to others. The frustrations and tensions that can result from problem-solving are not abnormal or unusual. They are an inescapable part of the process of living.

THE CONCERNS OF ADOLESCENTS

The Physical Self

Adolescents are concerned about the physical changes taking place in their bodies. Adolescence is usually a period of dramatic growth and change not quite like anything that has occurred before. Perhaps the most significant change is sexual maturing. With the girl's first menstruation and the boy's first seminal emission, comes the realization of a sexual potential, and with the realization may come anxiety, self-consciousness, and many other confusing feelings. Physical appearance, body image, and the opposite sex begin to occupy the thoughts of the adolescent.

Many adolescents experience concern regarding their body image. This is one dimension of the total self-concept we often overlook as a source of anxiety for youth. In adolescence the final edition of the physical self is being run off the press. Although in later years one may get heavier, lose or color hair, or change some aspect of appearance, the basic physical self — the skeletal structure and facial features — is in final form at the end of adolescence. The culture we live in accentuates concern about the physical self by promoting a stereotyped picture of the clean-cut all-American boy or girl with sparkling teeth, a clear face, and a firm, lean body. The media ideal becomes the standard by which adolescents measure themselves. For some it is difficult to bring together the physical self they see and the desired physical image projected on the screen.

The changing body becomes a symbol of new attitudes toward the self, others, and life in general. Growth and physical changes create many anxieties. Adolescents are often concerned lest they won't "measure up." Mary feels she is too plump. Joe worries because he isn't growing as fast as the other kids. Alice thinks she is too tall, Pete is bothered by the beginnings of acne. Gary worries because he thinks he isn't as strong as the others, and Mike is anxious because his genitals are not as developed as those of the other kids he sees in the shower room.

Physical growth creates a need in adolescents to form a view or a definition of their rapidly changing selves. Learning how to accept the physical self is an important developmental task, and it is one that can be made easier with the help of a self-actualized teacher.

Independence

Adolescents are striving for emotional independence from parents and other adults. They waver between the safety and security of dependence on their parents and the urge to discover what life holds for them as independent, fully functioning beings. They feel a strong need to assert themselves as persons. As one girl put it: "I don't want to be known as Mrs. _____'s daughter — I want to be known as Mary _____, a person in my own right." Adolescents are almost driven by the need to break away from adult authority. They vigorously pursue the right to make their own mistakes. They want to assume genuine responsibility for their own lives, and they often create issues with adults in order to demonstrate their independence. This may be reflected in how they wear their clothes, the music they listen to, their hair styles, or a special language unfathomable to all except their peers.

Adults are often embarrassed by adolescents and their tendency to make errors. It is much more helpful for adults to try and understand and be willing to suffer the occasional inconvenience that youthful errors can cause. One of the major objectives of education should be to provide pupils with the opportunity for personal growth and problem-solving experiences. Unfortunately, a number of educators deny their students appropriate learning experiences, out of a misguided sense of "promoting efficiency in the classroom" or a Pollyanna attitude of "let's not allow him to hurt himself." Individuals protected from making mistakes, for their own "good," are often held back from personal growth as well.

The need for opportunities to be independent and responsible is explained by Wilder:

> It is in this sense that responsibility is liberty; the more decisions that you are forced to make alone, the more you are aware of your freedom to choose. I hold that we cannot be said to be aware of our minds save under responsibility (1948:34).

Adolescents need encouragement and support for making decisions and for committing themselves to a "cause." Errors in judgment may be made, but the learning experience should lead to the exercise of better judgment. A permissive environment helps adolescents learn how to begin some activity, follow it through, and, if wrong, pick themselves up and start over again — that much further ahead for having tried something. Many adolescents do nothing, in order to avoid being wrong. Personal growth is sacrificed because they do not feel that they can afford to make mistakes and suffer the resultant pain. This attitude is due in part to a "better safe than sorry" adult attitude, which many adolescents integrate into their value structure. For many, error is seen as almost immoral (Friedenberg, 1962).

The right to have free choice carries with it the right to make a mistake. Learning conditions that do not permit mistakes limit the freedom of adolescents and makes them less willing to make their own choices. The process of growth and development requires the challenge of new experiences, of trying the unknown, and will often result in "mistakes." Humanistic education should facilitate the development of independence by providing a permissive atmosphere in which adolescents can explore new experiences, new ideas, and new thoughts without fear of penalty or embarrassment. In perhaps no other developmental period does one feel quite so strongly the need for the right to make mistakes, for, in essence, adolescence *is* a trial-and-error process.

Values

Adolescents are also concerned about acquiring a set of values and an ethical system to guide their personal behavior. They begin to question parental and adult concepts of good and evil, of right and wrong. They no longer accept without question the ideas and opinions of adults, who begin to appear as sadly human and fallible. Adolescents want to work out their own code of behavior. They have a growing need to come to their own conclusions on questions of consequence. In the process of developing their own values, they often come into conflict with parents, teachers, and other adults.

Adolescence is a process of defining oneself through *conflict* with society. "Adolescent conflict is the instrument by which an individual learns the complex, subtle, and precious difference between himself and his environment. In a society in which no difference is permitted, the word 'adolescence' has no meaning" (Friedenberg, 1962:34). Nowhere is this conflict more in evidence and less understood than in the schools. The inevitability of the conflict between the adolescent and the school is brought out quite clearly in the American School Counselor Association Policy Statement for Secondary School Counselors:

> Because the school is a democratic institution using group objectives and methods, and because learning, maturing, self-realization are inevitably individual processes, a paradox or conflict for the student is implicit within our educational structure (1963:196).

Although conflict with society is the instrument by which the adolescent defines himself, it does not follow that the conflict must be hostile. The desire to be unique, to break with tradition, and to question the strongest beliefs of the school and society are not necessarily hostile activities. The most significant way the young define themselves is by contrasting with social and cultural codes and values. If we place a small piece of black paper on a larger piece of black paper, it is extremely difficult to see the small black paper. If we place the same small piece of black paper on a larger piece of white paper, it is quickly and easily perceived. Adolescents do not change the background — society or the school — they challenge it and in doing so they find a way to stand out.

Adolescents who are permitted to question generally accepted values and shape their own without constantly having to defend them will probably develop integrity, self-respect, and an accurate perception of their place in the world. The importance of an independently established code of values is clear. Self-control is acquired on the new terms of "I do this because that's what I think is right." The adolescent may well come close to parental standards and values in the end, but he needs the feeling that he arrived there on his own. If this self-directive capacity is not developed during adolescence, the individual is likely to carry within himself a permanent feeling of inadequacy.

Our society is full of conflicting values, which does not make formation of a personal code of values an easy task. The values of the home, the church, the school, the community, the peer group, the various subcultures of society, and the mass media do not jibe with each other. In fact, often they are diametrically opposed. Demands on adolescents usually emphasize moral choices. Society demands that they ask themselves "Is it right?" before they consider "Do I want it?" The adolescent is usually highly idealistic, which makes it that much harder. Adults administer and interpret the culture in moral terms, but when adolescents apply these terms to the conduct of parents and other adults they find all too often that the ideal is lacking. Parents and teachers frequently ask for instant obedience, and yet they preach the American ideal of self-reliance. The ideals of altruism and concern for one's neighbor are contradicted by the overwhelming encouragement to compete, to outdo one another, to win. One type of behavior is rewarded by one's peers; the opposite type, by parents and adults. Adolescents also find conflict between their highly idealistic values and their need to be part of a group, which may espouse values that contradict their own. Establishing a set of personal values amid conflicting standards can be made easier by a teacher-learner relationship that permits the adolescent to be himself.

Adolescents who do not have to defend themselves, who do not feel threatened by moralizations, judgments, or critical evaluations are free to hold their own values. Being free to hold their values, they are also free to change them. And being free to change values, they are free to choose more personally enhancing values. As Rogers (1964) points out, when man is free to choose his values, he tends to select the ones that enhance himself, his community, and the society in which he lives.

Sexual Relationships

Prior to puberty, members of the opposite sex generally occupy a minor place in the life of the individual. But with puberty, problems concerning interpersonal relationships, dating, and sexual information emerge. As they develop a deepening interest in each other, adolescents become concerned with questions like how to overcome shyness, how to get attention from the opposite sex, whom to date, where to go, and how long to stay out. What are the rights and wrongs of heterosexual relationships? How far do you go? Petting, necking, and intercourse — what are appropriate attitudes? Adolescents have a pressing need for sex information, but it is a need that is seldom met by society, the schools, or the family.

In the matter of sex relations, our society abounds with contradictory messages. Despite the Puritan tradition, few cultures have provided more sexually arousing stimuli than our own, in movies, songs, and magazines. Few cultures provide easier opportunity for engaging in sex, with the availability of cars, birth-control information, and the absence of chaperones. Adolescents are given a setting for engaging in sex and then punished when they are discovered making the best of the opportunity.

Adolescents enjoy discussing problems about dating and potential marriage partners. From junior high school on, hetero-sexual relationships dominate the "bull sessions" of teen-agers. Because of the ambiguous standards of society and the repressive attitudes of adults regarding sexual relationships, adolescents find it extremely difficult to discuss their concerns with an adult. Here, education can fill the gap. Humanistic teacher-pupil relationships that are built upon trust, understanding, respect, empathy, and sensitive listening provide the much-needed opportunities to discuss concerns freely without fear of embarrassment, ridicule, or moralization.

Sex is an integral part of living, and in adolescence the sex drive is beginning to reach its peak. If we believe that the normal prob-lems of growth and development are within the legitimate sphere of education, how can any school justify the exclusion of sex from the curriculum? Indeed, where can conditions be more appropriate and positive for the rational discussion of sex than in the schools?

Social Relationships

During adolescence the individual becomes acutely aware of social pressures and relationships. One of the deepest needs of adolescents is to be supported and approved by peers. They are tremendously sensitive to social stimuli and greatly concerned about establishing themselves in their own society. Being popular and well-liked is one of the chief goals of the adolescent; the need to affiliate and communicate with others is extremely important. Adolescents find that their peer group provides them with the support they need to move away from dependency relationships with parents and to learn how to differentiate themselves as persons.

In their search for individuality, adolescents often find themselves in conflict with peer standards and values. The ambivalence can create a high level of discomfort; as a result, deviations of any kind from peer culture are extremely difficult. There are many individuals who enter adolescence with poorly developed social skills. They do not seem able to "get along with their peers." Education can provide experiences to help these adolescents develop a deeper sensitivity to and acceptance of others. Adolescents who are unable to relate effectively to others usually have a low self-concept. Self-esteem is crucial to social development. It is doubtful that there can be a self, except in relation to others, and to accept self implies the acceptance of others. Self-esteem engenders the opposite of the hostility that results from non-acceptance of self.

In their first encounter with humanistic education, some teachers question the emphasis on the development of individuality, particularly in regard to the adolescent. They see this emphasis as a philosophy that promotes sociopathic behavior among adolescents. But it is through humanistic education that adolescents become socialized in very healthy ways. Rogers says:

> When we are able to free the individual from defensiveness, so that he is open to the wide range of his own needs, as well as to the wide range of environmental and social demands, his reactions may be trusted to be positive, forward moving, constructive. We do not need to ask who will socialize him, for one of his own deepest needs is for affiliation and communication with others. When he is fully himself, he cannot help but be realistically socialized. We do not need to ask who will control his aggressive impulses, for when he is open to all of his impulses, his need to be liked by others and his tendency to give affection are as strong as his impulses to strike out or to seize for himself. He will be aggressive in situations in which aggression is realistically appropriate, but there will be no runaway need for aggression. His total behavior, in these and other areas, when he is open to all his experience, is balanced and realistic — behavior which is appropriate to the survival and enhancement of a highly social animal (1964:167).

Vocational Identity

Adolescents are concerned about their future, particularly in terms of selecting and preparing for an occupation. Preadolescents have general concerns about occupational goals, rather than the specific concerns that come in the later stages of adolescence. When children approach puberty, they begin to leave behind their fantasies regarding work. They begin to realize that their future will depend more on their abilities, interests, and opportunities than on early childhood dreams. In the movement from fantasy to tentative choices, young persons feel a need to find out more about themselves and the world they live in. It is a period of exploration, in which the individual embarks on a journey to discover who he is and how he relates to the world. Discovering who you are is essential to defining who you will become. Vocational identity is a reflection of one's self-concept. Adolescents need privacy and time for exploration; they need an emotional shelter from a world that seems to be saying, "Hurry up now, make up your mind!"

Tremendous pressure is exerted by parents, teachers, misguided counselors, and powerful social forces for adolescents to make major decisions about their futures. The concern about these "life choices" unfortunately encourages attempts by adults to manipulate the lives of students without due regard for the students' personal goals and desires. Young people want to talk about their dreams, goals, plans, and aspirations. But how does an adolescent communicate with an adult who already has the young person's future mapped out? How do adolescents talk to adults who perceive them as being unrealistic? An adult who listens is an oasis in the desert for the concerned adolescent.

Young people have never had it so good, or so bad. Today's adolescents are perhaps the best fed, best clothed, and best sheltered youth in the history of the world. But they are also confronted with a multitude of choices and pressures not felt by any preceding generation. Although it is true that other generations have had choices to make, there has never been such a range of choices available. Variety of choice intensifies the anxiety that accompanies decision-making, but it also makes the world and the future something to be excited about — a challenge that offers a greater opportunity to fulfill dreams.

Work is the avenue most adolescents expect to travel in order to find fulfillment. It is true that financial success, security, identity, recognition, and material acquisitions are most often provided through one's work. In survey after survey, adolescents speak of getting a "good job." They perceive the ideal self-concept (what I would like to be; how I would like to see myself) in terms of an occupation.

During adolescence, young people look about themselves and see what their parents and other adults have pursued. They often see faded hopes and dreams. They know they have the opportunity to reach out and grasp what has escaped so many of their elders, for whom time is running out. Adolescents have much more of a future than a past. Adults looking back to their own "Waterloos" feel obliged to tell young people not to risk, but to be careful and rational. "Avoid the mistakes I made," is common advice. Through their desire to protect youngsters, adults often create more anxieties instead.

Society asks adolescents to take more and more time to prepare for the future, but it is difficult to play the waiting game. They want to get on with the job of living. As a social process, adolescence is the "lift-off pad" to the future. Anxieties regarding that future can be reduced by a school environment that focuses on what the adolescents can become rather than on what they have been. Adolescents need the opportunity to tread new paths, the chance to make their own mistakes, the right to make decisions governing their future, and human relationships that will enable them to *become*.

Competence

Competence and excellence are highly esteemed among adolescents. "In a world as empirical as ours, a youngster who does not know what he is good *at* will not be sure what he is good *for;* he must know what he can do in order to know who he is" (Friedenberg, 1962:40). "Excellence is the best in the trade," says a Chicago high-school junior. "I'd even respect an excellent thief"(*Newsweek,* 1966:56). Feelings of adequacy and competence are a crucial aspect of the self-concept, and they are achievements, not gifts. The adolescent develops feelings of adequacy by being good at something. The human spirit does not thrive on failure, and adolescents as well as adults need the nourishment of success.

The school has enormous potential for developing feelings of adequacy and competence among adolescents. School is important to them. Adults who are not in daily contact with teen-agers consistently underestimate the importance of school life. It is widely believed that youngsters are indifferent to teachers and studies, and that educational institutions are regarded as minor annoyances in their lives. In truth, concern about school and teachers is high on the list of items which young folks mention. This is not surprising when we consider that a good half of their waking hours on weekdays are spent in activities linked to formal education.

School is a microcosm of the adult society in which an individual will live. Unfortunately, for a number of adolescents, it is an experience of inadequacy and failure. The school can contribute to the lowering of self-esteem because it demands success-oriented behavior. Often, however, the curriculum does not provide opportunities for the attainment of incremental successes for too many members of its captive population. As a middle-class institution that perpetuates middle-class values, the school's curriculum ordinarily represents one traditional academic avenue for success achievement. For the youngsters who cannot travel this avenue, school is an experience characterized by failure, shame, friction, and frustration.

When the formal curriculum does not provide positive experiences, the subliminal curriculum often reinforces the antithesis. The subliminal curriculum is a natural extension of the visible and formal curriculum. It is the way of life within the school, which sets the normative pattern of how to act and how not to act. Though hidden, it may be a formidable and effective aspect of the learning process. A pupil may gain status and prestige with peers by playing a truant role, by being a nonlearner, by being a discipline problem, or by being sexually promiscuous depending on the school

67

environment. Subliminal culture varies from school to school. In some schools, it may represent positive forces for social adaptation, but it often serves as a delinquency subculture that encourages acts of iconoclasm against the middle-class success ethic. For success-starved adolescents, socially aberrant behavior is one way to resolve their personal social failure. The reversal of values gives them a feeling of worth, at least in the eyes of peers. They achieve success by becoming successful failures. "Negative . . . kinds of experience force people to crawl deeper into their existing positions, to build shells around themselves and do not permit the open, outgoing exploration and discovery required for the production of a fully functioning positive self" (ASCD, 1962:105).

Our culture does not always offer enough opportunities for learners to develop the kinds of competencies necessary for feelings of adequacy and success. For some, adolescence is an existential vacuum, a social limbo that lacks meaning and purpose. They are walled off from the grown-up world just when they should be busy learning to live in it. Our society is a hard one to grow into; there are no easy gradients into the world of work and the whole of adult life. Adolescents crave significance and responsibility, and we offer only childhood. And so, delinquency and crime keep rising year by year even in "good" neighborhoods and rural areas; adolescents "clam up," and form private subcultures, or model on one another instead of mature adults. In their frustration, they join a formless rebellion against the world they yearn to belong to.

For both alienated and "normal" adolescents, feelings of adequacy and competence begin with human relationships in which difference is valued and uniqueness is prized. Adolescents learn who they are and what they are in the mirror of other people. Achievement and success are rooted in a positive view of self, and that view is learned. If a person trusts me, accepts me, respects me, likes me, understands me, and values me, I begin to feel trust-worthy, acceptable, respected, liked, understood, and valuable. The teacher-learner relationship is a human interaction that can tap the adolescent's well-springs of adequate and competent behavior. The teacher is the mirror in which the adolescent can see a positive image of self.

Undoubtedly, many problems can be solved just through the process of growth and living. Some problems may be at least partially solved by the adolescent alone; others will require the support of a helping relationship.

It is important to avoid creating a stereotype when discussing the problems of adolescence. Adolescence is not always characterized by trial, tribulation, and turmoil. Many individuals pass through adolescence with relative ease and comfort. One teen-ager we know, commenting on the picture of adolescent life portrayed in most textbooks, said, "When some of my friends and I read what adolescence is supposed to be we can't believe it. Life hasn't been so terrible or difficult as most of the textbooks say it is for the average teen-ager. Maybe we're not average but we enjoy being adolescents. Who are these kids the books describe?"

Adolescent behavior may sometimes be the operation of a self-fulfilling prophecy. Mass media, textbooks, and the expectations of adults seem to teach youngsters that when they enter adolescence, life will become burdensome and filled with troubles and anxieties. The picture may not be necessarily true for everyone, but many individuals begin to act the way they perceive their culture expects them to act. In other words, adolescent behavior mirrors the expectancies of the culture and its adult members.

Education must recognize the "humanness" of adolescents. An adolescent should not be viewed as an economic entity or an intellectual entity, but a whole person. People are rational beings, but they are also emotional beings. Rationality and emotionality are so inextricably interwoven that we cannot divorce one from the other. Alfred North Whitehead has stated in the *Dialogues:* "Intellect is to emotion as our clothes are to our bodies, but we would be in a poor way if we only had clothes without bodies" (1954:172). We in education cannot afford to act as though pupils were "clothes without bodies," considering the growing trend toward impersonality in today's schools.

ADOLESCENTS AND ADULTS

It is difficult for adults to understand or cope with the conflicts of adolescence because they rarely understand their own feelings about adolescence. As Friedenberg states:

> Adolescent personality evokes in adults, conflict, anxiety, and intense hostility (usually disguised as concern), colored by a whole complex of feelings, attitudes, and influential unconscious trends. . . . The most threatening feelings are certain to be deeply repressed into the unconscious, as a result, they are certain to influence action and perception with peculiar potency (1962:177).

Young people who have their lives ahead of them and who have not yet begun in earnest to make the most of their opportunities arouse mixed feelings in their elders. According to Friedenberg, one fear is that the adolescent will get beyond the adult's control and may disrupt situations that involve the adult. Adolescent spontaneity can be frightening and enraging to the adult. Another fear, particularly among American adults, is the fear of aging. Adolescents can also arouse envy, because it hurts to see someone who has the opportunity to grasp and hold what eluded you, or what you dared not touch and have dreamed of ever since. Friedenberg feels that fear of disorder and loss of control, fear of aging, and envy of the life not yet squandered lie at the root of much adult hostility. These repressed emotions account for much adult petulance, as well as the lack of genuine understanding and acceptance.

The conflict between youth and age has always existed, but it appears that a few generations ago there was more tolerance for youthful nonconformist behavior than there is in contemporary society. All too often, the harmless but rebellious behavior of adolescents is labeled "delinquent" by adults whose irritation level is low. There are adults in every community who are titillated by the nonconformist behavior of adolescents. They experience vicariously forbidden pleasures and impulses through reading sensational stories about adolescent escapades. Unconsciously, they experience strong gratification of unfulfilled desires, and attempt to deny them by condemning and punishing the youngsters who "make" them experience these forbidden thrills. The harsh indictment of youthful adventures is often a cloak that conceals the adult's hidden delight.

Adolescents also serve as a hostility target for the adult community, siphoning off the frustrations and tensions of living in a fast-moving, complex world. Adolescents are "handy," "convenient" and "respectable" scapegoats on whom the irritated adult can vent his pent-up aggressions without any feelings of guilt. The adult can resent adolescents with a vengeance and feel virtuous in doing so.

We believe that humanistic education provides a balance to these distorted adult-child relationships. It allows adolescents to perceive themselves more accurately, and to become sensitive to the causal anatomy of their actions and reactions. When adolescents reach this point, they become more self-actuating — more independent, responsible, self-sufficient; more able to do what they can do.

When adolescents are allowed to express themselves freely, more often than not they move from looking for an external cause for their concerns to evaluating their own involvement. Rationalization, projection, and other defense mechanisms only exist when there is a need for them. When people are free to be themselves, and when there is no need for self-defense, they can begin to look at themselves in relation to their environment with more accuracy.

The teacher who facilitates self-understanding and self-clarification within the adolescent operates on the principle that students are basically responsible for themselves and must retain that responsibility. The self-actualizing teacher focuses on the student rather than on the problem, accepts the adolescent's right to be different, and strives to help the adolescent understand himself within the context of society. It is important that the teacher not lose sight of the young person as he or she is. Farnsworth reminds us that we should always be aware that "students are important as much for what they are as for what they will become. A girl at Barnard College said, 'I'm sick and tired of being potential all the time.' While it is true that young people are on the road, that road is itself a place" (1966:33-34).

Self-actualizing teaching assists students in achieving self-understanding and self-management, and enables them to move in positive directions. Farnsworth (1965) spelled out these positive directions when he suggested that the task of education should include the following goals:

1. Respect for all persons, regardless of their race, sex, color, ethnic background, religion, or behavior at the moment.
2. Sufficient knowledge of other people to be able to judge in a general way what their needs are, the ideals they honor, the customs they practice, and the frustrations they endure.
3. Knowledge of the qualities of a person who can be at home with diverse groups of people and yet enjoy being alone as well.
4. A sensitive and perceptive awareness of one's own nature, including those qualities under the control of the will and those which are not.
5. Sufficient modesty and humility not to feel impelled to impose one's ideas on others.
6. The achievement of a proper balance between self-regard and concern for the welfare of others.
7. The ability to appreciate how one's self is perceived by others, thereby being able to modify actions in order to increase competence and the capacity to relate to others.
8. Being able to disagree with others without becoming angry; and gaining a conviction that differences of opinion should be settled by the power of rational authority rather than by verbal or physical force. However, the value, even the necessity, or righteous (or judicious) indignation should also be realized.
9. The habit of inquiry and doubt, practiced in such a way as to avoid becoming either a fanatic, who sees simple solutions to complex issues, or a cynic, who sees no merit in any constructive activity.
10. The capacity to formulate the nature of approaching problems along with some idea of how to plan the development of appropriate solutions.

Not all of these goals can be attained in adolescence; indeed, many of us will struggle to achieve them throughout our lives. However, by helping adolescents achieve a sense of who and what they are, and what the meaning and purpose of their lives can be, teaching can promote emotional maturity and make it more likely that such goals can be achieved.

REFERENCES

Association for Supervision and Curriculum Development, *Perceiving, Behaving, and Becoming.* Washington, D.C.: NEA, 1962, pp. 149, 238.

Bennet, Margaret E. *Guidance in Groups.* New York: McGraw Hill Book Co., 1955.

Erickson, Erik H. *Childhood and Society.* New York: W. W. Norton, 1950.

Farnsworth, Dana L. *Attitudes and Values of College Students.* Paper presented at 1966 Institute for Administrators of Pupil Personnel Services, Harvard University Graduate School of Education, July 25, 1966, pp. 33-34.

_____. *The Search for Identity.* The Edwardo Weiss Lecture, 1965-66. Series on Adaptation. DesPlaines, Illinois: American Hospital Association, Forest Hospital, September, 1965.

Friedenberg, Edgar Z. *The Vanishing Adolescent.* New York: Dell Publishing Company, 1962.

Newsweek. "The Teenagers," Vol. 67, No. 12, March 21, 1966, p. 56.

Renaud, Harold and Estess, Floyd. "Life History Interviews with One Hundred Normal American Males: Pathogenicity of Childhood." *American Journal of Orthopsychiatry,* October, 1961, No. 31, pp. 786-802.

Rogers, Carl R. "Toward A Modern Approach to Values." *Journal of Abnormal and Social Psychology,* vol. 68, February 1964, pp. 160-167.

"Tentative Statement of the ASCA Policy for Secondary School Counselors." *Personnel and Guidance Journal,* Vol. 43, No. 2, October, 1963, pp. 196-197.

Wilder, Thornton. *The Ides of March.* New York: Harper and Row, 1948.

Whitehead, Alfred N. *The Dialogues.* Boston: Little, Brown, 1954.

Part Three

Theory

We believe there can be no separation of theory and practice. The following chapters first develop the case for the integration of theory and practice. Then Rogers' theory of personality is translated into the teaching-learning context. Each proposition in Rogers' theory is specifically related to teacher and learner behavior. Finally, existential-humanistic concepts of motivation, adjustment, and interpersonal behavior are translated into humanistic principles and conditions of learning that provide the framework for equalizing the teacher-learner relationship.

6

Toward a Personal and Practical Theory of Teaching

A collective or personal theory is the basis for all of human behavior and certain psychological, cultural, social, and ethical assumptions influence the formation of that theory. When a nation engages in peaceful behavior that behavior is not accidental; it emanates from a governmental theory based upon certain assumptions that reinforce the importance of peace. When a nation engages in war, that behavior is not accidental; it emanates from a governmental theory based upon certain assumptions that reinforce the importance of war. When an individual decides to live an honest life, that behavior is not accidental; it is based upon certain assumptions that reinforce the importance of honesty. When an individual decides to steal, that behavior is not accidental; it is based upon certain assumptions that reinforce the importance of stealing.

Group and individual behavior emanates from an identifiable collection of assumptions and it is the arrangement of these assumptions which forms the theory that influences behavior. One's

77

ethical and practical behavior doesn't just happen. It is ignited and put into motion by one's theory.

When a person possesses a theory, and is able to identify the assumptions upon which it is built, that person is able to bring a certainty to his behavior because that behavior is congruent with his theory. That behavior is a natural outcome of a personal theory and is, therefore, an extension, reflection, and reinforcement of that theory (Boy and Pine, 1971; Cox, 1966; Frankl, 1963; Hoffer, 1968; Morris, 1966; Rogers, 1969; Toynbee, 1969).

THE INESCAPABLE USE OF THEORY IN TEACHING

In education there has been a certain aversion, and even hostility, toward theory. "Theory is all right for the ivory tower academician," "We've had enough of theory — now we want some answers," and "Theory can't help me in my situation," are statements expressed by a good number of student teachers and practicing teachers.

The basic assumption underlying this negative attitude is that theory and practice can be dichotomized into separate and distinct categories. On the abstract level this may be so, but on the concrete level, theory and practice cannot be neatly compartmentalized; they are inextricably intertwined. No matter how many times one attempts to divorce the two, one inevitably finds that practice rests upon theory. We believe that although many teachers may not have developed a formal, systematic theoretical statement as a foundation for their work — and indeed, may not be aware that what they do each day is based upon theory — they nevertheless operate from a theoretical base.

Teachers who think they can operate without theory and who assume an anti-theoretical position usually base their behavior on vaguely-defined but implicit theory. There is no other way that they can decide what to do. Intuition, which is often advanced as a substitute for theory, is but a crude type of hypothesizing. As teachers, we bring to our work certain assumptions. We have some underlying rationale (vague or implicit though it may be) for what we do, some hunches about what different students will do in different situations, and some general ideas about the teaching procedures that are apt to be effective.

We all have beliefs that guide our actions and help us to order the daily events of our lives. Under these informal theories our anticipation of daily events, though not scientifically precise, surrounds our lives with an aura of meaning. A theory enables us to view life as not wholly capricious, and prepares us to deal with each day's new experience in an orderly and somewhat consistent way. Instead of belittling theory and minimizing its importance, we need to devote more effort to defining and clarifying exactly the theory we hold.

THE FUNCTIONS OF THEORY

Through conscious examination and evaluation of the informal theory we hold, and through the study of more formalized statements of other theoretical positions, we can discover how useful theory is. Theory has a number of practical functions (Pine and Boy, 1975:124-125):

1. *Theory helps us to find relatedness, or some degree of unity, among diverse observations and experiences of human existence particularly as these occur in teaching and learning situations.* The teacher who relates to a diverse population of students each day who are learning at different rates, can bring unity to his teaching behavior if he conceptually identifies an attitudinal core which enables him to teach and students to learn. This attitudinal core can serve to synchronize the teaching-learning relationship so that there is a bond, a linkage, between what is being taught and what is being learned. But the teacher who desires to synchronize himself with the learner must expend full energy in identifying the theoretical constructs which enable such a linkage to take place.
2. *Theory may compel us to observe relationships that we had previously overlooked.* When a teacher feels that a theoretical base for teaching is unimportant, each day is merely a series of unrelated events. Sally cried, Ted shouted, Melissa fell asleep, Henry became more withdrawn, Debbie refuses to read, Bill taunts the others, Ann was truant again. A teacher who possesses a theoretical base sees these events as having a relationship to each other because his theory enables him to grasp the wholeness and interrelated meaning of these observations.
3. *Theory provides operational guidelines which help us in making provisional evaluations of the directions and desirability of our development as human beings and as teachers.* The teacher who possesses a theoretical base for his behavior moves himself toward decisions and

solutions which are logical outcomes of his theory. He never finds himself in a blind alley in the decision making process. He realizes that his theory will guide his decision if he gives that theory an opportunity to function. The practical solution will eventually be known if the theoretical base guiding that solution is given an opportunity to become energized.

4. *Theory focuses our attention on relevant data by telling us what to look for.* A person who functions from a theoretical base addresses himself to primary and substantive facts in order to reach a solution. Because he thinks conceptually, he is able to see the wholeness of a problem as well as the necessity of developing a whole solution. He seeks a more substantive solution for dealing with a rebellious student than merely isolating him from the group. He is able to conceptualize and behave in wholes because his theoretical base is whole.

5. *Theory may help us to construct new approaches to teaching and point to ways of evaluating old ones.* The person who possesses a theoretical base possesses an enlarged awareness of the impact of his teaching behavior. He is more free to be creative in his teaching behavior because his theory prompts him to be always seeking rather than being static and content. He either discards or revitalizes old approaches because as his theoretical base expands and evolves his practical behavior is also influenced to expand and evolve.

6. *Theory provides us with guidelines for helping students modify their behavior and learning more effectively.* The teacher who functions from a theoretical base is, intellectually and attitudinally, in continual motion. He is always seeking out better motivations, better approaches, and better results. He looks upon his teaching behavior as a tentative solution for assisting students because he is always aware that better solutions loom over the horizon if he can expand his theoretical awareness. He realizes that the more he expands his theoretical base the better will be his practical solutions to the ancient challenges of education.

Kelley points out that theory provides a basis for an active approach to living. It is not merely a means of contemplating the vicissitudes of life with detached complacence. "Theories are the thinking of men who seek freedom amid swirling events. The theories comprise prior assumptions about certain realms of these events. To the extent that the events may, from these prior assumptions, be construed, predicted, and their relative courses charted, man may exercise control and gain freedom for themselves in the process" (Kelley, 1963:22).

DEVELOPING A TEACHING THEORY

The beginning point in the development of a teaching theory is the teacher's attitude toward the individual, which is the cornerstone of one's philosophy of life. Teaching is a process that reflects the teacher's philosophy of existence. It is not a technique but a mode of existence, a way of living. Each teacher must resolve for himself certain basic questions regarding the nature of humanity and the world before he can communicate effectively with students.

In order to function effectively in helping students to realize their potentials, teachers must continuously evaluate five basic questions:

1. What is the nature of humankind?
2. What is the nature of human development?
3. What is the nature of the "good life" and the "good?"
4. What is the nature of the determination of the "good life" and who determines what is "good?"
5. What is the nature of the universe and what is our relationship to that universe?

In developing a theoretical framework, the teacher not only considers the philosophy behind teaching, but also considers the psychology of human behavior, which is a vital part of the teaching experience. For the teacher, this means asking himself questions about the nature and development of human personality, the conditions for and modes of behavior change, the dynamics of motivation, and the conditions and principles of learning.

From a philosophy of life and a psychology of human behavior, an approach to teaching emerges. The teacher begins to develop a construct that leads to some tentative, workable answers for the following questions:

1. What is the learner like?
2. How did the learner get that way?
3. What is the teacher doing during teaching?
4. What is the learner doing during teaching?
5. How do the teacher and learner interact during teaching?
6. How does the learner learn?
7. What is the relationship between (a) the learner's behavior *subsequent* to teaching and (b) the behavior of teacher and learner prior to and *during* teaching?

In searching for the answers to these questions, the teacher begins to formulate an explicit theoretical framework for teaching. With this framework he begins to see some "rhyme and reason" in the daily barrage of data and experience. He finds a point of departure for launching himself into teaching, and he can function with coherence in the different situations he is involved in. He does not have to grope for ways of facing new situations, because his theory enables him to react and respond with consistency. Even though he is not always able to translate his theory into full operation, it "raises his sights" and provides worthwhile goals for him. As he attempts to implement his theory, he will realize that the more his theory and practice agree, the more professional his work becomes. His teaching gains substance and depth because he knows the "why" of teaching as well as the "how."

The teacher's theory need not be a carte-blanche adoption of someone else's theory. Each teacher can adopt a theory tentatively and subject it to the test of practice. From such testing evolves a tempered theory, refined and modified in the light of the teacher's personal philosophy and psychology. If Mary Smith adopts Theory X, she adopts it in her own unique and personalized way, and she is "Smithian" in her teaching approach. And if John Jones adopts Theory Y, he may be more accurately perceived as "Jonesian" in his approach. It is the personalized assimilation and application of a theory that makes it meaningful and enables the teacher to teach more effectively. Theory does not become "butchered" in the personalized translation; rather it becomes more coherent and usable.

This personalized implementation of theory does not imply that one learns a set of rules and techniques to be applied mechanically and objectively in the classroom. The application of teaching theory is quite different from the application of theory in the physical sciences. Many scientific theories can be applied with little regard for the subjective element of human interaction, but teaching theory, which is applied amidst the give and take of a classroom, must be integrated into the teacher's personality. The teacher who applies theory in a rigid, mechanical way is seeing himself and his students as objects, thus ignoring the human element that so many see as essential in teaching. A teacher's theory of teaching should be a reflection of his personhood, not a banner to ride under. Shoben (1962) points out that aside from the internal consistency of a system of ideas, its comprehensiveness, or the degree to which it is clearly supported by evidence, it is quite possible that personal and temperamental factors may be the significant determinants in a choice of theory.

The effective teacher is philosophically and psychologically attuned to the theory that exemplifies what he is becoming and what he would like to become as a person. He forms a bridge between his teaching rationale and his self-identity. From his self-identity he produces a concept of his role that is the workable extension of basic concepts derived from his philosophical and psychological theory. His theory is not something he leaves behind in the school at the end of each day. It serves as the basis for *all* his relationships. He knows he functions most comfortably with people when there is a high degree of congruence between what he is as a person and what he holds to be philosophically and psychologically true.

The involvement of the self in a teacher's theoretical disposition may lead some to believe that the desired goal of a theoretical viewpoint is the personal comfort of the teacher. Certainly, a teacher should be comfortable with his theory. However, a teaching approach and theory should not be judged in terms of teacher comfort, but rather in terms of its effect on students. The humanistic teacher tries to be sensitive to the limitations of his theory. Although he is theory-oriented, he is not theory-bound. He is aware that a theory may blind him to the uniqueness of his students and that some teachers may try to make the student fit a theory tailored for the masses. The effective teacher realizes that such an application of theory is the opposite of open-minded humanistic practice.

One reason why a number of teachers have been unable to translate theory into practice may be the failure to understand and integrate into their own personalities the philosophical and psychological nutrients that have helped their theory grow. Without understanding and assimilation, teachers mire themselves in the quicksand of literal translation and purity of technique. Effective teachers are wary of this danger — they are not overly committed to dogma. They have a deep respect for theory, and have been able to personalize it and translate it into the cold reality of the working situation. They have learned that the most successful practitioners are theorists — and the most successful theorists are practical people.

REFERENCES

Boy, Angelo V. and Pine, Gerald J. *Expanding the Self: Personal Growth for Teachers.* Dubuque, Iowa: Wm. C. Brown Company, 1971.

Cox, Harvey. *The Secular City.* New York: Macmillan Company, 1966.

Frankl, Viktor. *Man's Search for Meaning.* New York: Washington Square Press, 1963.

Hoffer, Eric. *The Passionate State of Mind.* New York: Perennial Library, imprint of Harper and Row, Publishers, 1968.

Kelley, George A. *A Theory of Personality.* New York: W. W. Norton Company, 1963.

Morris, Van Cleve. *Existentialism in Education.* New York: Harper and Row, Publishers, 1966.

Pine, Gerald J. and Boy, Angelo V. "Teaching: Theory As A Guide to Practical Behavior." *The High School Journal,* Vol. LIX, No. 3, December, 1975.

Rogers, Carl R. *Freedom to Learn.* Columbus: Charles E. Merrill Publishing Company, 1969.

Shoben, Edward Joseph. "The Counselor's Theory as Personal Trait," *The Personnel and Guidance Journal,* 40:7, March, 1962.

Toynbee, Arnold J. "Why and How I Work," *Saturday Review,* April 5, 1969.

7

A Humanistic View of Behavior

A churchgoer who participates only in the rituals of religion never really knows what he believes or why he believes it. His participation is generally social in nature, and the whole matter of belief becomes a mixture of mysticism, auctions, bean suppers, and sweet-smelling flowers. The practices of a religion become mere routine unless based upon a substantial rationale. *Something* has to serve as a foundation, otherwise the practice of religion becomes a hollow activity. Religion based upon superficialities cannot hope to sustain a membership for long, because people need more than artifacts and rituals to achieve an internal feeling of belief. They need principles to enable them to meet the fundamental issues of life.

A teacher who functions without a theory of personality or a basic philosophy regarding people has much in common with the churchgoer who lacks an underlying substance or belief for his religion. Both function at a superficial level, paying attention to the inconsequentials rather than being sensitive to the fundamental issues that influence their overt functioning. A teacher finds substance in a theory of personality that serves as the basis for his behavior as a teacher.

ROGERS' PROPOSITIONS

Rogers presents a perceptive theory of the functional nature of human beings in the form of propositions. These propositions are not hardened rules to explain the motivational totality of human actions and reactions. Their validity is proportional to the degree that one assimilates their meaning and observes their expression in others. In this section we present our interpretation of Rogers' propositions as they apply to youngsters functioning in school settings. The translation of these propositions should help the potential or practicing teacher to develop greater sensitivity to the internal motivational factors that affect the pupil's overt functioning.

Proposition 1.   *Every individual exists in a continually changing world of which he is the center.* (Rogers, 1951:483)

There is a tendency to categorize students. Anyone who has worked in schools realizes that words like "good," "bad," "indifferent," "lazy," "sullen," "cooperative," "sick," etc., tend to be used as adjectives to indicate the totality of an individual. Teachers must realize that no two individuals are ever alike and that the human personality is so complex that any labeling of an individual is never accurate. After all, a person is a combination of many experiences and may react to a given situation in a variety of ways. The uniqueness of the individual is such that he can be known, in any significant sense, only to himself. The factors influencing his behavior may or may not be part of his awareness, but if his essence is to be understood in any meaningful way, the individual himself is the best source of information, having been the center of that experiencing self since birth.

No amount of labeling by school people can accurately render the essence of an individual. Although labels are simple and convenient symbols of a totality, they in no way express what a person is. The complexity of individuals often defies accurate categorization. True, the student may at times appear to be "lazy" or "sullen," but he is not totally these things. He may appear "lazy" and "sullen" to an observer and in fact be pensive and reflective; or he may appear to be pensive and reflective when in fact he is lazy and sullen. The categorization of individuals varies with the observer. Observers may see different things out of their own needs, in spite of trying to be fully objective. We tend to read meanings into comments and events that conform to our general needs or the needs of the moment. Thus, the uncovering of the perceptual world of the student must come from the student, who has been, and is, the center of an experiencing being who has rejected or assimilated past experiences into his self-concept.

Proposition 2.   *The organism reacts to the field as it is experienced and perceived. This perceptual field is, for the individual, reality.* (Rogers, 1951:484)

There is a tendency to think that what school people conceive as being reality is, in fact, reality. When a pupil looks at a certain situation and perceives its reality differently from the teacher or the administrator, his perception is often disregarded as incorrect.

Reality is in the eyes of the beholder, and the perception of reality is often closely related to what one *wants to perceive.* If a pupil perceives that the school is intolerant of minority opinions, no defensive statements by the school are going to change the pupil's belief. If a student perceives his mother as a possessive person who won't allow him to become an adult, no verbal disclaimers on her part will alter the student's perception.

Reality may be perceived in distinctly different ways by different people in the same situation. For instance, when student A describes the school principal, Mr. Smith, as a saint, and student B describes the same Mr. Smith as a sinner, what is Mr. Smith in reality? Is the reality of Mr. Smith achieved by adding up the positive reactions and weighing them against the negative reactions? Will the majority opinion determine Mr. Smith's reality? Let's say that we can fully and completely know the essence of Mr. Smith, and we find him to be a most saintly individual. Could we then present this reality to a student who is antagonistic toward Mr. Smith and expect him to assimilate this newer perception? Or will the student's perception significantly change only after he has had the opportunity to discover for himself that his perception was ill-founded? In general, the student's perception will change only after he has had the opportunity to examine his perceptions and decide that they need altering. Throughout all of this, Mr. Smith may indeed be a good, wholesome individual who was perceived as evil because of the student's need to see reality in a self-preserving fashion.

Proposition 3.   *The organism reacts as an organized whole to this phenomenal field.* (Rogers, 1951:486)

Teachers generally tend to look upon student's concerns as separate unrelated problems. If a student is doing poor work in school, is constantly in conflict with his peers, and is fighting with his father about a vocational decision, teachers tend to see these problems as three separate behaviors with independent solutions. They may proceed to recommend tutoring in order to improve the school work, change the student's classes so that he will not be in contact with antagonistic peers, and proceed to have a conference with both father and son to resolve their differences. However, people respond and react as total organisms rather than as segmented, atomistic beings. The teacher who works with student problems as if they are isolated from each other, will perhaps experience some degree of success. But this type of assistance affects only a small, overt part of a person's functioning. Later on, the same student may bring the teacher similar kinds of problems, only within a different context. The poor school work may appear improved based on the student's marks, but he may have developed the problem of uncertainty in classroom recitations. Instead of being in conflict with the new learning group, he is suspicious of their attempts to be friendly, and instead of being in conflict with his father about vocational choice, he now has to choose between Latin and French as an elective language.

Teaching must offer more than patchwork attempts to render assistance. Teachers need to be sensitive to the fact that improvement in one aspect of a student's functioning may have no great impact upon the total functioning of that individual. If a student is allowed to experience a learning relationship in which the existential totality of the individual can react and respond, growth will occur in many aspects of the student's life as he develops in a holistic manner. Instead of attempting to solve seemingly isolated problems, the teacher must create a learning atmosphere in which the student can be involved in the process of developing his total self. As the student learns to function better as a person and is able to perceive his functioning with more accuracy, superficial problems will be alleviated. The person who is self-actualized and who is more sensitive to why he functions as he does, will not only be able to handle current problems better, but, because of a global improvement of his functioning, he will be able to handle future problems in a more independent and knowledgeable manner.

Proposition 4.   *The organism has one basic tendency and striving — to actualize, maintain, enhance the experiencing organism.* (Rogers, 1951:487)

When a student reacts against authority in the school or at home, we see this proposition in action. Because the adult world is judgmental of the student's behavior and expressiveness, he proceeds to behave in ways designed to preserve the self. In order to maintain and enhance his self-structure, the young person may present a hard shell that seems to say to the adult world, "I dare you to try to change what I am. Young people are good and honorable and must defend themselves against the dominating forces of the adult world."

When a student is forced into a relationship with a teacher or other adult, he will often be defensive and feel that he doesn't have anything to discuss. As far as he can see, the "adult world" has more problems than he does because it cannot accept him and his mode of behavior. Sometimes this defensiveness is well-founded. However, students may take such positions simply because they seek a natural enemy to militate against as part of establishing their independence. Adults who respond to the bait furnished by the youngster are usually overly critical or caustic. If adults did not furnish youngsters with an extreme attitude to react against, the youngsters would be less antagonistic toward the authority group.

The student strives to preserve himself and because of his nature as a goal-directed human being, he also responds to the positive internal force that moves him toward actualizing himself. There is a general striving within the individual to become a more positively functioning person, to become more mature, and to improve his totality as a person. It is this basic force that has resulted in the ongoing process of building a better civilization. Each generation builds upon the accomplishments of the previous one as we attempt to perfect our functioning.

A good example of this positive movement is the contrast between the freshman and senior groups on any campus. The freshmen are characterized by dependence, uncertainty, and defensiveness. The seniors are generally autonomous, goal-directed, and more open. As a person moves toward an actualization of self — improving upon and perfecting what he is — he responds and reacts to a basic force within that is as much a part of him as his external physical characteristics.

The teacher is faced with a choice as he contemplates humanity. He can look at others from a fatalistic framework and see little good in human nature and have no hope that life can be better because external forces cannot be overcome — he must become a victim of these forces in order to survive. Or, he can view others as basically positive beings; individuals who can be self-enhancing and goal-directed if they achieve the internal freedom to become involved in the process of movement toward greater good.

The teacher must come to grips with the question of the nature of humanity. If the teacher is optimistic and sees people as involved in the process of reaching toward a perfected nature, his teaching will be more optimistic and dynamic. If the teacher sees humanity as a victim of itself or the environment, his approach will be unproductive; his message is that no matter how much we want to change things, we are doomed by our inadequacies.

Proposition 5.　*Behavior is basically the goal-directed attempt of the organism to satisfy its needs as experienced, in the field as perceived.* (Rogers, 1951:491)

Our behavior is often a reaction, not to objective reality, but to our perception of reality. Our perceptions may have a focus that is dependent upon our needs. For example, Mr. Brown is a skilled and communicating mathematics teacher who, by all standards, is a good and honorable individual. Brown's pupil, Johnny, has difficulty relating to male authority figures because his father always tells him what to do, when to do it, and how to do it. Johnny needs to be more independent of his father's will. He becomes involved in the process of moving toward the goal of a more independent existence. Because of the emerging need for independence on Johnny's part, Brown's innocuous correction of a mathematical error elicits a negative reaction from Johnny. His *perception of reality* is a reaction to a need. That is, Johnny's need for independence causes him to overreact because he feels Brown deprived him of his independence by correcting the error in mathematics.

Another student with a more dominant need to be dependent upon a male adult authority figure, sometimes makes mathematical errors on purpose, in order to bring himself into a closer relationship with Brown. This student perceives Brown not as someone who interferes with his independence but as someone whom he can be dependent upon, and he is interested in fostering that dependency relationship. Both pupils are looking at the same Mr. Brown, but each perceives him differently because of the underlying needs that influence their perceptions.

If we did not possess different needs, all reality would be objectively perceived in the same manner. But each of us functions according to his or her own needs, and, because our needs influence our perceptions, a Utopia School could be constructed on a grassy knoll, staffed with the best-qualified teachers, and furnished with the best of equipment, and still the youngster with a need to mistrust the motives of adults would see the school as an attempt to buy his loyalty and affection.

The teacher must be sensitive to the extent to which need-fulfillment influences behavior. If the teacher ignores this issue, he will become involved in the superficiality of looking at each student's behavior and judging whether it is "good" or "bad." In the learning relationship, the teacher must become involved in penetrating the students' needs and motives, which compel them to react as they do. When the teacher becomes sensitive to these needs he can help the student develop an awareness of their existence and their effect upon his functioning. This is part of professional teaching, and it is how the teacher assists the student to become more sensitive not only to how he *has* functioned but to how he *should* function in the future.

Proposition 6.   *Emotion accompanies and in general facilitates such goal-directed behavior, the kind of emotion being related to the seeking versus the consummatory aspects of the behavior, and the intensity of the emotion being related to the perceived significance of the behavior for the maintenance and enhancement of the organism.* (Rogers, 1951:492-493)

The extent to which our emotions are aroused and influence our behavior is proportional to the degree to which the self is involved. The self can be threatened or enhanced in proportion to the emotion one pours into a reaction. When the self is threatened and the threat is accompanied by a high degree of emotionality, the organism reacts negatively in a verbal or physical manner. Emotionality can also work to help an individual become more positive. That is, when a student perceives his behavior with accuracy and feels emotionally that he must change, a behavioral change of consequence occurs.

Youngsters have always been told to change their behavior, to become more constructive individuals. Such advice is usually blocked out because the youngster does not perceive the reality of his behavior as being wrong. Behavior is regarded as wrong by the student only when *he* perceives it as being wrong, and behavior changes only when the student becomes emotionally involved in desiring change. An attitudinal shift occurs when the student feels that he wants to change. Certainly, there are many examples of how youngsters have been coerced into proper behavior through fear of reprisals. Such coercion will result in an apparent orderliness designed to preserve the security of the person in charge, rather than to offer the student anything intrinsically valuable. Behavior becomes truly more positive when the individual is liberated by an atmosphere in which he can be emotionally involved in the process of change.

The student who is repeatedly told what he should do and who persistently proceeds to do just the opposite is not just insensitive to the needs that cause his behavior; he is also emotionally not committed to change. No amount of persuasion or coercion will result in a behavior change that is significant or has a long-term effect. When someone is internally motivated, emotionally and attitudinally drawn toward a behavior change, that change will occur. The teacher, then, must try to be sensitive to the student's emotions and feelings. He should respond to and internalize the student's negative feelings so that the student can perceive them and their consequences within the environment, and he should respond to any movement toward positive feelings so that the student can fully perceive the effect of his emerging positiveness upon the environment.

Proposition 7. *The best vantage point for understanding behavior is from the internal frame of reference of the individual himself.* (Rogers, 1951:494)

Teachers often must work with students who have received positive or negative external evaluations of their behavior, which they have taken for granted as being true. For example, if the school judges Sam to be an intellectually marginal student and there is consensus regarding this, Sam *is,* according to the school, intellectually inferior. Sam may see himself as a reasonably bright individual headed for a technological career. It is the student's perception of himself — his internal frame of reference — that the teacher must deal with, not the external perception of the student's abilities. The student's own perception of self is, in fact, him. The external frames of reference may be valiant attempts to describe Sam's essence, but they cannot be accurate because they are not part of Sam's conscious awareness of himself. Another student, Ann, may have been externally evaluated as intellectually superior. This external frame of reference means nothing to her if she personally feels that she is "dumb" and incapable of any worthwhile academic accomplishment.

The teacher works with the student's internal frame of reference not only to better understand the student's functioning, but also to present to the student a picture of himself that he can comprehend. It is only when this accurate self-picture, derived from an internal frame of reference, is presented to the student that other aspects of himself are allowed into his awareness. That is, when the student is confronted with a self-picture he himself has structured, the picture has far more significance for him than any externally conceived pictures of what he is.

Proposition 8. *A portion of the total perceptual field gradually becomes differentiated as the self.* (Rogers, 1951:497)

Youngsters are certainly aware of the functioning self. The process of self-identification may be accelerated as they undergo the changes associated with physical maturation. The pupil becomes more aware of the development of self because he is suddenly placed in a developmental level halfway between childhood and adulthood. He is still close enough to childhood to remember the freedom it allowed, and he is close enough to adulthood to be apprehensive about the responsibilities that will soon be his. He is torn between the two, displaying on one day the immaturity of childhood and on another the beginnings of adult behavior. He becomes more sensitive to his existence; more aware of the "I" or "me" aspects of his existence. The curious stratification of childhood, in which the child sees himself in a blurred fashion, gives way to the focusing process of growing up, in which the self is more

94

clearly defined. The evolving self becomes more unique, more consciously known.

The teacher who sees students as huge masses generally functioning in the same manner, will perhaps not bring as much skill and refinement to his work as the teacher who is aware of the uniqueness of each member of a student body. The categorization of students makes things easier for the teacher who prefers a life compartmentalized into neat sections. Such a teacher approaches students in a preconceived way, rather than with an openness that would allow him to discover the uniqueness of each individual and the particular manner in which each functions. If a youngster is in the process of discovering the uniqueness of his identity, it is imperative for the teacher to recognize this uniqueness. Unless he assimilates the uniqueness that makes Helen, *Helen,* his teaching will not give her the feeling that he has been able to empathize with her uniqueness.

Proposition 9.   *As a result of interaction with the environment, and particularly as a result of evaluational interaction with others, the structure of self is formed — an organized, fluid, but consistent conceptual pattern of perceptions of characteristics and relationships of the "I" or "me," together with values attached to the concepts.* (Rogers, 1951:498)

Proposition 10.   *The values attached to experiences, and the values which are part of the self-structure, in some instances are values experienced directly by the organism, and in some instances are values introjected or taken from others, but perceived in distorted fashion, as if they had been experienced directly.* (Rogers, 1951:498)

The youngster forms a self-concept as a result of his interaction with various persons or elements within the environment. Interactions develop values, which are formed directly or vicariously and become part of the self-structure. The evaluational nature of the environment directly influences the development of self. This may be related to the ancient psychological argument about the relative merits of punishment and reward. Under what circumstances does the psychologically healthy individual develop and thrive? A person values himself, his existence, and his contributions when he is in contact with others who value him and aid him in his development by providing an atmosphere that enables him to form a self-structure which neither denies or distorts experience. As we have pointed out earlier, when an individual feels no need to protect himself, he can learn to develop his self and look at both the positive and negative elements of his reactions. The student who denies certain threatening experiences will always be threatened by similar experiences until the original experience is allowed into awareness and discussed.

Students react against the evaluative nature of school because evaluation is usually structured as a negative experience. That is, the student's self-structure assimilates the attitude that "school is bad because it's always judging me to be good or bad." The teacher needs to be sensitive to the valuing process that occurs within school and to notice the effect of this process upon the students' self-structures. As students interact with the evaluative nature of the school environment, they may experience this evaluation directly, or they may experience it as an attitude that characterizes the school. In other words, although a student may not have been negatively evaluated, he may still live with the apprehension that some day this will occur.

These two propositions (9 and 10) indicate that the self is formed and assimilates values only through an interactive relationship with the environment. The teacher who atttempts to provide a facilitating learning relationship must provide the student with a non-evaluative relationship so that the student can freely involve and invest himself in the process of becoming.

Proposition 11. *As experiences occur in the life of the individual, they are either (a) symbolized, perceived, and organized into some relationship to the self, (b) ignored because there is no perceived relationship to the self-structure, (c) denied*

> *symbolization or given a distorted symbolization*
> *because the experience is inconsistent with the*
> *structure of the self.* (Rogers, 1951:503)

The youngsters, because of their sometimes defensive nature, seldom admit into their self-structures the negative reactions of adults. They often ignore such experiences because the adult who puts forth a negative evaluation of the youngster is presenting material that the youngster perceives as being totally unrelated to the self. The young person who is "lectured at" usually does not hear what is being said because he is unwilling to admit into his self-structure the "message" the adult is attempting to deliver. In order for the youngster to admit certain awareness into his self-structure, he must be involved in a relationship in which he can look at himself without the need to ignore the negative aspects of that self.

Youngsters may also ignore or give distorted symbolization to an experience because it is inconsistent with their self-structure. For example, the teacher who attempts to manage Sue's desire to attract boyfriends may be perceived by Sue as "picking on me." The student who flunks a test because he did not crack a book may distort the experience and say that, "I flunked because the teacher hates me." Such distortions are more common among students who have the feeling that the adult world is generally antagonistic. Because of this basic feeling, they may have a tendency to give distorted or self-enhancing symbolization to an experience that is, in fact, neutral. The teacher who tries to reflect distorted symbolizations to the student in an effort to assist him in seeing them for what they are, may find the effort rejected. The distortions are closely related to the need-structure of the individual, and usually, the result is that the student solidifies the distortion because of the threat represented by the teacher's attempt to point out "what really happened."

Proposition 12.   *Most of the ways of behaving which are adopted by the organism are those which are consistent with the concept of self.* (Rogers, 1951:507)

Assisting the student to develop a more positive self-concept will result in the student's movement toward more positive behavior.

In many schools, negative pupil behavior is simply punished, and the pupil's self-concept remains constant, the cause for norm-violating behavior. The pupil whom the environment feels is "bad," and who conceives of himself as "bad," has only one resource for his behavior — to *be* "bad." When the school disciplines, it is usually a punitive action, rather than a rehabilitative one. The school wants to make it known that the offender cannot flout authority or "get away with anything." The curious nature of punishment is that it provides the punisher with a catharsis totally unrelated to the ultimate goal of punishment — the rehabilitation of the offender.

Teachers who see themselves as working with "nice" youngsters, shun the school's behavior problems as if they were someone else's business (parent or administrator) rather than part of their responsibility. Certainly educators are aware of the professional rationale that supports the idea that a person cannot be both a punitive and rehabilitative agent. But some teachers use flimsy reasoning in order to avoid working with school behavior problems. Teachers who insist that they work only with normal individuals usually define normalcy as including those youngsters who intend to enter college. Some teachers would further restrict normalcy to include only those people who are like themselves! If behavior cannot change unless the self-concept is affected, the teacher must be committed to working with youngsters who are behavior problems, just as he is committed to working with the other youngsters who are in the school.

Some teachers may try to deal with the student's behavior in an attempt to change the student. If a student is cheating on exams, they might indicate the consequences of such behavior in an attempt to eliminate the cheating. The humanistic teacher might try to furnish the student with a non-threatening atmosphere in which he can safely discuss the internal motivations for his cheating. The student's behavior will change only after his self rejects cheating and embraces an attitude that values an internal concept of honesty. When honesty becomes part of the student's self-structure, honesty will become a part of his behavior pattern.

Proposition 13.   *Behavior may, in some instances, be brought about by organic experiences and needs which have not been symbolized. Such behavior may be inconsistent with the structure of the self, but in such instances the behavior is not "owned" by the individual.* (Rogers, 1951:509)

Public reaction to the effectiveness of teaching runs the gamut. Some people consider education useless, and others think that learning should turn people into superbly functioning individuals who are free from the tribulations of being human. They expect educated persons to function with highly positive consistency. Like anyone else, the educated person will have his moments of distress, weakness, and uncertainty. He may be better equipped to cope with the vicissitudes of life because of a more positive self-structure, but not all his behavior will be neat, even, or well-intended, no matter how educated he is. We are all subject to the frailties of being human, and we sometimes have trouble managing the behavior that comes from our complex natures. If we picture behavior as a line with peaks and valleys, after an effective learning experience the line would still be wavy but would have fewer peaks and valleys, and there would be a shorter distance between them. Behavior is never a consistently straight line. If it were, we would not be human. We try to bring some "straightness" to our behavioral lines in an attempt to reach for a better existence; an existence in which we try to transcend ourselves and reach for a perfection that seems always to be just beyond our grasp.

Proposition 14. *Psychological maladjustment exists when the organism denies to awareness significant sensory and visceral experiences, which consequently are not symbolized and organized into the gestalt of the self-structure. When this situation exists, there is a basic or potential psychological tension.* (Rogers, 1951:510)

Youngsters are confronted with experiences that are not allowed admission into the self-structure because of their threatening nature. The student who feels he is good and honorable will reject frames of reference that view him as bad and untrustworthy. When the external frame of reference is clearly rejected by the student, the self-structure remains intact. If an external frame of reference has some quality of truth, or if it is closer to the interior self than to the exterior self, the student may try to assimilate the ideas and this is when he may seek assistance. As the new ideas gnaw away at an apparently well-conceived and well-structured self, the student needs an opportunity to sift and weigh the relevancy of the opinions before he can reject or assimilate them. Tension occurs when the adolescent is apart from his reinforcing group or when he begins to admit into awareness the possibility that these external opinions about him may be accurate. For instance, the adolescent gang member is able to remain oblivious to the opinions of the adult world because, within the gang, he finds reinforcement of his self-structure. It is when the student is willing to consider the outside opinions that he needs a personal relationship with the teacher to help him bring about a resolution between what he thinks of himself and what other people think of him.

The ease with which adolescents deny certain experiences awareness is part of the defensiveness of the adolescent frame of reference. When an adult is confronted with external evaluations that contradict his self-structure, he *may* admit some of them into awareness because he has less need to be defensive. Adolescents are unwilling to accept the critical nature of the adult world's frame of reference. They feel, "If adults are always going to criticize me and what I do, then I'll just boot it back by criticizing them in return." The defensiveness of adolescents shows when they insist on defending not only themselves, but also the entire adolescent society and its mores!

Because of the adolescent's rejection of the adult world's perceptions, an encounter with a peer may be more significant than any exchange with an adult. If Mary's behavior has been called extreme by adults, and she has denied this perception awareness, she might be willing to accept the thought if it comes from a peer friend within the context of a group experience. Mary can reject the perception or assimilate it into her self-concept, but the chances are that she will be less defensive with a peer than with an adult. She may at least be willing to hear out a peer, whereas a negative evaluation by an adult usually gets tuned out in the first ten seconds.

Proposition 15.   *Psychological adjustment exists when the concept of self is such that all the sensory and visceral experiences of the organism are, or may be, assimilated on a symbolic level into a consistent relationship with the concept of self.* (Rogers, 1951:513)

The youngster who is generally defensive in his relationships with adults will probably display a similar attitude when beginning a relationship with a teacher. Experience has taught him that he cannot be himself in an evaluative adult world. If the youngster has always had to repress his feelings defensively, there is a buildup that keeps the youngster from ever really being himself. He is not freely expressive with adults because he has assimilated a reserved attitude that creates less likelihood of threat to the self-structure. The youngster is trapped inside himself, and as a result, he is less open when considering the self and its accompanying behavior. A person must be psychologically free in order to absorb a day's experiences, and to meditate on the experiences that have been denied entrance into the self.

The student involved in a freeing atmosphere with an empathic teacher is able to consider all experiences and their meaning to self. The student should be able to consider everything he has been or is experiencing, instead of having to be selective and consider only experiences that are self-protecting. When teachers suggest to students that only certain types of experiences should be allowed assimilation by the self, they condition them to deny awareness to threatening experiences. The repression of such experiences will lead to a partial awareness of self and will limit the degree of openness to self on the part of the student. The student's full assimilation of experiences is necessary if he is to symbolize adequately their relationship to the self.

In a relationship with a skilled teacher the youngster learns how to open himself up to feelings, attitudes, and reactions. He also becomes better able to absorb the totality of experiences outside the relationship. He is able to give meaning to experiences instead of denying their occurrence. He can discuss threatening relationships instead of repressing them and finding out later that repression and denial contribute to long-term malfunctions of the self.

Proposition 16.   *Any experience which is inconsistent with the organization of the self-structure may be perceived as a threat, and the more of these perceptions there are, the more rigidly the self-structure is organized to maintain itself.* (Rogers, 1951:515)

Teachers working with a student who has been classified as a behavior problem must be sensitive to the rigid, guarded responses of such a student. The student's self has been threatened so often that he has had to adopt a rigidly defensive attitude in order to maintain himself. Teachers involved in crisis situations with such students often have little success in their attempts at communication, especially if the student perceives the teacher as another threatening figure in a generally threatening world.

Many of the well-intended actions of school staff members tend to reinforce the defensiveness of difficult students. When the school attempts to coerce a problem student into accepting certain standards that are personally threatening and incongruent with the self, he is likely to rebel and become even more determined to continue his norm-violating behavior. The teacher must be non-threatening to the student. He must try to create a relationship in which the student feels that he is free to relax his defenses and discuss the aspects of his behavior that have not been accepted by the school. If the teacher poses a threat to a problem student, the student will only increase his rigidity.

In order for education to occur, there must be a framework of orderliness, but when, in the name of orderliness, the school insists on coercing students into "acceptable" channels of behavior, it must be willing to accept increasing student discontent with the total educational process. The more a school threatens its students, the more it moves away from the concept of a democratic existence in which the dignity of the individual is revered. The teacher who works in a school that insists on labeling large numbers of students as behavior problems is obligated to do more than just work with the youngsters. He should also be involved in a consultative role with school personnel in an effort to improve the school environment and to identify those aspects of the school experience that are detrimental to the psychological well-being of the students. Schools must become places in which the ideals of democratic living are fully expressed in the attitudes of staff members. A healthy school atmosphere reduces the threat to the individual student, thus reducing the degree of rigidity needed by students to maintain the self-structure.

Proposition 17. *Under certain conditions, involving primarily complete absence of any threat to the self-structure, experiences which are inconsistent with it may be perceived and examined, and the structure of self revised to assimilate and include such experiences.* (Rogers, 1951:517)

When a student and teacher are involved in a non-threatening relationship, the student is able to examine aspects of his behavior that are inconsistent with the self. In a nonthreatening relationship, the student classified as a behavior problem can begin to delve into actions and reactions that were previously not investigated because of their threat to the self. Instead of defending the self, he is able to investigate the degree to which he has contributed to his classification as a school behavior problem. He begins to recognize the behaviors that were self-protective rather than self-enhancing. He begins to realize, "I can keep blaming Mr. Jones for all the trouble I've gotten into, and I could do that forever . . . but it doesn't lead me anywhere. I'm beginning to see some of the things that *I* am doing . . . I mean, the things that *I* do to get me in trouble."

In a nonthreatening relationship the student becomes more sensitive to the self and the degree to which *he* is responsible for his behavior. The student typically enters a relationship with a teacher defensively because he sees the cause of his malfunctioning as totally

103

due to his environment. He feels that the environment is insensitive to his behavioral urges. Then, as he examines his behavior, he starts to develop a balanced view of the self and the environment. He does not indulge in self-mortification, but instead becomes increasingly aware of the transactional process that occurs between himself and his environment. He does not suddenly absolve Mr. Jones of all responsibility, in an antagonistic relationship. Instead he begins to examine the other-than-self side of the coin and becomes less egocentric and more responsive to the markings on that other side. He communicates deeply about experiences that previously were blocked from awareness because they posed a threat to the self.

Students are unwilling to investigate their behavior if the teacher places a value judgment upon the merits of that behavior. The student senses the threat of the teacher's judgmental reaction. The freer the student is from threat, the more he can investigate aspects of his behaving self that he was previously unwilling to admit to awareness. He defrosts hardened emotions because the teacher creates a nonjudgmental relationship. Students must have the right to *be* if they are ever to become involved in the process of *becoming*.

Proposition 18. *When the individual perceives and accepts into one consistent and integrated system all his sensory and visceral experiences, then he is necessarily more understanding of others and is more understanding of others as separate individuals.* (Rogers, 1951:520)

Acceptance of others begins with acceptance of self. The student who becomes involved in absorbing experiences into himself develops a functional autonomy, because self-awareness becomes linked to self-acceptance. But self-acceptance does not stop with the self; it extends beyond and embraces others. As one of our students put it, "Okay, I'm me and he's himself. Maybe he doesn't act the way I think he should, but that's him. We're different . . . he's got a right to be himself and I've got a right to be me."

The well-functioning self seeks to be in communication with others; it desires to mend rather than to remain tattered. The student who achieves self-acceptance — who has allowed into awareness both the positive and negative aspects of his functioning and has integrated them within the self — becomes involved with life. The student who was once a problem reaches out to people who previously bore the brunt of his malfunctioning, and communicates with people from whom he previously sought isolation. He becomes more confident of his abilty to communicate, and no longer needs to build a defensive wall around himself. His outgoing tendencies take on ease and clarity because he no longer feels the need to respond to others suspiciously. He senses an emerging trust in others because he senses a similar emergence within himself.

The extension of self-acceptance to an other-than-self acceptance appears to be a natural tendency of the human organism. At the beginning of a relationship with a teacher, the typical student sees little beyond himself and usually engages in diatribes against others in his milieu. As he begins to see the extent to which the self has contributed to his behavior, he becomes more sensitive to others — how *they* feel, how *they* respond. They are accepted as separate individuals, and their reactions to the student will change because the student has changed. The teacher often hears reports from students that relationships that were previously filled with conflict have become more positive because of the accepting attitude of the student. The student is able to affect his own functioning, and because of his accepting attitude toward others, a reciprocal attitude emerges from them. Behavior is no longer seen as determined by the environment; the student has developed an awareness that his own existential functioning can have an impact upon his environment and the persons in it.

Proposition 19.   *As the individual perceives and accepts into his self-structure more of his organic experiences, he finds that he is replacing his present value system — based so largely upon introjections which have been distortedly symbolized — with a continuing organismic valuing process.* (Rogers, 1951:522)

Schools are involved in introjecting values, the rationale being that if students are exposed to cultural values they will assimilate these values as their own. Certainly, schools are obligated to present values, but the values that have personal and visceral meaning are the ones a person discovers in the process of exploring his own self. The values of the adult world are meaningless to the young person. They may be generally accepted values for the adult, but they are not internalized by the pupil because they do not emerge from within. Instead, they are imposed by a frame of reference exterior to the pupil's self.

School staff members may value truth, honesty, and justice, but these concepts are mere terms unless the student has felt their visceral existence within himself. The emergence of personalized values among students is often discouraged because some adults fear that the emergence of individualized values among students would lead to anarchy. However, people tend to move toward values designed to perfect self and enhance others rather than toward values that are destructive to the self and to society. Human beings desire to enhance their existence — they move toward a greater good which perfects their existence within a societal context:

> Since all individuals have basically the same needs, including the need for acceptance by others, it appears that when each individual formulates his own values, in terms of his own direct experience, it is not anarchy which results, but a high degree of commonality and a genuinely socialized system of values. (Rogers, 1951:524)

The values that deeply affect behavior are the ones the student has perceived and assimilated into the self-structure. Externally imposed values have little meaning to the individual. The teacher who suggests appropriate behavioral values to students may be trying to avoid the guilt of not being a perpetuator of the school's values. But if he investigates how personally significant values emerge in individuals, he will discover that they emerge from within rather than from without.

Values that emerge from within do affect functional behavior. A student who values peer acceptance will behave in ways designed to gain that peer acceptance, although the behavior may not be in harmony with school standards. When he becomes involved in processing his own values within the context of a personal relationship with a teacher, he moves toward values that are more synchronized with the overall societal context in which he functions. That is, values become restructured; they come into a clear focus because of the individual's movement toward a more enhancing balance between himself and the environment.

Introjected values have only a temporary functional relevance. Students who are told not to cheat on exams will not move toward personal honesty unless they have viscerally come to grips with the question of honesty and have internalized a need to be honest. It is when the value of honesty emerges from within that it finds expression in the functional behavior of the student.

MOTIVATION AND ADJUSTMENT

The ideas of motivation and adjustment are the conceptual hinges on which the practice of teaching swings. The goals of teaching and the teaching-learning relationship itself are deeply affected by the teacher's operational theories of motivation and adjustment. Because these theories derive from one's view of personality and philosophy of teaching, it is important that they be examined in the light of Rogers' theory of personality and behavior.

A Theory of Motivation

In many respects, the core problem for the individual student, the teacher, the school is one of motivation. Much educational practice is based on the idea that motivation is a matter of student response to an external stimulus. Motivation is seen as a process of structuring external events to assist students in arriving at prior and "proper" ends; i.e., molding the student in "the way he should go." Behavior is a function of the forces exerted upon the individual. Reward, punishment, support, encouragement, and other reinforcements are called into play as a means of establishing stimuli external to the student that will elicit the correct response. The student is viewed as an organism to be made into something.

According to this approach, students cannot be trusted to decide what is good for themselves; someone else (the curriculum maker) must decide for them. Other people (teachers and administrators) must determine what force should be exerted to keep students moving through this "good experience." If some students develop ideas of their own about what is good and create problems, then another person (the school counselor) tries to help them adjust to the "good experiences" of the school. If the counselor is successful in providing effective reinforcements, the student's problem appears to be solved and he is ready to take full advantage of the curriculum (the "good experience").

Rogers (1951), Combs and Snygg (1959), Kelley (1951), Maslow (1954), and Leckey (1945), have pointed out that people are always motivated. They may not always be motivated to do what others would like them to do, but it can never truly be said that they are unmotivated. The general direction of motivation is towards health and growth. Our built-in thrust or will to health provides a need to become fully functioning or self-actualizing. There is a basic need to grow that does not have to be imposed by any external agent; it already exists — the internal response to self-generated stimuli. The natural drive of motivation can be observed in preschoolers and primary-grade children. They have a spontaneous urge to discover, to explore, to question, to find out about things. Their language is characterized by expressions like "let me try it," or "let me taste." The world surrounding them is their subject matter, and they learn about it in their own free and enthusiastic way. They are aware of their limited knowledge and experience and are hungry to taste the unknown. But, as children move toward adolescence, adults tend to assume more and more responsibility for determining what is to be learned, how it will be learned, and why it will be learned. Increasing emphasis is placed on "facts," "reality," "cognitive experiences," and "preparation for the life ahead," and less attention is given to what the children think, feel, and believe. The affective life of the child, which is an essential part of his self-hood, is relegated to a secondary position in deference to the rational cognitive elements of life. Spontaneity is discouraged, and sometimes children become afraid to be themselves. They cannot trust themselves, and they gradually learn to build their lives on the expectations of others; they lose their individuality and essences as persons.

108

Because of having been told so often "what to do," "when to do it," "where to do it," "how to do it," and "why to do it," the student relies less and less on his internal capacity for growth. Relationships with peers; evaluations from parents and other adults; and experiences in the community, society, and the classroom many times limit the opportunities for growth or feed the self-concept with images of inadequacy, failure, and incompetence. The will to health is blocked, and growth is arrested.

People around an individual form the climate and the soil in which the self grows. If the soil is fertile and the climate is wholesome, there is vigorous and healthy growth. If the climate is unwholesome and unkind, growth is stunted or blocked, and perceptual malnutrition occurs. The pupil nurtured in an unhealthy climate is compelled to build defenses, which also close out the food of healthy growth and thwart the inner self from emerging. Learning proceeds in the direction of self-protection rather than self-growth. The child who has failed, or has found himself condemned for his mistakes, will find it easier to take the punishment for not trying than to be ridiculed for being wrong. It is easier to pretend not to care than it is to let others know they have scored a hit. Non-learning or underachieving becomes a way of displacing hostility and striking back at parents and others who have been insensitive or rejecting.

Resistance to doing assigned work — non-learning, poor study habits, "inability" to follow directions, "inability" to concentrate — is a sign of perceptual malnutrition. This does not mean the student is unmotivated. He still has the potential for growth; the capacity to select what is good for the self. The natural thrust toward self-fulfillment — the will to health — is merely lying dormant. Through facilitative teaching the young person can discover and free this inner tendency. Facilitative teaching helps the individual to peel off the defensive layers so that the imprisoned self may again become expressive and exert its thrust toward adequacy.

A student moves toward more adequate functioning only when his current behavior is examined and found to be restrictive or inadequate. He cannot reject a certain mode of behavior until it has been allowed to exist and be perceived as being unfulfilling to the self. He is motivated to change because of the emergence of an inner force that enables him to reject an inadequate self in favor of an existence that enhances the self.

The self must be accepted as it presently exists in order to be freed for growth. Acceptance of the student means an acceptance of his values and standards as an integral part of him. The teacher does not have to accept the student's values and standards for himself, but he must be willing to let the student hold his own values. An individual is only free to change his values when he is free to hold them. When he feels his values are not condemned, judged, or labeled as "bad," he can then allow them to be explored by himself and by others. Change emerges from such an exploration and new values are developed, based upon new ways of perceiving. It is only in this free atmosphere that perceptions and behavior patterns change.

The freedom to have ideas, values, and beliefs — the permission to be oneself — exists in a learning climate marked by a deep respect for the individuality and uniqueness of the student. The discovery of self is a deeply personal matter. In the final analysis, each individual must discover his own unique being in his own way. An atmosphere where uniqueness is fostered and difference is valued makes possible the full discovery of self as an individual of dignity and worth. An accepting atmosphere provides protection from negative threatening experiences like attempts to change the behavior of the so-called "unmotivated." When we attempt to change the "unmotivated" pupil, what we are in effect doing is rejecting him. We are saying to him, "I will accept you, but I'll accept you with some reservation, on some conditions, that is, I cannot accept you as you are; you must change!" In the zeal to motivate students through the use of external stimuli, there is a very real danger that we communicate to the student that he is never acceptable as he is. If, for some reason, the individual has defined himself as a poor student, or sees himself as academically inadequate, the idea that someone wants to change him will be highly threatening and will reinforce his desire to maintain an unmotivated external posture.

The natural inner motivation can be uncovered in the "unmotivated" student through a teacher-learner relationship that encourages self-revelation rather than self-defense. The student learns that it is "all right to be me; my ideas and feelings can be looked at." Personal feelings, attitudes, ideas, doubts, fears, and anxieties may be openly brought to light and examined as the student begins to trust in his self. By giving the individual the feeling that he can try his wings and fail without fear of embarrassment or ridicule, the teacher creates an atmosphere in which the self can be safely ventured and explored.

The teacher who is professionally aware accepts differences in his students because he knows that when differences are not accepted, individuals cannot be. He promotes the existential, ongoing character of human growth by creating an atmosphere that gives the student the feeling that his worth and his contribution are held in high regard. The student feels that there is something he can contribute — his meanings, his feelings, and his ideas have value and significance. He will respond to the awareness that he can be more than he is because of an internally emerging stimulus. This is the core of motivation and the substance of more adequate student functioning.

Students will not move toward the positive because the teacher was victorious in a struggle of values. They move toward more adequate behavior because their attitudinal structure was internally challenged. They were allowed the right to be, so that they could involve themselves in the process of becoming. They are able to take a long, hard look at themselves, and reject values which inhibit their functioning. When allowed to be, students move toward values that are more personally satisfying and that enable them to function and behave in a more positive way.

The Concept of Adjustment

Teaching should be characterized by a deep respect for the idiosyncratic potential of each individual. Its focus should be enabling the student to free himself from environmental and emotional inhibitors that prevent him from learning and fully functioning. Adjustment is a word used frequently by psychologists, teachers, and administrators to describe the "harmonious interaction of the individual with his environment." Sometimes students are described as "maladjusted," "poorly adjusted," "not adjusting," etc. Basically these descriptions mean that the student is deviating from some behavioral norm. But is the student who deviates from average behavior, who does not conform, who is different, psychologically unhealthy?

Teachers are often the mediators of conflicts between teacher and student, student and curriculum, student and society, or student and parents. In mediating such conflicts, there is a tendency to stress the need of the student to adjust to school, teacher, society, or parents. The underlying assumption is that they "know what is best," "are always right," or "have the necessary answers." This implies that the student does not know what is best for himself; that he cannot be trusted to make mistakes. The individual is viewed as plastic material to be shaped and molded to fit the adult's concept of the world. If he questions the values of his learning experiences, tests his environment, or "rocks the boat" and refuses to fall neatly into line, he is often perceived as poorly adjusted. The student who trusts himself, who lives his own life according to his own values, is too often seen as "'unrealistic," "a troublemaker," someone who needs help. It is an old story. Examining the lives of four hundred eminent people, the Goertzels found that three out of five had experienced serious school problems. "In order of importance, their dissatisfactions were: with the curriculum; with dull, irrational, or cruel teachers; with other students who bullied, ignored, or bored them; and with school failure. In general it is the totality of the school situation with which they were concerned, and they seldom have one clear-cut isolated complaint" (1962:241).

As Maslow (1962) points out, the concept of adjustment comes into question when we ask, "what kind of culture and subculture is the 'well-adjusted' person well adjusted to?" A society, a school, a teacher, or a parent can be growth-inhibiting rather than growth-fostering. Certainly Goodman does not feel that our modern society is growth-fostering:

> Growth, like any ongoing function requires adequate objects in the environment to meet the needs and capacities of the growing child, boy, youth, and young man until he can better choose and make his own environment. It is not a "psychological" question of poor influences and bad attitudes, but an

objective question of real opportunities for worthwhile experience. It makes no difference whether the growth is normal or distorted, only real objects will finish the experience . . . It is here that the theory of belonging and socializing breaks down miserably. For it can be shown — I intend to show — that with all the harmonious belonging and all the tidying up of background conditions that you please, our abundant society is at present simply deficient in many of the most elementary objective opportunities and worthwhile goals that could make growing up possible . . . It is lacking in honest public speech, and people are not taken seriously. It is lacking in the opportunity to be useful. It thwarts aptitude and creates stupidity. It corrupts ingenuous patriotism. It corrupts the fine arts. It shackles science. It dampens animal ardor. It discourages the religious convictions of Justification and Vocation and it dims the sense that there is a Creator. It has no Honor. It has not Community (1960:12).

Although a number of educators would disagree with Goodman's indictment of society, they would perhaps agree that the school, the chief educational tool of society, is not always growth-fostering. If the school does not always facilitate growth, it is logical to assume that there may be many situations in which the "poorly adjusted pupil" is not poorly adjusted at all, but is rather dissenting and rebelling because there is a lack of meaning and value in the education he experiences. It is inevitable that conflicts between individual pupils and the school will develop. But how should the teacher handle the conflict? Certainly not in the way Arbuckle describes:

There is the reality of the group and the reality of the individual. The simple but questionable way in which many people have solved this questionable dilemma is to conclude that reality must be whatever the majority says it is; according to this view, the more the individual moves away from the concept of the group, the more odd or queer or the crazier he is (1965:302).

If teachers truly believe in human uniqueness and the idiosyncratic potential of individuals, it follows that they must value difference in human behavior. Personality as a norm cannot be conceived, and it would seem an essential part of the teaching ethic to value divergence in personality development and individual behavior.

REFERENCES

Arbuckle, Dugald S. *Counseling: Philosophy, Theory and Practice.* Boston: Allyn and Bacon, 1965.

Combs, A. W. and Snygg, D. *Individual Behavior: A Perceptual Approach to Behavior* (Rev. Ed.). New York: Harper, 1959.

Goertzels, Victor and Goertzels, Mildred G. *Cradles of Eminence.* New York: Little Brown, 1962.

Goodman, Paul. *Growing Up Absurd.* New York: Random House, 1960.

Kelley, E. C. *The Workshop Way of Learning.* New York: Harper, 1951.

Leckey, Prescott. *Self Consistency: A Theory of Personality.* New York: Island Press, 1945.

Maslow, A. H. *Motivation and Personality.* New York: Harper, 1954.

_____. in *Perceiving, Behaving, and Becoming.* Washington: Association for Supervision and Curriculum Development, 1962.

Rogers, Carl R. *Client-Centered Therapy.* Boston: Houghton Mifflin, 1951.

8

Principles and Conditions of Learner-Centered Teaching

This chapter discusses humanistic principles and conditions of learning that we believe can be translated into an educational process to enable people to expand the self in a variety of situations and circumstances. These statements refer to learning as it might occur in schools, churches, homes, business, or in any sphere of living. They refer to learning that incorporates and integrates humanistic theories of personality, motivation, and adjustment.

PRINCIPLES OF LEARNING

Principle 1. *Learning is the process of changing behavior in positive directions.*

By behavior we mean attitudes, ideas, values, skills, and interests. Positive directions are directions that enhance and expand

---

Adapted with permission from Gerald J. Pine, "Existential Teaching and Learning," *Education,* Vol. 95, No. 1, 1974, 18-24.

the self, other persons, and the community. The implicit goal of all learning is to enable individuals, groups of people, and communities to become more fully functioning, psychologically expanded, effective, and actualizing.

Principle 2. *Learning is an experience that occurs inside the learner and is activated by the learner.*

The process of learning is primarily controlled by the learner and not by the teacher (group leader). Changes in perception and behavior are products of human meaning and perceiving and not the result of any forces exerted upon the individual. Learning is not only a function of what a teacher does for or says to a learner; it is also something that happens inside the unique world of the learner. It flourishes when teaching is seen as a facilitating process that assists people to explore and discover the personal meaning of events.

No one directly teaches anyone anything of significance (Rogers, 1961). If teaching is seen as a process of directly communicating an experience or a fragment of knowledge, little learning will occur as a result of such teaching. The learning that does take place is usually inconsequential. People learn what they want to learn, they see what they want to see, and they hear what they want to hear. Learning cannot be imposed; when we try to impose ideas on people, we only train them. In an atmosphere where people are free to explore, nourish, and develop ideas, we truly educate them. Very little learning takes place without the personal involvement of the learner. Unless what is being taught has meaning for the individual, he will shut it out. People forget most of what they are "taught;" they retain only what they use in their work or what is personally relevant.

Principle 3. *Learning is the discovery of the personal meaning and relevance of ideas.*

People more readily internalize and implement concepts that are relevant to their needs. Learning is a process requiring the exploration of ideas in relation to self and community so that people can determine what their needs are, what goals they would like to formulate, and what they would like to learn. What is relevant and meaningful is decided by the learner, and must be discovered by the learner.

This means the curriculum as a set of experiences emerges from the learners. Rather than fitting people to externally prescribed programs of experiences, we need to provide a growth-fostering climate in which people are free to construct their own curriculum. No one person or agency can validly decide what must be learned by students as individuals or as members of a group. A curriculum consists of experiences freely chosen by free and responsible agents. The learners' choices of experiences define the curriculum.

Principle 4. *Learning (behavioral change) is a consequence of experience.*

People become responsible when they experience responsibility; they become independent when they experience independence; they become able when they experience success; they begin to feel important when they are important to someone; and they feel liked when someone likes them. People do not change their behavior merely because someone tells them to do so. For effective learning, giving information is not enough. People become responsible and independent, not from having other people tell them that they should be responsible and independent, but from having experienced authentic responsibility and independence.

Principle 5. *Learning is a cooperative and collaborative process.*

Cooperation fosters learning — "two heads are better than one." People enjoy functioning independently but they also enjoy functioning interdependently. The interactive process appears to "scratch and nick" people's curiosity, potential, and creativity. Cooperative approaches are enabling; through them, people learn to define goals, to plan, to interact, and to try group arrangements in problem solving. Paradoxically, as people invest themselves in collaborative group approaches, they develop a firmer sense of their own identity. They begin to realize that they count, that they have something to give and things to learn. Problems identified and delineated through cooperative interaction appear to challenge people to produce creative solutions and to become more creative individuals.

Principle 6. *Learning is an evolutionary process.*

Behavioral change requires time and patience; learning is not a revolutionary process. When quick changes in behavior are demanded, we often attempt to impose learning. Such learning is not likely to be lasting or meaningful to the learner. Implicit in all the principles and conditions for learning is an evolutionary model of learning. Learning situations characterized by open communication, active personal involvement, freedom from threat, and trust in the self are evolutionary in nature.

Principle 7. *Learning is sometimes a painful process.*

Behavioral change often calls for giving up the old comfortable ways of believing, thinking, and valuing. It is not easy to discard familiar ways of doing things and to incorporate new behavior. Sometimes it is downright uncomfortable to share one's self openly, to put one's ideas under the microscope of a group, and to genuinely confront other people, but if growth is to occur, pain is often necessary. However, the pain of breaking away from old patterns is usually followed by appreciation and pleasure in the discovery of an evolving idea or a changing self.

Principle 8. *One of the richest resources for learning is the learner himself.*

In a day and age when so much emphasis is being placed upon instructional media, books, and speakers as resources for learning, we tend to overlook perhaps the richest resource of all — the learner himself. Each individual has an accumulation of experiences, ideas, feelings, and attitudes which comprise a rich vein of material for problem solving and learning. All too often this resource is barely tapped. Situations that enable people to become open to themselves, to draw upon their personal collection of data, and to share their data in cooperative interaction with others maximize learning and personal development.

Principle 9.   *The process of learning is emotional as well as intellectual.*

Learning is affected by the total state of the individual. People are feeling beings as well as thinking beings, and when their feelings and thoughts are in harmony, learning is maximized. To create the optimal conditions for learning to occur in a group, *people must come before purpose* (Gendlin, 1968). If the purpose of a group is to design and carry out some task, it cannot be achieved if group members are fighting and working against each other. If the purpose is to discuss current issues and problems in a given field with reason and honesty, it cannot be achieved if people are afraid to communicate openly. Barriers to communication exist in people and before we can conduct "official business" we need to work with the people problems that may exist in a group. Regardless of the people problems that exist in a group, enough group intellectual capacity usually remains intact for group members to acquire information and skills. However, for maximum acquisition and internalization of ideas, the people problems should be dealt with first.

Principle 10.   *Learning fuses work and play.*

Joy in accomplishment is deeply rooted in human nature. Yet in learning values, one of the most confusing areas centers on the perceptions people have of work in the classroom. Several studies indicate that well-integrated, emotionally healthy people see little difference between work and play. For them, there is no dichotomy between the two. Likewise, young children are often so eager for accomplishment that it is impossible for them to draw a line between work and play. It is important to note that their work is usually of their own choosing; it has not been forced upon them.

We certainly stress the importance of work, but there is some question as to whether we as parents and teachers truly value work.

We often perceive it as a necessary evil. How familiar is the suggestion, "Hurry and finish your work so you can go out and play"? If work and play are repeatedly dichotomized in statements by teachers, a child will quickly come to feel that there is something negative about the word "work."

We can help people learn that play and work are on the same continuum by providing an atmosphere in which their learning evolves in accordance with their needs, capacities, and interests. Developing a learning climate that encourages the full use of each individual's unique abilities, makes work more meaningful. We can heighten the awareness of the pleasures of work by fostering cooperative interaction rather than competition in the classroom.

Many people believe that work is fatiguing, and play is refreshing. The fact is, however, that what is fatiguing or refreshing is more related to the attitude toward the task than to the actual energy expended on accomplishing the task. Learning that accentuates the discovery of the personal meaning and relevance of ideas and experiences may be strenuous at times, but it is enjoyable. It epitomizes the synthesis of work and play.

Principle 11. *Learning is a "religious" experience.*

Learning is an experience that expresses values. The data an individual chooses to internalize are a function of his values; what he chooses to exchange and share are reflections of what he deeply cares about. The questions he seeks to answer, the skills he wants to acquire, the values he weighs and ponders, and the ideas he develops are ultimately rooted in the deepest concerns inherent in his nature. "Who am I?" "What is my relationship to the world in which I live?" — these are "religious" questions that lie at the base of all human learning. Learning that deals explicitly and openly with these questions represents the highest and most relevant form of learning.

Principle 12. *The learner is a free and responsible agent.*

Existentially speaking, the learner is unable to avoid his way through life. He is a free agent; absolutely free to establish goals for himself. The setting of goals is the beginning point in learning and in creating values. The learner is also a responsible agent, personally accountable for his free choices as revealed in how he conducts his life (Morris, 1966). In living, the learner chooses his essence. He exists first and then defines himself through the choices he makes plus the actions he takes. Thought without action is meaningless. The learner *is* what he does.

At every moment we are free. We are free of external forces, and we are free of ourselves — of what we have been. According to existential thought, an individual's past life is history, it no longer exists *now*, in the present. A learner is influenced by external agents or by his past life only when he chooses to be influenced by these forces.

Accompanying our freedom is the awesome burden of responsibility. Each learner is responsible for what he is. He cannot give away his freedom and responsibility to the state, to his parents, to his teachers, to his weaknesses, to his past, or to environmental conditions. In choosing and acting he chooses and acts for all humanity.

Principle 13.   *The processes of problem solving and learning are highly unique and individual.*

Each person has his own unique style of learning and solving problems. Personal styles of learning and problem solving may be highly effective, not so effective, or totally ineffective. People must be aware of their own methods of learning and coping before they can become more effective in problem solving and learning. Once they recognize their own style, they can look at other people's models and refine or modify their own styles to make them more effective.

Principle 14.   *Teaching is learning.*

Since learning is defined here as the process of changing behavior in positive directions, it follows that teaching is learning. The problem with this statement is the word "teaching." In the traditional sense, it refers to a didactic procedure built upon an external stimulus-internal response idea of motivation, which regards learners as organisms to be made into something. This view suggests that learners cannot be trusted to decide what is good and relevant for themselves. Someone else (the curriculum maker) must decide, and then some other people (teachers) must determine how to keep learners moving through this "good experience." People are seen as pupils or students, but they are not necessarily learners.

An enhancing learning situation is characterized by a curriculum defined by the learners' choices of good and relevant experiences, and by the presence of a teacher who is a learner. Learners are free and responsible persons who bring to any interaction an accumulation of experiences, ideas, feelings, attitudes, and perspectives. Learning occurs when free and responsible people are open to themselves, and can draw upon and share their personal collection of data in cooperative interaction. As a learner, the teacher shares his data when they are needed by others and in turn draws upon the data of others for his own growth and development. It is unfortunate that so many think teaching is just the direct dissemination of ideas, facts, and information in a structural relationship that permits little or no feedback from learners. This kind of "teaching" mainly attempts to alter behavior in order to accomplish an objective formulated by agents or agencies external to the learning group. That is training, not teaching.

CONDITIONS THAT FACILITATE LEARNING

Condition 1. *Learning is facilitated in an atmosphere which encourages people to be active.*

The learning process thrives when there is less domination by the teacher (group leader) and more faith that people can find alternatives and solutions which are satisfying to themselves. Listening to people and allowing them to use the teacher (group leader) and the group as a resource facilitates the active exploration of ideas and possible solutions to problems. People are not passive receptacles into which we can pour the "right" values, the "right" answers, and the "right" ways of thinking. They are active and creative beings who need the opportunity to determine their own goals, the issues to be discussed, and the means of evaluating themselves. They learn when they feel they are a part of what is going on, when they are personally involved. Learning is not poured into people; learning emerges from people.

Condition 2.   *Learning is facilitated in an atmosphere that facilitates the individual's discovery of the personal meaning of ideas.*

This means that the teacher (group leader), rather than directing or manipulating people, helps them discover a personal meaning in ideas and events. He creates a situation in which people are free to express their needs instead of having their needs dictated to them. Learning becomes an activity in which the needs of the individual and the group are considered in deciding what issues will be explored and what the subject matter will be.

No matter how permissive or unstructured a learning activity may be, there are always implicit goals in the activity itself — a group leader (teacher) is never goal-less. Learning occurs when the goals of the leader accommodate, facilitate, and encourage the individual's discovery of personal goals and meanings. The art of helping people change requires the development of goals that provide room for individuals to explore and internalize behavior satisfying and growth-producing to themselves.

Condition 3.   *Learning is facilitated in an atmosphere that emphasizes the uniquely personal and subjective nature of learning.*

In such a situation, each individual has the feeling that *his* ideas, *his* feelings, and *his* perspectives have value and significance. People need to realize that not everything to be learned is outside or external to themselves. They develop that awareness when they feel their contributions and their value as people are genuinely appreciated.

Condition 4.   *Learning is facilitated in an atmosphere in which difference is good and desirable.*

Situations that emphasize the "one right answer," the "magical solution," or the "one good way," to act or think or behave, limit exploration and inhibit discovery. If people are to look at themselves, at others, and at ideas openly and reasonably, they must have the opportunity to express their opinions, no matter how different they may be. This calls for an atmosphere in which different ideas can be *accepted* (but not necessarily agreed with). Differences in ideas must be accepted if differences in people are to be accepted.

Condition 5.   *Learning is facilitated in an atmosphere that consistently recognizes the right to make mistakes.*

If mistakes are not permitted, the freedom and willingness of people to make choices are severely limited. Growth and change are facilitated if errors are accepted as natural. The learning process involves meeting the challenge of new and different experiences, and therefore, necessarily involves making mistakes. If people are to learn, they need the opportunity to explore the unknown without being penalized or punished for mistakes. The teacher (group leader) who feels and acts on the need to always be right creates a limiting and threatening condition for learning.

Condition 6.   *Learning is facilitated in an atmosphere that tolerates ambiguity.*

In a rigid, defensive atmosphere, people feel they cannot take time to look at many solutions. They feel highly uncomfortable without answers, and they feel there is more concern for "right" answers than for good ones. The open, fearless exploration of solutions calls for time to explore alternatives without feeling pressure for immediate answers.

Condition 7.   *Learning is facilitated in an atmosphere in which evaluation is a cooperative process with emphasis on self-evaluation.*

If learning is a personal process, then people should have the opportunity to formulate criteria to measure their own progress. Criteria established by the teacher (group leader) are mostly artificial and may be irrelevant to some individuals. Usually behavioral change and growth are measured by the ability to regurgitate what has been presented by the teacher. Anyone can play the game of "giving the teacher what he wants," but a more viable and meaningful evaluation occurs when students are free to examine themselves and the roles they play with other people. Self-evaluation and peer evaluation enable them to really judge how much they have learned and grown. For example, audio or video recordings of behavior allow people to see themselves in the process of learning. The recordings provide tangible and concrete evidence of progress, and they provide a rich source of learning material for the group. New insights evolve as people see themselves as they really are. For learning to occur, the individual in the group needs to see himself accurately and realistically. This can be best accomplished through self and group evaluation.

Condition 8.   *Learning is facilitated in an atmosphere which encourages openness of self rather than concealment of self.*

Problem solving and learning require that personal feelings, attitudes, ideas, questions, and concerns be brought to light and examined. To the degree that an idea, thought, feeling, or attitude is held back and not openly expressed, the processes of learning and discovery are inhibited. People need to feel that they can try something and fail, if necessary, without being humiliated, embarrassed, or diminished in any way. Openness can only occur in an atmosphere free from psychological threat. People invest themselves fully in the collaborative and interactive process of learning when they know that no matter what they say, there will be no psychological punishment or penalties.

Condition 9.   *Learning is facilitated in an atmosphere in which people are encouraged to trust in themselves as well as in external sources.*

People become less dependent upon authority when they open up to the self and feel that *they* are a valuable resource for learning. It is important for people to realize that they have something to bring to the learning situation. Learning is *not* just the acquisition of facts and knowledge passed on by some external agent for use in the future. People learn when they begin to see themselves as the wellsprings of ideas and alternatives to problems. Learning improves when people begin to draw ideas from themselves and others rather than relying on the teacher (group leader) for everything.

Condition 10.   *Learning is facilitated in an atmosphere in which people feel they are respected.*

If high value is placed on the individuality of group members and on the relationships that exist within the group, people learn that someone cares for them. A genuine expression of caring from the teacher (leader) and a warm emotional climate generate an atmosphere of safety in which people can explore ideas and other people without any threat. Confrontations and differences of opinion become constructive forces in a group if group members know that they are respected as persons. A safe atmosphere need not exclude personal confrontations; they are often effective catalysts for learning.

Condition 11.   *Learning is facilitated in an atmosphere in which people feel they are accepted.*

People are free to change when they feel that change is not being imposed upon them. It is paradoxical, but the more we try to change people, the more resistant they become. A person must *be* before he can *become.* Accepting a person means that we allow him to hold his values and to be himself. When a person does not have to defend himself or his values, he is free to evaluate himself and to change his ideas. An insistence on change by an outside agent contains an implicit note of rejection: "I can't accept you as you are; you must change." People need to feel they have the option to change or not to change. They will develop this feeling if they experience that they are accepted for who they are. If they feel they are being attacked, they will naturally defend themselves, and people who are busy defending themselves are not free to learn.

Condition 12. *Learning is facilitated in an atmosphere which permits confrontation.*

A non-threatening psychological climate that encourages free and open communication, allows the unique self of each person to be expressed. It is inevitable that individuals will confront each other and that ideas will challenge ideas. Confrontations facilitate learning; they provide opportunities for people to see their ideas and themselves from the perspective of other people in the group. No one learns in isolation from other people. Behavior is changed and ideas are modified on the basis of feedback from other people. Confrontation allows people to test ideas to be synthesized, to discover new ideas, and to change their behavior and values.

Condition 13. *The most effective teacher creates conditions by which he loses the teaching function.*

By creating an appropriate atmosphere and setting up facilitating conditions, the teacher gradually moves away from dispensing information toward functioning as a resource person and learner. He enables group members to emerge more strongly as vital human resources and active learners. The conditions the teacher tries to foster include: communication, productive confrontation, acceptance, respect, freedom from threat, the right to make mistakes, self-revelation, cooperation and collaboration, active personal involvement, shared evaluation, and responsibility. Successful teaching "succeeds by doing itself out of a job. It succeeds by becoming unnecessary, by producing an individual who no longer needs to be taught, who breaks loose and swings free of the teacher and becomes self-moving" (Morris, 1966:153).

The teacher creates the learning climate by viewing *himself* as a learner and by behaving as learner. He reveals himself as an inquiring, valuing person who conveys spontaneity, curiosity, warmth and empathy. He *listens* to others, he conveys acceptance and respect, he understands affective as well as cognitive meanings and intents, and he confronts others in a genuine and caring way. He creates an atmosphere in which these qualities can be internalized by members of the group. To the degree that the teacher becomes a facilitator and a vibrant learner learning will be enhanced. He who teaches least, teaches best.

REFERENCES

Gendlin, Eugene T. and Beebe, John. "Experiential Groups," *Innovations to Group Psychotherapy,* George M. Gazda (ed.). Springfield, Ill: Charles C. Thomas Company, 1968.
Morris, Van Cleve. *Existentialism in Education.* New York: Harper & Row, 1966.
Rogers, Carl R. *On Becoming a Person.* Boston: Houghton Mifflin, 1961.

9

Equalizing the Learning Relationship

Equalizing is the process through which any human relationship is brought into balance, accord, parity, bilateral symmetry, or mutuality. A relationship that is equalized has the potential to be productive. A relationship that is not equalized has the potential to be nonproductive. For example, an effective marriage is basically equalized. Both partners share rights and responsibilities and have developed an intuitive understanding of the process whereby the relationship is kept in balance. When this sort of balance exists, marriage is a personally rewarding and a positive experience for both partners. If the relationship is not balanced, the marriage is likely to deteriorate. Similarly, when the relationship between labor and management is equalized, the work incentive and level of productivity is higher than when the relationship is not equalized. Both labor and management behave productively if there is a balance between the groups in terms of trust, positive regard, and concepts of justice. Also, when the relationships among nations are equalized there is a tendency toward peaceful coexistence. If the relationships among nations are not equalized, there is a tendency toward distrust that may eventually lead to war. When nations are economically, territorially, politically, and militarily equalized, they possess the psychological security to deal with each other in an atmosphere of mutual trust.

The equalizing principle is of paramount importance in determining the effectiveness of any relationship. Whether the relationship is between friends, worker and supervisor, marriage partners, learner and teacher, or nations, it is the equalizing principle that helps the relationship move toward the positive and the productive. This is especially true in the teacher-learner relationship. When students sense that the relationship with the teacher is equalized, they invest themselves in moving toward more positive behavior. This movement occurs because students sense that they are respected participants in the process of learning. They feel accepted, understood, and trusted, and are motivated to communicate honestly and to identify aspects of the relationship with the teacher that need modification. The teacher is perceived as someone who is equally involved in the process and outcomes of the relationship. Because the teacher is perceived as an equal, students sense a co-ownership of the relationship and have no need to be evasive, defensive, or vague.

The mission of the teacher, then, is to create a learning environment in which the relationship with a student, or group of students, is equalized. Each of the participants should contribute equally to the goals, process, and outcomes of the relationship. The teacher contributes to this by not controlling or manipulating the relationship or the students. Once the teacher internalizes the importance of equalizing the learning relationship and sees the positive effect such a relationship has on the outcomes of learning, he can begin to identify the *pre-learning procedures* and *in-learning attitudes* that contribute to equalizing the relationship.

PRE-LEARNING PROCEDURES

1. *Develop an orientation to learning.*

A student usually wants to know what to expect before he enters a learning relationship. This is quite understandable. People like to know what they are getting into before they move ahead with any experience, and teachers have an obligation to satisfy the students' curiosity. Students want to know who the teacher is, what he has to offer, what the context for learning will be, what and how content will be treated, what the parameters are for student activity and involvement, and how students will contribute to the development of a facilitative learning atmosphere. The teacher's expectations should be freely and directly communicated. An equalized learning relationship is not a one-way street. Students *and* teachers are co-participants in the learning relationship. The teacher cannot abandon personal identity, expertise, pedagogy, expectations, knowledge, and other professional and personal attributes if learning is to occur. Students expect teachers to bring something to the relationship, and the teacher who behaves as if he or she has little to offer comes across to students as patronizing, condescending, and unauthentic. Both teacher and students are members of a group of learners and every teacher has a responsibility to share personal resources and expertise with that group. Too often, under the guise of freeing students to learn, teachers deny who they are and abdicate their responsibilities for sharing knowledge, experience, and insights.

Teachers can satisfy students' right-to-know by developing a student orientation regarding what transpires in the learning relationship. Through such an orientation the student is able to gain a vicarious sense of what sort of behaviors to expect from the teacher and what the goals and aspirations of the teacher are. When students are able to sense and internalize the equalizing dimensions of the learning relationship, they feel more comfortable with the learning process. No student wants to be part of a relationship in which he is merely told what to do or how to do it. Students need to be involved in a relationship in which their human rights and integrity as persons are respected. In such a relationship, students sense more personal power and have the opportunity to exercise their unique rights.

2. *Develop learning experiences in which students will be inclined to become voluntarily involved.*

131

An equalized learning relationship can occur more easily if the student is voluntarily involved. When students make the decision to enter a learning relationship, their sense of being equal to the teacher is enhanced. A voluntarily involved student is not cast into a subservient role; his position is more equalized because he retains personal rights in the relationship. This is not the case when a student is required to engage in learning. In required relationships, the student is usually antagonistic toward the teacher because he had no part in the decision to enter the learning relationship. Such an involuntary association with a teacher will lead to an unequalized and nonproductive relationship for both parties.

3. *Demystify learning.*

If potential clients see learning as a complex and mysterious undertaking with an authority figure, and if the teacher's behavior reinforces such perceptions, any hope of equalizing the learning relationship is lost. Through orientation to learning, students should perceive learning as an equalized relationship between persons who invest themselves in the process of learning. Learning is a relatively simple process and should be represented as such to students so that they will feel that it is not a threatening experience with an all-powerful teacher. The history of the teaching profession has certainly contributed to the public's ideas about teacher control and forced learning. Today's teacher must dispel student fears about education and help them realize that learning is a vibrant human relationship in which their personhood will be treated with dignity.

4. *Develop a positive image of the teacher as a facilitative person.*

Students prefer to associate with teachers who possess attitudes that contribute to the progress of the learner. Students feel more comfortable in a relationship with a teacher who has faciltative attitudes. In the name of professionalism, some teachers inhibit the feeling of equalization on the part of the student. They are too official in their attitudes and behavior, and are perceived by students as the gatekeepers of institutional policy. Students do not feel that they can have an equalized relationship with such a teacher.

5. *Tend toward a theory of learning that has potential for equalizing the learning relationship.*

Some theories of learning give the teacher too much power in the learning relationship. They say that the teacher is in the best position to determine student values, behavior, and learning goals. These theories place the student in a relationship that is decidedly biased in favor of the teacher. When a teacher espouses such a theory, there is little hope that an equalized relationship can develop.

Students covertly or overtly rebel against an authoritarian teacher because they sense that their personal rights and powers are being ignored. They know they really cannot communicate with the teacher because he has a preconceived notion about how people learn. In such an unequalized relationship, the student engages in a struggle to resist the certainty of the teacher's answers. When student and teacher are engaged in a power struggle, they are involved in a win-lose confrontation that has little potential for a mutually positive outcome. If a teacher expects to move toward an equalized relationship with students, he should study and incorporate the more productive theories of humanistic teaching.

IN-LEARNING ATTITUDES

1. *The teacher's awareness of authenticity.*

The teacher's authenticity is a quality that allows the learning relationship to become equalized. When the teacher is able to communicate authentically, he creates an atmosphere that prompts the student to behave authentically. When both teacher and student behave authentically it tends to equalize the relationship.

When students enter the learning relationship, they are typically not authentic, in that the self is obscured. Learning helps them uncover the self and move away from self-referent statements toward the more personally meaningful authentic self-statements. In the past, students have learned to live by adopting conventional unauthentic patterns of response. Their environment has taught them to muffle rather than to express; to delude themselves rather than to be personally honest. The learning atmosphere should provide students with the safety they need to take a long look at themselves and rid themselves of false characteristics in their behavior. The teacher's authenticity is the quality that prompts the student to function with a higher degree of clarity and personal congruence. When both the student and the teacher are behaving authentically, the result is an equalized relationship.

The evolvement of authenticity is not reserved for the relationship between teacher and student. It should be a commitment for all persons, regardless of the role in which they function. They must remove the facade — the persona — that separates the authentic self from the world. The teacher's authenticity influences the student to be authentic, resulting in an equalized relationship. It is the equalized relationship that prompts the student to learn.

2. *The teacher's sense of presence.*

When teachers possess a sense of presence they influence students to develop a sense of presence. If both the student and teacher achieve a sense of presence, their relationship has the potential to be equalized. The teacher's sense of presence is essentially an awareness of who he is, where he is, what he is doing, how he is doing it, and why he is doing it. He has a cognitive and visceral sensitivity to involvement with the student in the student's learning perceptions and to involvement with the student in the process of becoming a more adequate learner.

Teachers who achieve a sense of presence are able to give of themselves. Effective teachers become involved with the learning of students because they, as persons, exist. To exist means more than sitting and waiting for the student to pause so that the teacher may interject a judgment or moralization of the student's struggle with learning. It means being empathetically attuned to the student's feelings, to his hopes, desires, frustrations, fears, defenses, and anxieties. It means recognizing the personal characteristics that make a student unique, different from any other learner who has existed or will ever exist. This type of involvement demands a giving of self many teachers have yet to experience. They must put aside their own motivational desires so that the relationship exists for the evolvement of the student's personalized learning.

All too often teachers are unable to achieve a sense of presence because they hold preconceived notions about the ingredients of an effective learning relationship. They introduce information from external frames of reference, make superficial suggestions, criticize the student's proposed plan for learning, or ask irrelevant questions. Whenever teachers act in such mechanical ways, they diminish the possibility of total presence. Presence is not limited to the mechanical actions that flow from the self; it is also an involvement of the teacher's existential self with the existential self of the student. The involved presence is not dependent on mechanistic activities, for a teacher who is deeply involved with a student is not consciously planning what they will say or do next. He responds to the *student's* learning needs, and his sense of presence makes the use of predetermined remarks or devices impossible. A teacher who senses his presence in the student's learning and is not hesitant about being there, finds it existentially impossible to retreat into a pattern of trivial questioning and information-rendering. When a teacher is deeply present in the student's learning process, his own needs are all but lost because of the depth of the involvement with the student. In the words of Marcel:

> ... there is a way of listening which is a way of giving and another way of listening which is a way of refusing (1963:40).
>
> To be incapable of presence is to be, in some manner, not only occupied but encumbered with one's own self (1963:42).

In describing the effectively communicating person Maslow shows his sensitivity to the concept of presence:

> [The person] must be able to listen in the receiving rather than in the taking sense in order to hear what is actually said rather than what he expects to hear or demands to hear. He must not impose himself but rather let the words flow in upon him. Only so can their own shape and pattern be assimilated. Otherwise one hears only one's theories and expectations (1965:182).

135

There is a proportional relationship, then, between the teacher's sense of presence and the degree to which the relationship with a student is equalized.

3. *The teacher's sensitivity to emergence.*

When student and teacher are more authentic, have a greater sense of presence in their relationship, and have an awareness of the process whereby learning emerges, the relationship tends to equalize and become more productive. Emergence is a mode of learning in which there is an increased awareness of one's motivation and the degree to which motivation can influence learning. Emerging persons develop a more adequate, enlightened way of learning that frees them of the bonds that previously restricted them. They develop more creative ways of becoming involved in learning because they are free enough to consider the various alternatives. They no longer must rely on a mode of learning that is superficially cognitive rather than personally integrative and satisfying. Emergence is evolutionary in nature. It occurs in a gradual way, with the person continually building a more perceptive and strengthened pattern of learning. It is through this internal emerging that the person is able to truly become involved in the process of learning.

Emergence cannot be brought about by the teacher tugging at the student from without. It is achieved from within, as a result of learning relationships that encourage students to ask themselves why they do or do not look within for the causes of their pattern of learning. If the student is to emerge as a learner, he must exist in a relationship that encourages the inner view. The teacher must create an atmosphere in which the student is able to explore the individuality of the learning process.

Allowing students to discover their own learning process can be a monumental task for a teacher, because we have been conditioned to sit in judgment of the people we associate with. The teacher who holds a rigid value system for learning is often insensitive to students whose learning values are quite different from his own. The mark of a competent teacher is not his ability to deal with students who hold the same values he does; rather, it is his ability to communicate with students who hold learning values that are vastly different from his own. Teachers must prize the right of other persons to *be* before they can ever become involved in a process that will encourage the emergence of those individuals.

If the student is to emerge as a learner, he must be allowed the right to be — the right to hold learning values different from the teacher's. Some teachers give lip service to the right to be, and attempt to cover up their internal frustrations with students who are different from themselves. Students are great at sensing a fraud, and will assume a psychological posture to defend their learning values, thereby retarding their development as learners. A false relationship usually evolves into something serving the teacher's need to be victorious, and the teacher loses all sight of his responsibility to create a learning atmosphere that encourages the emergence of the student as a learner.

Allowing a person the right to be will result in the emergence of that person:

> Whether one speaks to mathematicians, physicists, or historians, one encounters repeatedly an expression of faith in the powerful effects that come from permitting the student to put things together for himself, to be his own discoverer (Bruner, 1962:82).

The emergence of the student as a learner occurs as a result of effective teaching. An essential task for the teacher is to determine how he can facilitate this emergence, how he can create a learning atmosphere that furnishes students with an inner feeling that they can become determiners of their own learning destiny. If he does his work well, students will gain the feeling that they can go beyond the dimensions of their current learning and move toward a more adequate personally satisfying learning pattern. When both teacher and student engage in the process of emergence, their relationship becomes equalized and tends to be a more mutually productive learning experience.

EQUALIZED LEARNING RELATIONSHIPS: THE CLASSROOM

We believe that equalized learning relationships are most easily achieved in a classroom where:

137

1. Each student is allowed to progress at his or her own pace. The student's work is assessed within the framework of what he or she is able to accomplish and according to the demands of the discipline as interpreted by the teacher.
2. A large variety of learning activities can occur simultaneously. Students progressing at different levels and rates of speed are engaged in individualized and small-group learning situations designed to meet individual needs and interests.
3. The ability of a student to become concerned and committed is an important gauge of growth. Concern and commitment lead to engagement and involvement in the learning process and are significant benchmarks in assessing growth.
4. Students initiate much of the classroom activity. They set learning goals and design activities with teacher assistance and guidance.
5. Time, space, and materials are manipulated to meet the needs of students and enhance their learning. Students are not manipulated to fit predetermined restraints of time, space, and materials. The time and means required for learning vary greatly among individuals.
6. Opportunities for wonder, imagination, and humor are part of the classroom. Spontaneity, laughter, curiosity, and vitality are prized and nourished.
7. The student's unique style of learning is recognized and used, so that emphasis is placed on learning by the student, rather than on teaching by the teacher.
8. Students learn from each other. Students are recognized as human resources for each other and peer teaching and learning are encouraged and facilitated.
9. The teacher raises questions for students to respond to concerning their personal roles and responsibilities in learning. Students are encouraged to follow through on their commitments to themselves and others.
10. Students behave in ways that least interfere with the activities of others students and the teacher. Mutual respect, enhancement, and cooperation characterize the classroom.

11. Students have formulated learning goals and selected approaches for accomplishing their goals. Goals are challenging but not frustrating.
12. The teacher is an active resource person who provides materials, shares knowledge and understanding, listens carefully, gives encouragement, and effectively uses time, space, and materials to develop a facilitative learning climate.

REFERENCES

Bruner, J. S. *On Knowing: Essays for the Left Hand.* Cambridge: Harvard University Press, 1962.

Marcel, G. *The Philosophy of Existentialism.* New York: Citadel Press, 1963.

Maslow, A. H. "Cognition of being in the peak experiences." *The Self in Growth: Teaching and Learning.* D. E. Hamachek (Ed.). Teaneck, New Jersey: Prentice-Hall, 1965.

Part Four

Research and Practice

In the preceding chapters we developed our perspectives and views on learner-centered teaching, focusing on the teacher, the learner, and the theories of personality and motivation that illuminate the teacher-learner relationship. We also discussed the implications of our views for the practice of teaching. Here we would like to share with you two research studies that provide empirical data on the relationship between reading achievement, self concept, and informal education, and the writing process as it occurs among learners in informal and formal classroom settings. We believe that these studies are important because the heart of the informal open-classroom approach is learner-centered teaching. The "hard" data and scholarship of these studies are intellectually provocative and ought to "scratch and nick" the thinking of everyone interested in the improvement of teaching and learning.

10

Reading, Self-Concept and Informal Education

*Mary A. Pine**

SELF-CONCEPT THEORY

In the study of human behavior, many terms have been used to describe the phenomenon of the self. It is necessary to understand the meaning of the term "self-concept" vis-a-vis other terms related to self in order to develop a more adequate conceptual base for planning research, facilitating communication, and improving teaching practices. Perhaps the most common definition of the self-concept is that it is referent to the pronoun, "I" (Helper, 1955). However, many psychologists offer more specific definitions.

Perkins defines the self-concept as those "perceptions, beliefs, feelings, attitudes and values which the individual views in describing himself" (1958:226). The individual's self-concept consists of the persisting ways he sees himself in the life situations that he faces or might face. According to Kehas, "The self-concept is the organization of the system of generalizations a person has about himself,

---

*Mary A. Pine is Assistant Professor of Education, University of Maine at Portland-Gorham, Gorham, Maine.

the cluster of the most personal meanings a person attributes to himself" (1964:44). McDonald (1967) suggests that the self-concept is an individual's conception of his integral unity as he moves from role to role — the way he sees himself, the set of characteristics he associates with himself, and the set of inferences drawn from self-observation in different situations that describe his characteristic behavior patterns.

Most personality theorists consider the self-concept to be an important factor underlying the individual's behavior. Wylie points out that "all the theories of personality which have been put forth within the last two decades assign importance to the phenomenal and/or nonphenomenal self-concept with cognitive and motivational attitudes" (1961:129).

As James (1890) pointed out many years ago, the individual has many selves. He might conceive of the self he really believes he is, the self he aspires to be, the self he hopes he is now, and the self he fears he is at present. According to Brownfrain (1952), the self-concept is a configuration of those and other possible self-definitions, and the stability of the self-concept is derived from the interrelations among these various ways of defining self. Allport (1937) says that the "proprium of personality," which is comprised of awareness of self and other activities gives stability and consistency to evaluations, intentions, and attitudes.

Mead (1934) considers the self as an object of awareness. She claims that the individual responds to himself with specific feelings and attitudes as others respond to him. He becomes aware through the way people react to him as an object. Lewin (1936) gives Mead's self a functional process of causality that is dynamically active, through what he calls the "life space." According to Lewin, the self-concept is represented by a life-space region that determines present beliefs about the self. The life space includes the individual's universe of personal experience. It is a complex internal mechanism which produces behavior. Lundholm's (1940) theory of the self is similar to Mead's, in that he believes the self is primarily an object of awareness. He makes no mention of the functional, motivational, or process dynamics of the self. The subjective self is mainly what a person comes to think about himself. Symonds (1951) incorporates

144

the social philosophy of Mead. He sees the ego as a group of processes and the self as the manner in which the individual reacts to himself. Although the ego and self are distinct aspects of personality, there is considerable interaction between them.

Cattell conceives of the self both as an object and a process. He considers the self the principal organizing influence on the individual, giving him stability and bringing order to his behavior. The sentiment of self-regard is the most important influence. Cattell states that sentiments are the "major acquired dynamic trait structures which cause their possessors to pay attention to certain objects, or class of objects, and to feel and react in a certain way with regard to them" (1950:161). Here he is discussing selective perception as it relates to self-concept. He also introduces the process of self-observation in describing the real self and the ideal self. Murphy (1947) expands the objectified self. He defines self as the individual as known to the individual. It is derived from a person's conceptions and perceptions of his total being. He says that the major activities of the ego are to defend and enhance the self complex.

Rogers (1951) stresses the self-concept as the principal determiner of behavior. He believes in the discontinuity of the conscious and unconscious. People behave in terms of the ways in which they see themselves — a conscious activity. He allows for the probability of an unconscious, but implies that only when information about the self and the environment is "admissible to awareness" does it influence behavior:

> As long as the self-Gestalt is firmly organized, and no contradictory material is even dimly perceived, then positive self-feelings may exist, the self may be seen as worthy and acceptable, and conscious tension is minimal. Behavior is consistent with the organized hypotheses and concepts of the self-structure (1951:191).

Rogers describes the self-concept:

> as an organized configuration of perceptions of one's characteristics and abilities; the percepts and concepts of the self in relation to others and to the environment; the value qualities which are perceived as associated with experiences and objects; the goals and ideals which are perceived as having positive or negative valence (Wylie, 1961:174).

145

As would be expected, in the early stages these theories were comparatively crude and unsophisticated. However, as interest in the field grew, more carefully defined, detailed thinking evolved. The work of Combs and Snygg (1959) is presently one of the clearest representations of self-concept theory. They describe the self-concept as the organization of all that the individual refers to as "I" or "me." It is himself from his point of view. The self-concept is not the sum of isolated concepts of self, but a patterned inter-relationship of all these concepts. The self-concept has a degree of stability and consistency that gives predictability to an individual and to his behavior. How a person behaves is the result of how he perceives the situation and himself at the moment of action. Awareness directs behavior; how a person feels and thinks determines his course of action.

Combs states:

> The self is composed of perceptions concerning the individual and this organization of perception in turn has vital and important effects upon the behavior of the individual (1963:470).

Combs and Snygg give us a self that is both an object and a process, thereby avoiding semantic differences. The self-concept is an inference about the self. It is useful in helping us understand ourselves and it enables us to deal with a complex function that is not directly observable. The fact that it is an inference does not make it invalid. To the individual, his perceptions of self have the feeling of reality; his self-concept seems to him to be what he truly is.

THE RELATIONSHIP BETWEEN SELF-CONCEPT AND BEHAVIOR

Generally speaking, there are two aspects of self-concept theory that most psychologists appear to agree on:

1. An individual's self-perceptions include his view of himself as compared to others, his view of how others see him, and his view of how he wishes he could be.

2. An individual's self-perceptions are largely based upon the experiences he has had with people who are important to him.

A fundamental thesis of this perceptual point of view is that behavior is influenced not only by the accumulation of our past and present experiences but also by the personal meanings we attach to our perceptions of those experiences. In other words, our behavior is not only a function of what happens to us from the outside, it is also a function of how we feel on the inside.

The idea that behavior and learning are functions of the self-concept has been fully developed in the work of Combs and Snygg (1959), Maslow (1959), Kelley (1951), and Rogers (1951). In essence, they believe that the adequate person has an essentially positive view of self developed not only from many successful experiences but also from an inner feeling of self-worth and the ability to cope. The person of high self-concept looks on life and its challenges as an adventure. If he experiences failure, he keeps it in perspective. He recognizes that he has failed in this particular instance, but does not feel that he *is* a failure. He continues to see himself as an able human being and confronts each new experience from this vantage point. Because he feels he can cope, he generally does. Therefore, he accumulates many successes, and his internal reactions to these successes support and enhance his already positive self-concept.

People who are relatively inadequate tend to view themselves quite negatively. Lacking a feeling of self-worth, they tend to perceive themselves as unliked, unwanted, and unable to cope with problems. Their tendency to focus on inadequacies causes them to lose touch with their strengths and abilities. When they encounter situations, they expect not only insurmountable difficulties but also failure. The self-fulfilling prophecy continues, each failure bringing about others, with the accompanying feelings of inadequacy, helplessness, and inferiority. The result is a further lowering of self-concept. Purkey states:

> Perhaps the single most important assumption of modern theories about the self is that the maintenance and enhancement of the perceived self is the motive behind all behavior. Each of us constantly strives to maintain,

147

protect, and enhance the self of which he is aware. It therefore follows that experience is perceived in terms of its relevance to the self and that behavior is determined by these perceptions (1970:10).

Psychologists and educators are becoming aware that how a person views himself is closely connected to how he behaves and learns (Hamachek, 1971). Why is it that some children with high IQ scores do not receive correspondingly high academic grades? Have they learned to see themselves as incapable? And why is it that some children with average intelligence scores perform remarkably well in the academic world? Is it because they see themselves as able, coping individuals and perform accordingly? "Research is teaching us that how a student performs depends not only on how intelligent he actually is, but how intelligent he thinks he is" (Hamachek, 1971:174).

THE RELATIONSHIP BETWEEN SELF-CONCEPT AND READING ACHIEVEMENT

As the child enters school, the major task confronting him is learning to read. Our society places a high value on reading ability and the child quickly senses that his parents and teachers consider this accomplishment vital. As the first major academic situation that he must master, the task adds a significant dimension to his definition of self. How will he function? Will his self-concept be affected by his success or failure in accomplishing the task? From our knowledge of the relationship between self-concept and human behavior and learning, we can hypothesize that the child with a positive self-concept will have greater success than the child with a negative self-concept. We can also expect a low reading score to have a negative effect and a high reading score to have a positive effect on the child's self-concept.

For years reading has been taught in a very structured, almost grim manner. Emphasis has been on methods, materials, word games, drills, purple dittos, and workbooks. In most instances the overall instructional program of the classroom is determined by the teacher, and the children must adjust themselves to the curriculum with few, if any, opportunities to make choices and focus on their own interests. Despite the emphasis on teaching reading, many children have either failed to accomplish this task or are reading at levels far below their capacity. I believe that one of the principal reasons for this lack of achievement is the lack of consideration given to the affective dimensions of the child and the affective aspects of learning.

Many studies have investigated the relationship between self-concept and reading achievement. Hallock (1959) tested 926 students in grades four, six, and eight, using a factorial design including variables for sex, intelligence, reading achievement, and personality, and found self-reliance and a feeling of personal worth among the measures most significantly related to reading achievement. Hamachek (1962) found that high achievement and intellectual self-image were related to reading age among a group of 100 children. The belief that self-image as a reader would correlate significantly was substantiated by Sopis (1965). In a study of self-concept and verbal mental ability in kindergarten children, Giuliani (1968) determined that the two variables were significantly related to reading readiness.

After evaluating the personality adjustment of fifteen under-achieving and fifteen over-achieving eighth- and ninth-grade pupils on the basis of their performance on the *Rorschach,* the *Thematic Apperception Test,* and the *Mental Health Analysis,* Blackman (1965) found that underachievers had significantly poorer mental health than overachievers. Differences that approached statistical significance were immaturity, emotional instability, and feelings of inadequacy. Bodwin (1959) studied the relationships between self-concept and certain disabilities for children in grades three through six. He investigated 100 pupils with no educational disabilities, and found a relationship between immature self-concept and reading disability. The correlation was .72 at the third-grade level and .62 at the sixth-grade level. Lumpkin (1959) found not only a significant relationship between self-concept and reading achievement, but also that "with this particular group (underachievers) the self-concept which the individual has influences his behavior in academic work as well as his social relationships." Studying some eighth-grade boys Bricklin (1963) found that the group with

149

comprehension and word-recognition problems had more negative self-concepts than either the achieving group or the group with only comprehension problems.

In an investigation of the relationship between personality adjustment and attitudes toward achievement, Zimmerman and Allebrand (1965) determined that the good reader was more likely to consider himself well-adjusted and be motivated by internalized drives. Using the *California Test of Personality,* Lockhart (1965) obtained coefficients of .45 for boys, .30 for girls, and .35 for a total group of first-grade children when she correlated the perceptual adjustment scale with the *Metropolitan Readiness Test.* Schwykart (1967) found evidence of negative self-concept patterns among 35 retarded readers, and Toller (1968) found a significant difference in favor of achievers in the areas of acceptance, adequacy, personal and social self-security, and consistency of view of self.

Other investigations of children in grades three through nine support the finding that a relationship exists between self-concept and reading achievement: Spicola, 1961; Williams and Cole, 1968; Hake, 1969; Cummings, 1970; and Swartz, 1972. These researchers have concluded that children who are successful in reading have positive self-concepts; the antithesis is true of unsuccessful readers. Only two investigations conducted around the same time with children of the same age levels refute these findings: Nicholson, 1965; and Sederat, 1968.

The number of investigations using younger children as subjects is minimal, and their findings are in conflict with the results of larger number of studies conducted with older children. Both Ruhly (1971), who worked with second graders, and Lewis (1974), who used first graders as subjects, failed to find a significant difference between the self-concept scores of successful and unsuccessful readers.

Two longitudinal studies have suggested the possibility of a cause-effect relationship between self-concept and reading achievement. Investigating the relationship between children's self-perceptions in kindergarten prior to reading instruction and their subsequent achievement in first grade, Lamy (1963) found that self-perception scores correlated as highly with reading achievement as intelligence scores did. Together, the scores were found to be better predictors of reading success than either score taken separately. In concluding her study, Lamy suggested that the perceptions a child has about himself and his world may in fact be causal factors in his future reading achievement. Wattenberg and Clifford (1964) conducted an exploratory study to determine whether self-concept or reading disability was the antecedent phenomenon. Measures of kindergarten children's self-concepts were made on the basis of self-reference statements obtained as the children drew pictures of their families and as they responded to incomplete sentences. The scores were then related to reading achievement in the second grade, and the results showed that the measure of self-concept obtained at the kindergarten levels was, in fact, predictive of reading achievement two and one-half years later.

The results of these earlier studies were not supported by Williams' 1973 study. She hypothesized that self-concept scores of children were positively correlated with reading achievement in first and second grade, and that self-concept scores would add to the prediction of reading-achievement scores beyond intelligence and reading-readiness scores. For two successive years, Williams drew subjects from three first-grade classrooms and administered an adaptation of the "Coopersmith Self-Esteem Inventory" and the *Metropolitan Reading Readiness Test.* At the end of both first and second grade, she administered the *California Achievement Test* to these children. Results revealed that self-concept failed to add to predictability of either first- or second-grade reading achievement beyond the prediction of intelligence or readiness scores.

The studies of Carter (1953) and Wood (1972) do not support, or only partially support, the hypothesis that self-concept and reading achievement are related. Carter failed to find any significant difference in reading achievement for seven-year-old children who were rated high, medium, or low on personal, social, and total adjustment. Wood analyzed 585 fifth graders and found that boys with higher reading-comprehension scores had higher self-concepts than boys with average or lower reading-comprehension scores. However, the correlations did not hold for girls in the same study. Moreover, Wood's findings also indicated that neither boys nor girls who scored high in word meaning had higher self-concepts than those who scored average or below.

Although most of the studies reported suggest that there is a persistent relationship between self-concept and reading achievement, caution must be exercised before generalizing these findings. The research cited assumes that the self-concept is unidimensional, yet many theorists now agree that the self-concept is not a unitary phenomenon. In fact, an individual has many different self-attitudes connected with such things as his physical, psychological, and social characteristics.

> The implication of this for the classroom is that the individual's self attitudes relating to achievement will be complex; instead of, or in addition to, a general conception of his academic ability, he will have self attitudes regarding the various subjects and requirements of the school (Johnson, 1970:87).

None of these studies, however, has investigated the child's self-concept as a reader.

One must also be careful about the question of whether the self-concept determines reading achievement or whether reading achievement shapes the self-concept:

> It may be that the relationship between the two is caused by some factor yet to be determined. The best evidence now available suggests that it is a two-way street, that there is continuous interaction between the self and academic achievement and that each directly influences the other (Purkey, 1970:23).

It is quite possible that one of the "factors yet to be determined" is classroom organization. Certainly it is a current concern and its effect on self-concept and reading achievement should be explored. However, the effect of classroom organization cannot be investigated without considering the effect the teacher has within the organizational structure. He not only determines the use of time, space, and materials for instruction, but he also determines the emotional climate of the classroom and the expectations children hold for themselves.

THE TEACHER AND THE CHILD

The child enters school with "psychological bags" packed with a wide assortment of ideas about himself and his abilities. However, he is by no means a fixed personality with singular traits, feelings, ideas, and attitudes. He arrives with a pliable self-image that has resulted from many past experiences. We could say that at this time, the self-concept is still in process, subject to the effects of every experience, including those in the classroom. Combs comments: "Outside the child's own family, no institution in our society is in a better position to affect the growth and development of an individual's self-image than our public schools" (1958:315-316).

Unfortunately, not all teachers recognize the influence they have on children. A teacher's attitudes, though perhaps only subtly expressed, are transmitted to children and in turn influence behavior (Moustakas, 1966). Teachers need to view students in essentially positive ways and hold favorable expectations for them. The perceptions the teacher has of the child affects the child's perceptions of himself; if he sees a child bright and capable, the child will perceive himself as bright and capable and this perception will govern his behavior. Several studies have supported this idea. The classic study of Rosenthal and Jacobson (1968), *Pygmalion in the Classroom,* showed that teachers often adjust their behavior to respond to a child's IQ. The researchers chose some names of first-grade children at random and informed their teachers that these children would grow dramatically in scholastic as well as mental ability during the coming school year. Subsequent testing showed that the experimental group of children gained an average of 12.2 IQ points compard to an average gain of 8.4 IQ points for the control group. Interestingly enough, the experimental children were viewed by their teachers as being better adjusted, happier, and possessing a better chance for academic success than the control children. Rosenthal and Jacobson concluded that the teacher, through her verbal and nonverbal behavior, subtly helped the experimental group learn. They summarized their study with the conclusion that "children who are expected to gain intellectually by their teachers in fact do show greater gains after one year, than do children of whom such gains are not expected" (1968:221).

Beez (1970) also conducted an interesting investigation on teacher expectancies. In his study, sixty children ranging in age from 5½ to 6½ were taught the meaning of a series of symbols. Half of the teachers who worked with the children individually were led to anticipate good symbol learning, but the other half were led to expect poor achievement. When the data were analyzed, the results showed a dramatic difference in learning. Twenty-three percent of the children alleged to have poorer intellectual potential learned five or more symbols, while 77 percent of the children alleged to have better intellectual potential did fifty. The effect of expectation upon teacher effort was equally astonishing. Eight or more symbols were taught by 87 percent of the teachers expecting better performance, while only 13 percent of the teachers expecting poor performance tried to reach that many symbols. The teachers of the lower expectancy group not only rated their children as having lower social competency and intellectual ability, but also spent more time on each task, repeated it more frequently, and engaged in many more non-teaching activities with the child.

Kranz (1970) and her associates conducted a study to determine whether there were significant differences between substantive positive appraisal, negative appraisal, and the managerial behaviors a teacher exhibits toward pupils depending on his perception of their academic potential and achievement level. Subjects were 11 urban elementary teachers and their 258 pupils. Data were collected on the teacher's verbal behavior as well as their perceptions of the relative academic potential and achievement level of each child. In general, the findings suggest that relationships do exist between the perceptions a teacher has regarding a pupil and the kinds and frequency of teaching behaviors she directs toward the child.

Several studies indicate that the child's academic achievement is also affected by the personal feelings the teacher holds toward him. Davidson and Lang (1960) studied the relationship between students' perceptions of their teachers' feelings toward them and their academic performance, classroom behavior, and self-perception. A "Check List of Trait Names," which consisted of thirty-five descriptive terms, was administered to 114 boys and 89 girls in grades four, five, and six of a New York City public school. The children were also rated by their teachers on achievement and a number of behavioral characteristics. When the data were analyzed, the researchers found that:

1. There was a positive and significant correlation between children's perceptions of their teachers' feelings toward them and the children's self-perceptions.
2. The more positive the child's perception of his teacher's feelings toward him, the higher his academic achievement and the more desirable his classroom behavior.

The favorable bias that teachers may have towards more physically attractive children and its corresponding effect on teacher expectations has been explored by Clifford (1972). She gave teachers a fifth-grade student's report card to which was attached a photo of either an attractive or unattractive child. The teachers completed an opinion sheet indicating their appraisal of: (1) the child's IQ; (2) his peer relationships; (3) the parental interest in the child's academic achievement; and (4) the student's potential educational attainment. Results indicated that on all four dependent variables, the teachers' expectations were significantly higher for the attractive child.

It is imperative for the first-grade teacher to view each child as capable of achieving to the fullest and that his behavior, both verbal and non-verbal, convey this message to the child. He should provide opportunities for success as well as an atmosphere of warmth, respect, and challenge. This is critical in light of the research findings regarding the first-grade teacher's ability to predict reading success.

In order to determine the comparative predictive value of a reading readiness test and the teacher's judgments of reading readiness, Henig (1949) administered the *Lee-Clark Reading Readiness Test* to 98 beginning first-grade pupils. He also asked their teachers to rank the relative likelihood of their success in learning to read. The test scores and teacher rankings were then compared to the children's reading grades at the end of first grade. Although the scores made on the readiness test did forecast student progress for the first year with a substantial degree of success, Henig found that the rankings made by experienced teachers well-versed in readiness techniques were equally efficient predictors of success. These findings have been substantiated by the work of Karlen (1957), Annesley and others (1970), and Koppman and LaPray (1962).

Perhaps the most significant research dealing with the teacher's impact on how children learn to read are *The First Grade Reading Studies* (Bond, 1966). This massive piece of research, consisting of 27 independent studies planned, directed, and implemented by nationally known leaders in the field of reading, was an attempt to explore the effects of various approaches on children's reading development. The results suggest that the methodology employed is comparatively incidental. Commenting on this study, Bond says: "As would be expected, there was greater variation between the teachers within the method, than there was between the methods" (1966:468).

THE ACTIVITY-CENTERED CLASSROOM

Many people believe that changing from the traditional classroom organization and its approaches to a more child-centered format would enhance students' cognitive and affective development. The philosophical basis for this assumption is that all human beings have potential and want to learn. However, the atmosphere in which learning occurs is extremely important. Learning can best be facilitated by an environment in which:

1. Instruction is carefully personalized in an attempt to meet the individual needs, interests, and abilities of children, thus providing maximum opportunity for success and lessening the possibilities of threat to the ego.
2. The materials provided are perceived as meaningful and relevant to the child.
3. There is freedom to peruse personal interests, raise questions, make decisions, explore, and discover.
4. Provocative interest centers and materials that demand

interaction and constant investigation are provided to help bring about self-initiated learning.

5. An attitude of competitiveness need not exist; each child is appreciative of the value of his own personal growth and development.
6. The child has the freedom to make mistakes and still feel competent.
7. Opportunities are provided for the child to grow socially, emotionally, and intellectually through working as an individual, and as part of a wide variety of group and peer learning situations.
8. Respect, trust, love, and concern for one another are nurtured.
9. The teacher's role is facilitator of learning rather than disseminator of information.

If this atmosphere and learner-centered teaching were provided for children, would their self-concepts be enhanced? Would this increase in self-concept help each child to see himself as an achiever in reading? Would this feeling of effectiveness be reflected in increased reading achievement? Or, would the comparative lack of structure in the activity-centered classroom produce a decline in self-concept and have a negative effect on reading achievement?

In the typical traditional classroom atmosphere, the child is forced to work on imposed tasks, and as a result there is little opportunity for him to experience psychological success, which is a major factor in determining self-esteem. According to Lewin (1944:335) psychological success occurs when:

1. The person is able to define his own goals.
2. The goals are related to his central needs and values.
3. The achievement of the goals represent a realistic level of aspiration for the person.

This definition is synonymous with the goals of the activity-centered classroom.

Many children enter first grade with positive self-concepts; others come with negative perceptions of self. The facilitating atmosphere of the activity-centered classroom, with its learner-centered teaching approach, should not only enhance the self-concept but also increase the reading achievement of all the children.

There is a paucity of research on the topic of reading achievement in activity-centered classrooms that follow the British Infant School model. Most of the available research comes from England, where informal education has been in existence since the end of World War II: Silberman, 1970; Goddard, 1969; Southgate, 1973; Wallen and Travers, 1963; and Weiner, 1974.

The Central Advisory Council's review of primary education in England, *Children and Their Primary Schools* (1967), contained data on standardized reading achievement tests administered periodically from 1948 to 1964. The data showed a steady and consistent upward trend in reading scores. Thus, this study substantiated the findings of the earlier, more limited, investigations of Gardner (1950 and 1966) and Warburton (1964), who concluded that children attending informal schools surpassed their peers attending formal schools in reading.

Although more recent research by Harckman (1972) supports this conclusion, the findings of three other investigators did not corroborate the results. Morris (1959) analyzed the test results of children seven to eleven years of age and concluded that good reading achievement is associated with a formal approach to reading and a particular emphasis on phonics. After analyzing the reading test scores of children who attended twelve different infant schools located in deprived areas, Cane and Smithers found that "initial success does not prove to be associated with what are sometimes loosely considered to be progressive methods (1971:182). As a result of this study, they conclude that the major difference between schools that were successful in teaching reading and schools that were unsuccessful is "the lack of systematic instruction in the unsuccessful schools" (1971:182). Finally, a National Foundation Reading Survey (Start and Wells, 1972) indicated that in contrast to the earlier statements of the Central Advisory Committee about reading achievement, average test scores are now falling off. As a result of these findings the Secretary of State of

Education created a special committee to investigate the teaching of reading (Southgate, 1973).

Many have stated that an informal approach to education enhances the total development of the child (Brown and Precious, 1968; Rogers, 1969; Silberman, 1970; Weber, 1971; Barth, 1972), but there has been no research investigating the nature of the relationship between self-concept and informal education or the nature of the relationships between self-concept, informal education, and reading achievement. Nonetheless, some American educators are incorporating the informal approach modeled after the British Infant Schools without really knowing what effect it will have on the child's self-concept or his reading achievement. The informal approach has attracted considerable public attention. In this age of accountability, with critics of informal education demanding that we go "back to the basics," research must be conducted within the context of American education to discover the effectiveness of the activity-centered approach versus the traditional approaches to teaching young children. An empirical comparison of the two approaches would also help generate new perspectives on the teaching of reading and the enrichment of children's self-concepts.

The most recent research comparing the effects of informal and formal education in Great Britain is the four-year study conducted by Neville Bennett (1977). On the basis of preliminary surveys and a typology of teaching styles Bennett and his colleagues assigned 37 teachers to one of three categories: "informal," "mixed," or "formal." Nine hundred and fifty fourth-year students in their classrooms were tested for achievement in reading, mathematics, and English before and at the end of the school year. Pre and post test scores were obtained on a battery of personality tests. Each student wrote an imaginative and a descriptive story for analysis and the classroom behavior of 100 students was observed and analyzed.

The results of the study indicated that the effect of teaching style was statistically and educationally significant in all the areas of achievement tested. In reading, pupils of the formal and mixed teachers progressed more than those of informal teachers three to five months. In mathematics, formal students were superior to both

159

mixed and informal students by four to five months. Formal students showed gains of three to five months in English over students in both mixed and informal groups. No differences were found among the three groups in creative writing. Personality tests showed that teaching style did not affect students' self-concept or esteem. Informal classrooms were found to produce more motivation and anxiety. Students in formal classrooms spent more time in work activity but also fidgeted more.

The design of Bennett's study has been criticized by Divoky (1977) on several points. Students were not matched on ability, social background, or past school experience. Although children in the formal classrooms had higher pre test scores, this factor was not accounted for in the study. The study made no judgment about whether a teacher was a good model of formal or informal teaching. The students' entire academic experience up to the point at which they entered the study was not accounted for.

PRE SELF-CONCEPT, READING ACHIEVEMENT, AND CLASSROOM ORGANIZATION

I would like to share with you the results of a study I carried out on the question of the relationship between self-concept, informal education, and reading achievement. The study focused on the following questions:

1. What is the relationship between pre self-concept and reading readiness?
2. What is the relationship between pre self-concept and reading achievement?
3. What is the interaction effect of pre self-concept and classroom organization on reading achievement?
4. What is the relationship between reading achievement and post self-concept?
5. Will there be a difference between the post self-concept scores of children in the activity-centered classrooms and the post self-concept scores of children in the traditional classrooms?
6. Will there be a difference between the post self-concept scores of children with high reading-achievement scores

and the post self-concept scores of children with low reading-achievement scores?
7. What is the interaction effect of classroom organization and reading achievement on post self-concept?

Sample

Twelve first-grade classrooms located in New Hampshire and Maine were selected. Of the twelve classrooms, six were organized according to traditional patterns, and six were activity-centered. Traditional classrooms were defined as classrooms in which the curriculum and the instructional program was determined and prescribed by the teacher, so that the children had to adjust themselves to the curriculum. These classrooms were more curriculum-oriented than child-centered. The teachers in these classroms identified themselves as traditional teachers and were regarded by their school principals as excellent teachers. Activity-centered classrooms were defined as classrooms in which instruction was carefully geared to meet the individual needs and abilities of children; in which play was perceived as a valuable learning experience; in which the child had freedom to pursue his own interests, make decisions, explore, and discover within a curriculum designed to meet his needs. These classrooms are frequently referred to as informal and are modeled after the British Infant Schools. The teachers in these classrooms were well-prepared in the activity-centered approach. Each of them had received a graduate degree in Early Childhood Education that emphasized informal, activity-centered learning. Teachers in both groups were matched on the basis of age and experience. Of the total sample of 257 children, 124 were in the traditional classrooms and 133 were in the activity-centered classrooms. There were no significant differences between the two groups of children on the variables of age, sex, and IQ. The total sample of 257 children were given the following tests:

1. The *Murphy-Durrell Reading Readiness Analysis* (Murphy and Durrell, 1965). This was administered at the beginning of the school year. Scores at or above the fiftieth percentile

were defined as high; scores below the fiftieth percentile were defined as low.

2. *The Thomas Self-Concept Values Test* (Thomas, 1969). This was given at the beginning of the school year (to obtain a pre self-concept measure) and at the end of the school year (to obtain a post self-concept measure). Scores at or above the fiftieth percentile were defined as high; scores below the fiftieth percentile were defined as low.

3. The reading subtests of the *Metropolitan Achievement Tests* (Durost et al, 1970). These were administered at the end of the school year in order to obtain a reading-achievement score. Scores at or above the fiftieth percentile were defined as high; scores below the fiftieth percentile were defined as low.

4. *The Pintner Cunningham Primary Test* (Pintner, 1964). This was given in order to obtain an intelligence quotient measure.

To control the data for the variables of teacher personality and materials available for purposes of reading instruction, each teacher completed a pre and post testing on the *Adjective Check List* (Gough and Heilburn, 1952), and an inventory of the types of materials in his classroom or available in the school for purposes of reading instruction. There were no differences between the two groups of teachers on these measures. In addition, the investigator made two informal and three formal observational visits while the study was in progress in order to make sure that each teacher was adhering to his organizational structure.

The quantifiable data were analyzed through Pearson product-moment correlations, analysis of variance, and analysis of co-variance. Garrrett's table, "F-ratios for .05 and .01 levels of significance" (1965:451-454) was used to determine significance between means.

Findings

1. There was no significant relationship between (a) pre self-concept and reading readiness; (b) pre self-concept and

reading achievement; or (c) post self-concept and reading achievement. Correlations ranged from –.17 to +.04.

2. There was no significant difference between the post self-concept scores of children with high reading-achievement scores and the post self-concept scores of children with low reading-achievement scores. However, the data did indicate a significant difference at the .05 level between the post self-concept scores of children in the activity-centered classrooms and the post self-concept scores of children in the traditional classrooms (F = 4.48, 5.63, and 5.35). These data favored the activity-centered classrooms.

3. Although there was no significant difference between the observed reading-achievement scores of children in either type of classroom, the data did indicate that children in activity-centered classrooms obtained slightly higher reading-achievement scores (57.81-55.52) when reading readiness was held in control. A similar difference, favoring the activity-centered classrooms (57.88-55.81), was found when pre-self-concept was the covariate.

4. There was no significant interaction effect of classroom organization and pre self-concept on reading achievement. However, the data indicated that pre self-concept has a relatively strong effect on reading achievement with a P = .09, F (1,252) = 2.87.

5. Although there was no significant interaction effect for classroom organization and reading readiness on reading achievement, the variable of reading readiness had a significant main effect at the .005 level of reading achievement: F (1,252) = 7.957.

6. There was no significant interaction effect for classroom organization and post self-concept on reading achievement. However, the interaction effect of classroom organization and a post self-concept had a strong effect on reading achievement with a P = .09 favoring the activity-centered, high post self-concept group, which showed the higher adjusted mean reading-achievement score: F (1,252) = 2.89. Classroom organization was also found to have a strong

effect with a P = .13 favoring the activity-centered classrooms, which showed the higher adjusted mean reading-achievement score: $F (1,252) = 3.78$.

7. There was a significant interaction effect at the .05 level for classroom organization and reading achievement on post self-concept: $F (1,252) = 4.97$. The variable of classroom organization was found to have a significant main effect on post self-concept at the .05 level: $F (1,252) = 3.78$. These data favored the activity-centered classroom.

Conclusions and Implications for Teaching

This investigation tends to support the hypothesis that activity-centered, informal education enhances the self-concept and produces reading-achievement scores equal to or slightly higher than those obtained by children in traditional classrooms, and first-grade teachers may consider this approach to classroom organization a viable alternative. Certainly the data suggest that a learner-centered teaching approach is effective with young children.

It must be recognized, however, that the activity-centered classrooms observed in this investigation were carefully planned, well-organized, and functioned with a high degree of excellence. Their effectiveness was due, at least in part, to the teachers in these classrooms, who were not only committed to the philosophy of informal education, but also knowledgeable of a wide variety of approaches that could be implemented to translate the theory into practice. In addition, I consider it extremely important that these teachers voluntarily chose to implement the informal approach and availed themselves of a university program that assisted them in the endeavor.

Teacher educators who wish to help teachers use this alternative in their classrooms should consider:

1. Providing field-based programs to offer teachers an opportunity to gain expertise and skill in this area. These programs should be modeled on activity-centered education themselves.

2. Forming an informal education advisory service of faculty members to be available to public school teachers who want to implement informal education but do not wish to enter a degree program. Assistance would be provided on site and supplemented on campus when appropriate.
3. Helping teachers to develop as persons and actualize their own potential.
4. Helping teachers develop a sensitivity to and an awareness of the child's self-concept. Facilitative approaches and materials to enhance the child's image of himself and his sensitivity to others should be integral parts of teacher-education programs.

REFERENCES

Allport, Gordon W. *Personality: A Psychological Interpretation.* New York: Holt, Rinehart and Winston, Inc., 1937.

Annesley, Fred, et al. "Identifying the First Grade Underachiever," *Journal of Educational Research,* 63 (July-August 1970), pp. 459-462.

Barth, Roland S. *Open Education and the American School.* New York: Schocken Books, 1972.

Beez, Victor W. "Influence of Biased Psychological Reports on Teacher Behavior and Pupil Performance," *Learning in Social Settings,* Matthew W. Miles and W. W. Charters, Jr. (ed.). Boston: Allyn and Bacon, 1970.

Bennett, Neville. *Teaching Style and Pupil Progress.* Cambridge: Harvard University Press, 1977.

Blackman, G. J. "A Clinical Study of the Personality Structure and Adjustment of Pupils Underachieving and Overachieving in Reading." Unpublished Doctoral dissertation, Cornell University, 1965.

Bodwin, Raymond. "The Relationship between Immature Self-Concept and Certain Educational Disabilities," *Dissertation Abstracts,* XXIX (1959).

Bond, Guy L. "First Grade Reading Studies: An Overview," *Elementary English,* XLIII (May 1966), pp. 464-470.

Bricklin, Patricia. "Self-Related Concepts and Aspiration Behavior of Achieving Readers and Two Types of Non-Achieving Readers." Unpublished Doctoral dissertation, Temple University, 1963.

Brown, Mary and Precious, Norman. *The Integrated Day in the Primary School.* London: Ward Lock Educational Publishers, 1968.

Brownfrain, John. "Stability of the Self-Concept as a Dimension of Personality," *Journal of Abnormal and Social Psychology,* XLVIII (October 1952), pp. 594-597.

Cane, Brian and Smithers, Jane. *The Roots of Reading.* Slough: National Foundation for Educational Research in England and Wales, 1971.

165

Carter, Cleo D. "The Relationship between Personality and Academic Achievement of Seven Year Olds." Unpublished Doctoral dissertation, Indiana University, 1953.

Cattell, R. B. *Personality: A Systematic, Theoretical, and Factual Study.* New York: McGraw-Hill Book Co., 1950.

Central Advisory Council for Education (England). *Children and Their Primary Schools,* Vol. 1. London: Her Majesty's Stationery Office, 1967.

Clifford, Margaret M. *The Effect of Physical Attractiveness on Teacher Expectations:* Final Report. ERIC No. ED 056 348. Bethesda, Maryland: ERIC Document Reproduction Service, 1972.

Combs, Arthur W. "New Horizons in the Field of Research," *Educational Leadership,* 15 (February 1958), pp. 315-319, 328.

_____. "Snygg and Combs' Phenomenal Self," *Theories of Personality,* Calvin Hall and Gardner Lindzey (eds.). New York: John Wiley and Sons, Inc., 1963.

Combs, Arthur W. and Snygg, Donald. *Individual Behavior: A Perceptual Point of View.* New York: Harper and Brothers, 1959.

Cummings, Ruby N. "A Study of the Relationship between Self-Concept and Reading Achievement at the Third Grade Level," *Dissertation Abstracts,* 31. Ann Arbor, Michigan: University Microfilms, A Xerox Company, 1970-1971, p. 5195-A.

Davidson, Helen and Lang, Gerhard. "Children's Perceptions of Their Teachers' Feelings toward Them Related to Self-Perception, School Achievement and Behavior," *Journal of Experimental Education,* XXIX (February 1960), pp. 107-118.

Divoky, Diane. "War on Open Classrooms." *The Chronicle of Higher Education,* Volume XIII, No. 2, February 14, 1977, p. 12.

Durost, Walter N., et al. *Metropolitan Achievement Tests,* Revised Edition, Primary I, Form F. New York: Harcourt Brace Jovanovich, Inc., 1970.

Gardner, Dorothy E. M. *Long Term Results of Infant School Methods.* London: Methuen, 1950.

_____. *Experiment and Tradition in Primary Schools.* London: Methuen, 1966.

Garrett, Henry E. *Elementary Statistics.* New York: Longmans, Green and Company, 1965.

Giulani, George A. "The Relationship of Self-Concept and Verbal Mental Ability Levels to Levels of Reading Readiness Amongst Kindergarten Children," *Dissertation Abstracts,* XXVIII (1968).

Goddard, Nora L. *Reading in the Modern Infants School.* London: University of London Press Ltd., 1969.

Gough, Harrison G. and Heilburn, Alfred B. *The Adjective Check List.* Palo Alto, California: Consulting Psychologists Press, 1952.

Hake, James M. "Covert Motivation of Good and Poor Readers," *The Reading Teacher,* May 1969, 22, pp. 731-738, 741.

Hallock, George A. "Attitudinal Factors Affecting Achievement in Reading," *Dissertation Abstracts,* XVIII (1959).

Hamachek, Don E. "Study of the Relationships between Certain Measures of Growth and the Self-Image of Elementary School Children." Unpublished Doctoral dissertation, University of Georgia, 1962.

————. *Encounters with the Self.* New York: Holt, Rinehart and Winston, Inc., 1971.

Harckman, Laura D. *The Effect of Informal and Formal British Infant Schools on Reading Achievement.* Bethesda, Maryland: ERIC Document Reproduction Service, ED 062 011, 1972.

Helper, Malcolm. "Learning Theory and the Self-Concept," *Journal of Abnormal and Social Psychology,* LI (May 1955), pp. 184-189.

Henig, Max S. "Predictive Value of Reading Readiness Tests and Teacher Forecasts," *Elementary School Journal,* L (September 1949), pp. 41-46.

James, William. *Principles of Psychology.* New York: Holt, Rinehart and Winston, 1890.

Johnson, David. *The Social Psychology of Education.* New York: Holt, Rinehart and Winston, Inc., 1970.

Karlen, Robert. "The Prediction of Reading Success and Reading Readiness Tests," *Elementary English,* 34 (May 1957), pp. 320-322.

Koppman, Patricia S. and LaPray, Margaret H. "Teacher Ratings and Reading Readiness Scores," *The Reading Teacher,* 22 (April 1962), pp. 603-608.

Kehas, Chris. "An Analysis of Self-Concept Theory and the Application of the Findings to the Study of Achievement in School." Unpublished Master's thesis, University of Illinois, 1964.

Kelley, Earl C. *Education for What Is Real.* New York: Harper and Brothers, 1951.

Kranz, Patricia L., et al. *The Relationship Between Teacher Perception of Pupils and Teacher Behavior Toward Those Pupils.* ERIC No. ED 038 346. Bethesda, Maryland: ERIC Reproduction Service, 1970.

Lamy, Mary. "Relationship of Self-Perceptions of Early Primary Children to Achievement in Reading," *Dissertation Abstracts,* XXIV (1963).

Lewin, Kurt, et al. "Level of Aspiration," *Personality and Behavior Disorders,* J. M. Hunt (ed.). New York: Ronald Press, 1944.

Lewin, Kurt. *Principles of Topological Psychology.* New York: McGraw-Hill Book Co., 1936.

Lewis, Ruth W. "The Relationship of Self-Concept to Reading Achievement," *Dissertation Abstracts,* 34. Ann Arbor, Michigan: University Microfilms, A Xerox Company, 1974, p. 3839-A.

Lockhart, Hazel M. "Personality and Reading Success," *Illinois School Research,* 2 (1965), pp. 9-11.

Lumpkin, Donovan, "The Relationship of Self-Concept to Achievement in Reading," *Dissertation Abstracts,* XXIX (1959).

Lundholm, Helge. "Reflections upon the Nature of the Psychological Self," *Psychological Review,* XLVII (April 1940), pp. 110-127.

McDonald, Frederick. *Educational Psychology.* Belmont, California: Wadsworth Publishing Co., 1967.

Maslow, Abraham. *Motivation and Personality.* New York: Harper and Brothers, 1959.

Mead, G. H. *Mind, Self and Society.* Chicago: University of Chicago Press, 1934.

Morris, Joyce M. *Reading in the Primary School.* London: Newnes, 1959.

Moustakas, Clark. *The Authentic Teacher.* Cambridge, Massachusetts: Howard A. Doyle Publishing Co., 1966.

167

Murphy G. *Personality: A Biosocial Approach to Origins and Structure.* New York: Harper and Row, Publishers, 1947.

Murphy, Helen A. and Durrell, Donald D. *Murphy-Durrell Reading Readiness Analysis.* New York: Harcourt, Brace & World, Inc., 1965.

Nicholson, Liston O. "The Relationship between Self-Concept and Reading Achievement," *Dissertation Abstracts,* XXV (1965).

Perkins, Hugh. "Factors Influencing Change in Children's Self-Concepts," *Childhood Development,* XXIX (April 1958), pp. 224-227.

Pintner, Rudolph: Cunningham, Bess V.; and Durost, Walter N. *Pintner-Cunningham Primary Test* (Rev. ed., Form A). New York: Harcourt, Brace & World, Inc., 1964.

Purkey, William W. *Self-Concept and School Achievement.* Englewood Cliffs, New Jersey: Prentice-Hall, Inc., 1970.

Rogers, Carl R. *Client-Centered Therapy: Its Current Practice, Implications and Theory.* Boston: Houghton Mifflin Company, 1951.

_____. *Freedom to Learn.* Columbus, Ohio: Charles E. Merrill Publishing Company, 1969.

Rosenthal, Robert and Jacobson, L. *Pygmalion in the Classroom: Teacher Expectations and Pupils' Intellectual Development.* New York: Holt, Rinehart and Winston, Inc., 1968.

Ruhly, Velma M. "A Study of the Relationship of Self-Concept, Socio-Economic Background and Psycholinguistic Abilities to Reading Achievement of Second Grade Males Residing in a Suburban Area," *Dissertation Abstracts,* XXXI (1971).

Schwykart, F. K. "Exploration of the Self-Concept of Retarded Readers in Relation to Reading Achievement." Unpublished Doctoral dissertation, University of Arizona, 1967.

Sederat, Nassir. "Relationship of Achievement Motive, Ego Strength and Certain Aspects of Word Association to the Reading Ability of Intellectually Superior Pupils," *Dissertation Abstracts,* XXVIII (1968).

Silberman, Charles E. *Crisis in the Classroom.* New York: Random House, 1970.

Sopis, Josephine. "The Relationship of Self-Image of a Reader to Reading Achievement." Unpublished Doctoral dissertation, New York University, 1965.

Southgate, Vera. "The Language Arts in Informal British Primary Schools," *The Reading Teacher,* 26 (January 1973), pp. 367-373.

Spicola, Rose Frances. "An Investigation into Seven Correlates of Reading Achievement Including Self-Concept," *Dissertation Abstracts,* XXI (1961).

Start, K. B. and Wells, B. K. *The Trend of Reading Standards.* Slough: National Foundation for Educational Research in England and Wales, 1972.

Swartz, Darlene J. *The Relationship of Self-Esteem to Reading Performance.* Bethesda, Maryland: ERIC Document Reproduction Service, ED 006 723, 1972.

Symonds, P. M. *The Ego and the Self.* New York: Appleton-Century-Crofts, 1951.

Thomas, Walter L. *The Thomas Self-Concept Values Test* (Rev. Ed.). Grand Rapids, Michigan: Educational Service Company, 1969.

Toller, Gladys. "Certain Aspects of the Self-Evaluations Made by Achieving and Retarded Readers of Average and Above Average Intelligence," *Dissertation Abstracts,* XXVIII (1968).

Wallen, Norman E. and Travers, Robert M. "Analysis and Investigation of Teaching Methods," *Handbook of Research on Teaching.* Nathaniel L. Gage (ed.). Chicago: Rand McNally and Company, 1963.

Warburton, Frank W. "Attainment and the School Environment," *Education and Environment,* Stephen Wiseman (ed.). Manchester: Manchester University Press, 1964.

Wattenberg, William and Clifford, Clare. "Relation of Self-Concepts to Beginning Achievement in Reading," *Child Development,* XXXV (June 1964), pp. 466-467.

Weber, Lillian. *The English Infant School and Informal Education.* Englewood Cliffs, New Jersey: Prentice-Hall, Inc., 1971.

Weiner, Roberta. "A Look at Reading Practices in the Open Classroom," *The Reading Teacher,* 27 (February 1974), pp. 438-472.

Williams, Jean H. "The Relationship of Self-Concept and Reading Achievement in First Grade Children," *The Journal of Educational Research,* April 1973, 66, pp. 378-380.

Williams, Robert L. and Cole, Spurgeon. "Self-Concept and School Achievement," *Personnel and Guidance Journal,* 46 (January 1968), pp. 478-481.

Wood, Joan M. "The Relationship of Self-Concept to Reading Comprehension, Word Meaning, and Intelligence." Unpublished Master's thesis, University of New Hampshire, 1972.

Wylie, Ruth. *The Self-Concept.* Nebraska: University of Nebraska Press, 1961.

Zimmerman, Irla and Allebrand, George. "Personality Characteristics and Attitudes toward Achievement," *Journal of Educational Research,* 59 (September 1965), pp. 28-30.

11

Writing and the Self: An Examination of the Writing Processes of Seven Year Old Children

*Donald H. Graves**

The complexity of the writing process and the interrelationships of its components have been underestimated by researchers, teachers, and other educators, because writing is an organic process that frustrates approaches to explain its operation. Three major "Needs for Research" summaries in the last eleven years reflect specific concern for dealing with the issue of complexity (Braddock, 1963; Parke, 1960; Meckel, 1963). All three recommend extensive investigation of developmental issues, issues that focus much more on individual differences than on the "procedural-methodological" matters which have historically received research emphasis.

A review of research since the summaries indicates that most efforts have focused on correlative studies or the examination of the effects of single or multivariate interventions. The data from these separate studies make it difficult to produce a sound, organic

*Donald H. Graves is Assistant Professor of Education, University of New Hampshire, Durham, NH. Reprinted with permission from *Research in the Teaching of English,* Vol. 9, No. 3 (Winter 1975), pp. 227-241.

understanding of what is even involved in the writing process. Furthermore, only two studies seem to have involved the actual observation of the behaviors of writers while they are in the process of writing. One of these studies (Emig, 1969) involved the composing processes of twelfth graders and the other (Holstein, 1970) was primarily concerned with the use of metaphor by fifth-grade children.

This investigation was undertaken to explore the writing processes and related variables of a group of seven-year-old children. Through the gathering of data in a case study procedure, an analysis of broad samples of writing, and the naturalistic observation of children while writing in two types of classroom environments, formal and informal, the study sought to avoid both a fragmentary approach and teacher intervention. From this study a profile of writing in the early years emerges sufficient in depth and scope to make effective research hypotheses and recommendations.

In recent years new focus has come to the case study approach as a means to investigation of the variables involved in new areas of research. Indeed, the case study approach in the field of comparative research is most often recommended when entering virgin territory in which little has been investigated. Because of a lack of studies on the writing process or the actual observation of children while actually writing, the use of the case study to investigate the writing processes of children was considered as one of the appropriate methodologies.

The emphasis in this report of the study of the writing processes of seven year old children will be placed on a detailed description of the procedures used, and the conclusions and hypotheses formulated from the findings. This was done because the complexity and extent of the actual findings from case studies, small and large groups precluded their reporting in short space.

PROCEDURES

The Sample

Two formal and two informal second level (second grade) classroms in a middle-class community were chosen for the principal focus of a five-month investigation. The classrooms selected met specific criteria that identified them as being either formal or informal. These criteria concerned the degree to which children were able to function without specific directions from the teacher and the amount of choice children had in determining their learning activities.

Figure 1 depicts the makeup of the sample for the different phases of data gathering in the study. The First Phase involved ninety-four children (forty-eight boys and forty-six girls) with a mean age of seven years and six months at the beginning of the study. In Phase II fourteen seven-year-old children (eight boys and six girls) from each of the four rooms were observed while they were writing. In Phase III, seventeen seven-year-old children (nine boys and eight girls) from each of the four rooms were interviewed as to their views of their own writing and concepts of the "good writer." Finally, in Phase IV, eight children (six boys and two girls), two from each of the four classrooms, were chosen for case study investigation. The eight children selected were considered by teachers and administrators as representative of "normal" seven-year-old children; thus pupils of unusually high intellectual capacity and those with learning or emotional problems were excluded.

Data Collection Procedures

Throughout the data collection period from the first week of December, 1972, to the middle of April, 1973, the primary emphasis was placed on gathering case study data on two children in each of the four environments. Secondary emphasis was placed on gathering data from larger groups in the same four classrooms. Data were collected from: (1) the logging of five categories of information secured from the writing of ninety-four children; 1,635 writings were logged for theme, type of writing, number of words, use of accompanying art, and teacher comments; (2) the naturalistic observation of fourteen children while they were writing in their classrooms; (3) the interviewing in four different sessions of the eight case study children as to their views of their own writing and of seventeen children as to their concepts of "a good writer"; (4) the gathering of full case study data about eight children through parent

Phase IV — Case Study
Michael
N-1

Phase III — Interviews
Interviews on children's views
of their own writing and concept of the "good writer."
N-17

Phase II—The Writing Episode
The observation of fifty-three writing
episodes.
N-14

Phase I — The Writing Folder
1. Thematic choices of children
2. Writing frequency
3. Types of writing (assigned — unassigned)
N-94

Formal Classrooms		Informal Classrooms	
Room A	Room B	Room C	Room D
N-24	N-25	N-24	N-21

FIGURE I
Study Phases and Procedures

interviews, testing, assembling of educational-developmental history, and observing the children in several environments. The
purpose of this form of data gathering and reporting was to provide
a range of cross-validation of data to support the findings and, thus,
to add power to the research recommendation and instructional
hypotheses posed. This approach made it possible to follow findings
from the several larger settings to an individual case and, con-
versely, from the case and/or small group findings to all-class
profiles and to the entire group of seven-year-old children studied.

Phase One: The Writing Folder

Writing folders were kept by all children in each of the four classrooms in the study. The purposes of having all children keep a writing folder were the following:

1. to reduce focus on the eight children chosen for case study work;
2. to provide background data of a total classroom nature in order to view the writing of the eight children with greater objectivity;
3. to assess the general writing habits of the children in terms of writing frequency, assigned-unassigned writing, use of illustrations accompanying writing, writing length, and the thematic interests of children.

The definition of writing that was employed to determine paper selections was as follows:

> Any writing intended to be at least a sentence unit that was completely composed by the child.

Teachers distinguished between two types of writing — assigned or unassigned — when they reviewed the writing folders. Assigned was defined as writing that children were required to attempt and for which completion was expected. Unassigned writing was defined as unrequired writing. In this situation the child chose on his own initiative to write. There was no expectation by the teacher that specific work would be completed. Thus the child made choices as to mode, length of writing, and the disposition of the writing product.

Phase Two: Writing Process Observation (The Writing Episode)

In this stage of the investigation, fifty-three writing episodes of fourteen seven-year-old children (mean age — 7:7), made up of eight boys and six girls from all of the four rooms were observed. Writing of the children in the episodes was observed within the classroom in order to gain a more valid view of their writing processes. Writing episodes were not structured by the researcher. Rather, recordings of the children's writing behaviors were made when they chose to initiate writing in assigned or unassigned work. For this reason, approximately 250 hours were spent observing children while waiting for them to enter into a writing episode.

Within each of the four environments two children were chosen as case studies. These eight children were the prime focus of classroom observation. Because these cases were not always engaged in writing, were absent, or were working with the teacher, it was possible to record some of the writings of other children in the rooms. Twelve of the fifty-three writing episodes recorded were from six children who were not case studies.

There is more to a writing episode than the children's act of composing and writing down words. The observation of writing at only one point in time limits an analysis of the writing process and may result in conclusions which overlook important variables. Therefore, a single writing episode was considered to consist of three phases of observation: prewriting, composing and post-writing. Definitions of these phases and the factors in each phase for which data were obtained are given.

Prewriting phase. This phase immediately precedes the writing of the child. Examples of factors related to writing observed in this phase were the contribution of room stimuli to thematic choice, art work behaviors, and discussions with other persons.

Composing phase. This phase begins and ends with the actual writing of the message. Examples of phase factors were spelling, resource use, accompanying language, pupil inter-actions, proofreadings, rereadings, interruptions, erasures, and teacher participation.

Postwriting phase. This phase refers to all behaviors recorded following the completion of writing the message.

Examples of these behaviors were product disposition, approval solicitation, material disposition, proofreading, and contemplation of the finished product.

Recording of the episode

Whenever the researcher noted that a child was structuring materials for a writing episode, he moved close to the child and usually seated himself directly in front of his desk or table. Although the researcher was viewing the child's work in the upside-down position, it was the best location to record behaviors accompanying the writing episode. In this way the child's body posture, use of overt language, and rereading could be better observed.

For many children drawing was a major step in the prewriting phase. Michael, the case study chosen for reporting, apparently needed to draw before he was able to write in the composing phase. As he drew he would talk, often making appropriate sound effects to go along with the figure being drawn at the moment. While drawing the dinosaur referred to in Table I, Michael made growling noises to simulate the dinosaur's presence. To aid the recording of such data the observer reproduced the drawing, at the same time numbering each operation to indicate the sequence in which the picture evolved. Notable behaviors that accompanied each step were also recorded.

As soon as Michael completed his drawing, he started to write about information contained in the picture. At this juncture he began the composing phase. The researcher immediately recorded the time in the center column (Table I). When the child completed his writing the time was also recorded at the bottom of the column. In this way, the length of time the child was engaged in the composing phase could be computed.

The procedure for recording behaviors in the composing phase is contained in Table I. The left column records exactly what Michael wrote. The sequence of the writing and significant acts are indicated by the numerals. Since specific behaviors were noted from time to time by the observer as the writing was done, reference is made to these by circled numerals, with explanations of them given in the right column. For example, the circled eleven in the left column is explained following the eleven in the right column. That is, as Michael wrote dinosaur, he copied the word from the dictionary. Other behaviors were recorded during the composing phase and noted in the right hand column. To assist the summary of these behaviors, lettered symbols were placed in the center column from the key below to indicate the classification of the child's behaviors in the episode. For example, in the center column opposite the numeral twenty in the right column, the symbol "OV" was recorded. This symbol indicates that in step twenty Michael voiced words as he was writing them.

In the key at the bottom of the page in Table I the range of behaviors monitored when a child engaged in a writing episode were listed. Teacher involvement (T) was any form of teacher interaction with a child during his writing episode. Interruptions (IS-IU) were monitored for their effect on the continuance of the child's writing.

TABLE I
Example of a Writing Episode

A whale is eating the 1 2 3 4 5	10:12 R	9—Gets up to get dictionary. Has the page with pictures of animals.
men. A dinosaur is 6 7 8 ⑨⑩ ⑪ 12		
triing to eat the whale.	IU	10—Teacher announcement.
13 14 15 16 17 ⑱	R	11—Copies from dictionary and returns book to side of room.
A dinosaur is frowning ⑲ ⑳ ㉑ 22 23 ㉔		
a tree at the lion. and		18—Stops, rubs eyes.
25 26 27 28 29 30 31 32	RR	19—Rereads from 13 to 19.
the cavman too. the men	OV	20—Voices as he writes.
33 34 35 ㊱ 37 38	OV	21—Still voicing.
are killed. The dinosaur	IS	24—Gets up to sharpen pencil and returns.
39 40 41 42 43		
killed the whale. The	RR	25—Rereads from 20 to 25.
44 45 46 47 49 ㊽	RR	36—Rereads to 36. Lost starting point.
cavmen live is the roks.		48—Puts away paper, takes out again.
50 51 52 53 54 55 ㊶		
	RR 10:20	56—Rereads outloud from 49 to 56.

KEY: 1-2-3-4 — Numerals indicate writing sequence. ④ — Item explained in comment column on the right. //// — erasure or proofreading. T — Teacher involvement; IS — Interruption Solicited; IU — Interruption Unsolicited; RR — Reread; PR — Proofread; DR — Works on drawing; R — Resource use. Accompanying Language: OV — Overt; WH — Whispering; F — Forms letters and words; M — Murmuring; S — No overt language visible.

Two other behaviors, rereadings and proofreadings (RR and PR) were important indices of other writing habits. Rereadings were the child's rescanning of writing composed prior to the current word being written whereas proofreading was defined as an adjustment of a previously composed writing operation. In a number of instances children would adjust a picture to go with a new idea in the text (DR). The use of resources to aid writing (R) such as word banks, phonic charts etc. were recorded during the observations. Finally, the range and type of language used to accompany the actual writing was recorded. This language behavior ranged from full voicing (overt — OV) to the absence of any visible or aural indication of accompanying language (covert — S).

From time to time the researcher would intervene and elicit information from the child as he was engaged in a writing episode. The purpose of this procedure was to gain understanding of the child's rationale for a previous operation or insight into his

TABLE II
Examples of Interventions Made By Observer
During Writing Episodes

Phase in Episode	Setting at Time of Intervention	Observer's Objective	Observer's Questions or Statements
Prewriting Phase	1. The child was about to start drawing his picture.	1. To determine how much the drawing contributes to the writing.	1. "Tell me what you are going to write about when you finish your drawing."
	2. The child has finished his drawing.	2. To determine how much the drawing contributes to the writing.	2. "Tell me what you are going to write about now that you have finished your drawing."
	3. The child has finished his drawing.	3. To determine in less direct fashion how the drawing contributes to the writing.	3. "Tell me about your drawing."

Table II (continued)

Phase in Episode	Setting at Time of Intervention	Observer's Objective	Observer's Questions or Statements
Composing Phase	1. The child is about to start writing.	1. To determine the range of writing ideas possessed before child writes.	1. "Tell me what you are going to write about."
	2. The child attempts to spell a word.	2. To determine the child's understanding of the resources available for spelling help.	2. 'That seems to be a hard one. How can you figure out how to spell it? Tell me all the different ways you can figure out how to spell it."
	3. The child has written three to four sentences.	3. To determine the range of ideas possessed after the child has started writing.	3. "Tell me what you are going to write about next. Tell me how your story is going to end."
Postwriting Phase	1. The child is starting to put his paper away.	1. To check the child's oral reading in relation to the actual words written by the child.	1. "Would you please read outloud what you have just written."
	2. The child is starting to put his paper away.	2. To check the child's feelings or value judgments about work that has been completed.	2. Question series: "Which sentence do you like best? Tell me about it." "Is there anything you would change to make it better?" "Pick out two words that you felt were the most difficult to write."

strategies for future operations. The type of intervention varied with the phase of the episode. Examples of interventions and their settings and objectives are shown in Table II. Although there were many types of interventions they were infrequently employed to minimize the observer's effect on the child's writing.

180

Phase Three: Interviews

Two types of interviews were used to record children's views of their own writing and writing in general. The first included individual conversations with the eight case study children about the writing in their folders. The purpose in employing the writing folder interview was to gain a profile of the child's view of his own writing. This profile was constructed from the child's rating of papers from his folder, the rationales for such ratings, and his responses to other statements and questions about the papers. In the interview the child was asked to rate writings in his folder from best to poorest and to state a rationale for his choice of the best paper. The second interview consisted of asking questions as to the child's conception of what good writers needed to be able to do in order to write well. The questions were asked of seventeen children, seven of whom were the case study children.

Phase Four: Case Study (Michael)

At the conclusion of the data gathering, a decision was made to report only one case study, Michael, but to use all of the writing observations and interviews of the other cases, as well as the additional information gathered on other children in the four classrooms. The procedures used for gathering case study data involved all of those used in the first three phases, plus additional procedures unique to case study research. The additional procedures were the interviewing of parents throughout the study, the individual administration of test batteries in reading, intelligence, and language; the gathering of the child's educational-developmental history, and the extended observation of the child in areas other than writing at home and in school.

CONCLUSIONS

The findings in this study led to conclusions in five areas: learning environments, sex differences in writing, developmental factors and the writing process, the case study, Michael, and the procedures used in the study. These conclusions are reported below.

Learning Environments

Since the study distinguished two types of environments, conclusions relative to writing in each are possible. These are the following:

1. Informal environments give greater choice to children. When children are given choice as to whether they write or not and as to what to write, they write more and in greater length than when specific writing assignments are given.
2. Results of writing done in the informal environments demonstrate that children do not need motivation or supervision in order to write.
3. The formal environments seem to be more favorable to girls in that they write more, and to greater length, than do boys whether the writing is assigned or unassigned.
4. The informal environments seem to favor boys in that they write more than girls in assigned or unassigned work.
5. In either environment, formal or informal, unassigned writing is longer than assigned writing.
6. An environment that requires large amounts of assigned writing inhibits the range, content, and amount of writing done by children.
7. The writing developmental level of the child is the best predictor of writing process behaviors and therefore transcends the importance of environment, materials and methodologies in influence on children's writing.

Sex Differences in Writing

Differences in boys and girls were examined in three areas: writing frequency, thematic choice, and their concept of the "good writer." Warranted conclusions relative to these appear to be the following:

1. Girls write longer products than do boys in either formal or informal environments.
2. Boys from either learning environment write more unassigned writing than do girls. Unassigned writing seems

to provide an incentive for boys to write about subjects not normally provided in teacher-assigned work. Teachers do not normally assign work that includes themes from secondary and extended territory, the areas most used by boys in unassigned writing. (Secondary territory is defined as the metropolitan area beyond the child's home and school. Expanded territory is defined as the area beyond the secondary which would include current events, history and geography on a national and world scale.)

3. Boys seldom use the first person form in unassigned writing, especially the *I* form, unless they are developmentally advanced.
4. Boys write more about themes identified as in secondary and extended geographical territories than do girls. The only girls who write in these areas are those who are more developmentally advanced than others.
5. Girls write more about primary territory, which is related to the home and school, than do boys.
6. Boys are more concerned than are girls with the importance of spacing, formation of letters, and neatness in expressing their concept of "the good writer."
7. Girls stress more prethinking and organizational qualities, feelings in characterizations, and give more illustrations to support their judgments than do boys in expressing their concept of "the good writer."

Developmental Factors and the Writing Process

Such factors as a child's sex, the use of language, and problem solving behaviors, all of which have developmental roots, are involved as a child writes and interacts in various ways to produce two distinctive types of writers, identified by this study as *reactive* and *reflective*. These characteristics and behaviors are summarized in the following statements:

1. *Reactive:* Children who were identified as reactive showed erratic problem solving strategies, the use of overt language

to accompany prewriting and composing phases, isolation that evolved in action-reaction couplets, proofreading at the word unit level, a need for immediate rehearsal in order to write, rare contemplation or reviewing of products, characterizations that exhibited general behaviors similar to their own, a lack of a sense of audience when writing, and an inability to use reasons beyond the affective domain in evaluating their writing.

2. *Reflective:* Children who were identified as reflective showed little rehearsal before writing, little overt language to accompany writing, periodic rereadings to adjust small units of writing at the word or phrase level, growing sense of audience connect with their writing, characterizations that exhibit general behaviors similar to their own in the expression of feelings, and the ability to give examples to support their reasons for evaluating writing.

The reactive writer was most often a boy and the reflective writer was most often a girl. The reactive and reflective writers, however, were each composite profiles of a general type of child. Identification of either the reactive or the reflective writer was not dependent on the observation of a single behavioral trait. Rather, the characteristics exist in varying degrees in all children, and can emerge under different types of writing conditions, but they gain greater visibility when viewed at the extremes of the high and low ends of a developmental continuum. The identification of a cluster of traits over a period of time from any one behavioral type (reactive or reflective) can be useful in predicting other writing behaviors of children and thereby be of assistance to teachers in adjusting instruction to their needs.

The Case Study, Michael

The chief conclusion drawn from the case study of Michael was that many variables contribute in unique ways at any given point in the process of writing. Although the contributions of these variables were specific to each child, the identification of them appears to be transferable to the study of the writing of other children. Table III reports several factors identified as contributing to various components of Michael's writing and writing processes. Findings from the case study data made it possible to chart the influence of four main variables on factors identified as important in the process of writing. In Table III the influence of four main variables, family and home, teacher — room D, Michael's developmental characteristics, and a peer, Kevin, can be viewed in relation to their effect on such writing process factors as writing cause, thematic origin of writing, prewriting, composing, and postwriting. Each of these variables should be viewed in relation to its influence on the writing process. For example, in investigating what causes Michael to write, one can view specific contributions of a positive nature from the family and home, the teacher, the satisfaction of personal need, and the support of Kevin. Any one of these factors alone, or in combination with others could be the cause of Michael's choosing to draw and then write.

The influence of these variables on the thematic origin factor can be both direct and indirect. Examples of a direct factor in Table III is seen in the home's influence on Michael's writing about King Arthur, sports, ghosts and witches. An example of a multiple, and less direct origin, is seen in Michael's drawing in the prewriting phase. Michael may draw because of Kevin's suggestion, extra time given by the teacher, a desire to express a favorite theme, or the need to prepare ideas for writing. Thus, the following conclusions appear to be significant concerning the case study.

1. At any given point in a writing episode, many variables, most of them unknown at the time of composing, contribute to the writing process.
2. Children write for unique reasons, employ highly individual coping strategies, and view writing in ways peculiar to their own person. In short, the writing process is as variable and unique as the individual's personality.

Procedures Used in the Study

Because the use of the case study combined with data gathering from both large and small groups produced particularly striking

TABLE III
General Contribution of Specific Variables To Michael's
Writing and Writing Processes

	Family and Home	Teacher Room D	Michael Developmental	Peers (Kevin)
Writing Clause	Family is generally supportive of his work.	Provides mostly positive feedback.	Writes in order to draw.	Boys write up a joint project.
	Gives Michael encouragement with his drawing.	Provides help with self-direction.	Writes in order to play.	Kevin makes suggestion to write.
	Provides Michael with extra materials for drawing and writing at home.	Provides freedom of choice, time, and activity.		
Thematic Origin	King Arthur, sports ghosts and witches, camping and hunting, fires and explosions	Apollo 17, groundhogs, whales	Secondary and extended territorial use. Use of third person male, no females. Little use of first person. Need to express aggression.	Mutual interests: Kevin: "Let's write about fires." Request for Michael to draw and write on a subject to help Kevin with ideas and drawing models.
Writing Process — Prewriting Phase	Rehearses for ideas in family discussions. Provided materials and encouragement for drawing.	Provides materials that permit art work before writing. Provides freedom to to discuss materials and	Needs to draw to rehearse ideas for writing. Interested primarily in drawing.	Two boys discuss what they will draw.

186

Table III (continued)

	Family and Home	Teacher Room D	Michael Developmental	Peers (Kevin)
	Draws at home.	content.	Exhibits action-reaction style of drawing ideas. Demonstrates playing behaviors with sound effects.	
Writing Process — Composing Phase	Vocabulary backgrounds. Speech interference problems.	Teaching of: spelling reading punctuation proofreading Provision of resources: Phonic charts Pictionaries Word blanks	Generally reactive behaviors. Letter reversal problems Speech interference problems. Speech interference with spelling. Speech interference with writing syntax.	Minimal contribution to ideation. Some spelling assistance. Affects pace and structure by saying to Michael, "Hurry up, let's paint."
Writing Process — Post-Writing Phase	Unknown	Attempts to teach proofreading.	Quickly disposes of writing product by placing in folder or desk.	Kevin sometimes is in a hurry for Michael to do another activity and may subvert proofreading.

findings, a number of conclusions related to the procedure are warranted. First, the case study is an effective means of making visible those variables that contribute to a child's writing. Through the unity of one child's life, the constant focus in observation, interviewing, and testing makes it possible to hypothesize concerning the variables that contribute to the child's writing. In a broad interventive-type inquiry involving many children such speculation would not have been possible. Many of the variables discussed in larger group findings became apparent as a result of the intensive case study. In this sense case studies serve principally as surveying expeditions for identifying the writing territories needing further investigation. Some of the areas identified through case study and reported in larger group findings are the following:

1. The use of first and third person reported in thematic choices.
2. The identification of secondary and extended territoriality reported in thematic choices.
3. The identification of the prewriting, composing, and post-writing phases in the writing episode.
4. The identification of the components making up profiles for assessing developmental levels of children.

Whereas the case study contributed to the identification of variables in the larger group data gathering activities, large-group data provided a means for additional testing of the suitability of certain research hypotheses and directions. For example, large-group data were of assistance to analyzing the case study findings in the following areas:

1. Combining all of the fifty-three writing episodes made it possible to develop and hypothesize about the range and relationship of the developmental variables deemed significant to the writing process.
2. The larger group data confirmed the significance of assigned and unassigned writing and thereby contributed to the recognition of the need to pursue the area with the case study children.
3. The larger group data made it possible to view the differences in boys' and girls' writing shown in the case studies with greater objectivity. Writing frequencies, thematic choices, use of assigned and unassigned writing, and responses to the question on the "good writer" in larger

groups are examples of these differences which were observed.

QUESTIONS TO BE RESEARCHED

The main purpose of this study was to formulate instructional and research hypotheses concerning children's writing. The most significant of these hypotheses grouped into related categories appear to be the following:

Assigned and Unassigned Writing

1. If given the opportunity in an environment providing the freedom to exercise choice in activities, will children produce more writings on their own than if the teacher gives specific assigned tasks?
2. Will unassigned writing be longer than assigned writing, show greater thematic diversity, and be used more by boys than girls?
3. Will boys in comparison with girls, exhibit distinctive choices with respect to the use of primary, secondary and extended territory as well as first, second, and third person in their writing?
4. Will a survey of teacher-assigned writing in the primary years show that girls are favored through the assigning of topics chiefly concerned with primary territory?

Concepts of the "Good Writer"

5. Will distinctive responses to the "good writer" question be noted with respect to: boys and girls in general, those rated high and low developmentally, and specific writing strengths and limitations of the respondents?

Developmental Factors

6. Will two distinct groups of seven-year-old children be judged high and low developmentally as a result of the

demonstration of consistent behaviors related to writing in the following categories: word writing rate, length of proofreading unit during writing, concept of an audience who may read their papers, spelling errors, rereadings, proofreading after writing, range and complexity of ideas expressed before writing, and in reasons expressed in rating their own writing?

General Factors

7. Will general behaviors exhibited by the child in his writing episodes be determined principally by his developmental level and be changed only slightly by the classroom environment?

NEEDED RESEARCH DIRECTIONS

To date the need for developmental studies related to children's writing has been virtually ignored. Direct contact and extended observation of the children themselves are necessary to reach conclusions relating to developmental variables involving the behaviors of children. In fields such as psychiatry, child development, or anthropology, the investigation of behaviors would be unthinkable without the direct observation of the persons to be studied.

With the exception of a few studies, researchers have been removed from the direct observation of children at the time of their writing. Furthermore, the scope of even the direct observation at the time of writing needs to expand to include other behaviors in the environment. Such studies, however, cannot be conducted without the successful development of procedures that effectively record the full-range of child behaviors in their natural environment.

In order to improve both procedures and study scope, future research in writing should continue to explore the feasibility of the case study method. Further studies are needed to investigate the developmental histories of different types of children in relation to writing and the writing process. In a profession where there is a basic commitment to the teaching and understanding of the individual child, it is ironic that research devoted to the full study of single individuals is so rare.

REFERENCES

Braddock, Richard, Lloyd-Jones, Richard, and Schoer, Lowell. *Research in Written Composition.* Champaign, Illinois, NCTE, 1963.

Emig, Janet A., "Component of the Composing Process Among Twelfth Grade Writers." Unpublished doctoral dissertation, Harvard University, 1969.

Holstein, Barbara I. "Use of Metaphor to Induce Innovative Thinking in Fourth Grade Children." Unpublished doctoral dissertation, Boston University, 1970.

Meckel, Henry C. "Research on Teaching Composition," *Handbook of Research on Teaching,* American Education Research Association. Chicago: Rand, McNally and Co., 1963.

Parke, Margaret B. "Composition in Primary Grades," *Children's Writing: Research in Composition and Related Skills.* Champaign, Illinois, National Council of Teachers of English, 1960.

Part Five

Professional Concerns

Teachers who lack a deep commitment to learners and the teaching-learning relationship will probably seem to have few problems. They usually function at a superficial level and fail to recognize problems, or they succumb to environmental pressures that compel them to behave in a mechanical fashion. Teachers who think in terms of cause and effect, who ask, "Is what I am doing as a teacher consistent with what I believe in?" will find it much more difficult to settle into a frame of mind that makes them insensitive to problems. They face the problems of their profession because if they retreat into complacency their work becomes shallow, and they cannot easily live with a superficiality that is antithetical to their convictions and essences as persons. They are compelled to search for solutions that will enable them to be truthful with themselves, the learners in their classrooms, and the calling of teaching. In the next six chapters we share with you our views on the issues we have grappled with and consider vital problems for learner-centered teachers.

12

Teaching: Freedom and Responsibility

In the past decade, our American society has undergone an accelerated and significant cultural revolution. Traditional values have been discarded and there is an increasing tendency toward more personal freedom in the areas of human rights, sexual behavior, personal appearance, the communications media, and flexible time patterns for job attendance.

Americans today are freer in their personal ethics, values, and life styles than ever before. Divorce, once considered a personal failure, is now accepted as a commonplace occurrence. Premarital sex, once associated with the undisciplined people in society, is now an accepted part of a relationship. Honoring God and country, once common to the average American, now seems to be an attitude reserved for a minority of citizens. Physicians who previously responded to the 2 a.m. telephone call for assistance, now use their freedom to have a full night of uninterrupted sleep. The examples could be continued, but the trend is clear. At no time have citizens of any modern nation achieved such an expanded range of personal freedom in all phases of their lives.

The schools of our country have always followed cultural trends, patterns, and changes. In colonial times, when society decided that reading, writing, and arithmetic were essential for survival, they were taught. When the first colleges were formed in the European liberal arts tradition, and attendance at these colleges became the mark of an educated person, school curricula were expanded as mini-introductions to the experience of a liberal education. The advent of the industrial revolution prompted schools to develop vocational curricula so that students not attending college would be prepared to work in the emerging factories of our nation. When Russia launched Sputnik in 1957, the United States responded by pouring billions of dollars into space technology, and schools expanded and refined their science curricula in an effort to produce scientists, engineers, and technicians capable of helping us compete with Russia in the race to harness space.

Schools are but reflections of the desires and trends of society, and today they also participate in the movement toward more freedom. Students are freer than ever to choose courses of study, determine which learning experiences they want to have, and to decide how they will dress, how they will behave, and how they will live. Open classrooms, schools without walls, and alternative schools have added to the students' movement toward more freedom.

Teachers are also freer, actively moving toward more permissive teaching styles, expanding the range of learning experiences available to students, and reducing the emphasis on academic rigor in the classroom. They are freer in their lives, as well.

Accompanying the dramatic changes in social and cultural values, personal life styles, and educational approaches has been another change that is generating considerable national concern: students appear to be learning less. The evidence for less learning comes from the results of three nationally administered tests. Scores on the *Scholastic Aptitude Test,* used as part of college entrance requirements, have been declining for well over a decade. The

National Assessment of Educational Progress has results indicating that students knew less about basic scientific concepts in 1973 than they did in 1970, and that the writing skills of 13-year-olds in 1974 were more awkward, more simplistic, and less coherent than they were in 1970. The Department of Health, Education, and Welfare has evidence showing that the reading levels of students have been declining since the mid-1960s. Colleges must now offer remedial courses for the many students who have difficulty with grammar, spelling, reading, and computation. Textbook publishers have had to lower the reading levels of textbooks for them to be understood by college students. One city university has established eighth-grade competence in reading and mathematics as a new admissions standard. Data from several studies indicate that illiteracy is increasing despite massive educational efforts supported by billions of local, state, and federal dollars.

Educational analysts have offered several hypotheses to explain this disturbing phenomenon. Some of the explanations for the apparent dramatic decline in learning are (CEMREL, 1976):

1. Students are taking fewer academic courses. Enrollment in typical college preparatory courses such as algebra, first-year foreign languages, physics and English are down by fifteen percent since 1970.
2. Data indicate that there has been an increase in student absenteeism nationally.
3. By the time a student is fifteen he or she will have invested more time watching television than attending school. Television encourages a passive as opposed to an active approach to information processing. It transmits visual and impressionistic data and offers little opportunity for sustained analysis and reflection.
4. There has been a loss of school instruction due to shortened school days and increased student suspensions.
5. There is a drop in the perceived importance of schooling and more people are questioning the economic benefits of education.

6. With the increase of households in which both mother and father work, there has been a decrease in attention given to the intellectual and emotional development of children.
7. Intellectual and educational values are not especially prized by adults. Only one adult out of every eleven in the United States reads a newspaper. A relatively small number of adults are consistent readers. Adults do not model reading and writing behaviors.
8. The technology of communication has placed a lower premium on writing skills. Long distance telephone calls have replaced letter writing; copying machines have reduced the need to summarize and analyze written material.
9. Achievement tests measure things that are not now as significant as they once were in education.

The issue of student learning and achievement is a complex problem that will not be solved by simplistic answers and rhetoric. It has forced us to reconsider the concepts of freedom and responsibility in education. It appears that we may be faced with the dilemma of choosing between the two. Proponents of either choice are carrying on a vigorous argument with each other, and each group believes their choice must become supreme and exclude the other.

Democracy, the process of blending divergent viewpoints into a workable whole, seems highly applicable in the current confrontation between proponents of freedom and responsibility. A country dedicated to expanding human freedom must have models for that freedom in the education provided by the schools. A country that is dedicated to the importance of responsible citizenship must have models for that sense of responsibility in the schools. We must not foster freedom at the exclusion of responsibility, and we must not foster responsibility at the exclusion of freedom. Choosing to promulgate one at the exclusion of the other would result in a student who is only partially educated. Freedom and responsibility are not independent, unrelated, or mutually exclusive concepts. They are synergistic concepts that expand and enrich each other. They are synergistic because each requires the existence of the other in order to produce a total positive effect, and they are synergistic because a fusion of these concepts in the educational process develops a far more complete student than fostering one of the concepts alone. More heat than light will be generated if the proponents see no viewpoint but their own. In fact, when one viewpoint prevails, the catalytic influence of the other to affect, enrich, expand, and improve the prevailing viewpoint has been lost.

Personal freedom is a time-honored right to Americans, whether that freedom involves religion, self-expression, values, or personal behavior. That sense of freedom should continue to be nurtured in our schools, but individuals need a counter-balancing sense of responsibility if a synergistic relationship between the two is to be maintained.

Part of the magnificence of a true democracy is the attainment of the highest level of personal freedom for all citizens. But that freedom must have boundaries beyond which it cannot go; the boundary that necessarily limits freedom is the responsibility of respecting and attending to the rights of others. A truly free person engages in behaviors that expand and enrich the self but his personal expressions of freedom are accompanied by a counter-balancing sense of responsibility toward others. We may be free to light a fire in order to stay warm, but we also have the responsibility to keep that fire under control so that sparks do not destroy a neighbor's home. We have the right to vote for an elected official but that freedom is balanced by the responsibility to vote for the best-qualified candidate. We are free to earn a living, but we also have a responsibility to assist neighbors who are physically unable to work. We do have the freedom to speak but we also have the responsibility of not engaging in lies or slander. Personal freedom does have limits and those limits are reached when personal freedom is an encroachment upon the intellectual, physical, economic, social, or psychological freedom of another person. The truly free person must possess *both* a sense of freedom and a counterbalancing sense of responsibility.

If persons are to develop a sense of freedom and responsibility, it seems logical that the schools must furnish a basis for such development. A school that promulgates either personal freedom *or* responsibility alone has only half educated its students. A school that promulgates *both* freedom and responsibility has exposed its students to a total educational experience.

In order for schools to provide the correct learning atmosphere, its teachers must possess an intellectual and visceral sense of the importance of both concepts; they must be free and responsible individuals themselves.

Their sense of freedom will allow them to provide a classroom model of respect for individual freedom. The learning environment will encourage pupils to freely engage in the learning process because the teacher embodies attitudes that foster the emergence of personal freedom and initiative among students. The teachers' sense of responsibility will enable them to provide a model of respect for the importance of knowledge in the life of a fully educated person. They can demonstrate the importance of reading, writing, and computation as tools that help a person acquire academic knowledge. Academic knowledge should be presented within the context of freedom to enhance the student's existence as a positive and productive person.

Structure, responsibility, and freedom are not incompatible. Learner-centered teaching does mean that the teacher cannot develop structure and organization or present traditional information. In *Freedom to Learn,* (Rogers) cites the example of a college professor, Volney Faw, who gives freedom within limits:

> When the central focus is upon learning rather than teaching, there is no doubt that some teachers fear they will be left out, that they no longer have a place on the stage. Faw has handled this, in my estimation, realistically and well. The instructor in no way denies his own interests. He recognizes his desire to instruct, to teach. Like the student, he chooses those things he wants to present, and takes the initiative in making his place in the life of the class (1969:52-53).

A student in Faw's class commented:

> I had taken another course in which the instructor met with us and then said, "What would the class like to do?" Well we spent the main part of the course spinning our wheels. It was pretty disorganized. But in *this* course there was a well defined organization which gave me a feeling that the instructor knew what he was doing but still permitted me the maximum of freedom . . . to work on something I wanted to work on (Rogers, 1969:13).

One of the roadblocks to implementing humanistic education is the teacher's denial of self. We have observed teachers in a variety of situations who try to use an "open education" approach and after two or three months wind up throwing their hands in the air, completely frustrated and angry with their students. What has usually occurred is that the teacher bent over backwards to meet the needs of students and forgot that he was also a member of the learning group and entitled to full participation in the group's activities. The teacher who holds back ideas, knowledge, understandings, feelings, and information is not congruent, responsible, or involved. Glasser (1965) defines responsibility as the ability to fulfill one's needs, and to do so in a way that does not deprive others of the ability to fulfill their needs. Just as student needs should be met, so also should the teacher's.

The direct dissemination of knowledge and ideas from the teacher and the open expression of his feelings are consistent with learner-centered teaching. He is knowledgeable and has been prepared to teach the subject matter, and it would be the epitome of naivete to assume that students and parents do not expect him to communicate that knowledge and those ideas. The teacher is human, and there will be times when students will have to give way to the teacher if he really behaves in authentic and genuine ways. The "laissez faire, let them do what they want" approach to teaching reflects a lack of caring for students, a lack of engagement and involvement, and a lack of commitment. Under the guise of unstructured learning, open education, or humanistic education, some teachers have tried to escape responsibility and avoid commitment. Open education and humanistic education require time, energy, thoughtful planning and organization, and, above all, freedom with responsibility. As Glasser points out:

> Responsibility is not a one way street. Reasonable rules are part of a thoughtful, problem-solving education. Educational effectiveness cannot be increased by irregular class attendance. Teachers have the responsibility to make education relevant and interesting; students have the responsibility *to attend class, to study, and to learn* (1969:201).

And he clarifies responsibility when he says:

> The teacher must under no circumstances accept any excuse for a commitment not being fulfilled. If she takes an excuse, she breaks the

involvement because the student then knows she really doesn't care. Involvement ceases because a person who makes a commitment and is then allowed to excuse himself out of it knows that he is being harmed; he cannot continue to be involved with anyone who lets him harm himself. *Teachers who care accept no excuse* (Glasser, 1969:23).

For more than fifty years studies have been demonstrating the effectiveness of non traditional school programs (Jennings and Nathan, 1977:568-572). However whether in traditional or non traditional programs caring teachers know that reading, language, and computational skills are instruments that assist people in gaining access to the economic, material, political, and educational resources of society. Caring teachers expand and enrich personal freedoms in the classroom, but they nourish those freedoms within a framework that acknowledges the counterbalancing responsibility to help students acquire the basic knowledge and skills that will enable them to be fully capable persons in all phases of their current and future existences.

REFERENCES

Achievement Test Score Decline: Do We Need to Worry? Chicago, Illinois: CEMREL, Inc., Suite 3045, 875 N. Michigan Avenue, 1976.

Glasser, William. *Schools Without Failure.* New York: Harper and Row, 1969.

Jennings, Wayne and Nathan, Joe. "Startling/Disturbing Research on School Program Effectiveness" *Phi Delta Kappan,* 58, March 1977, pp. 568-572.

Rogers, Carl R. *Freedom to Learn.* Columbus, Ohio: Charles E. Merrill Company, 1969.

13

The Teacher
As a Student Advocate
and Change Agent

Within the literature of education there is a clear and unavoidable recommendation that the teacher should invest time and energy in working as an advocate for students. According to this viewpoint, a teacher can prevent students from being victimized by the school by functioning as an intermediary between the students and the institution. The teacher represents students in the school and transmits their grievances in an effort to influence the institution to behave more justly towards students. The idea that teachers can function as agents for institutional change is supported by Bennis, Benne, and Chin (1969), Havelock (1970), Sarason (1971), Schmuck, Runkel, and Blondino (1970), and Watson (1967).

The need for institutional change has been especially important to writers who are concerned with the needs and rights of culturally different persons within our society: Aragon and

Ulibarri, 1971; Kincaid, 1973; Spang, 1971; Sue and Sue, 1973; Szasz, 1970. These writers believe that culturally different persons have been denied distributive and retributive justice by institutions that cater to the needs and rights of the cultural majority. Distributive justice is based upon the legal concept that all persons should have equal access to the services and advantages offered by an institution. Retributive justice is based upon the legal concept that justice should be rendered to those persons who have been previously denied justice by institutions which purport to serve human needs.

If the teacher possesses any sense of personal and professional commitment, he must function as an advocate for the rights of the student in the institutional setting. The idea of the teacher as an agent of change is easy to think about, write about, and read about. It is logical because teachers are supposed to be committed to servicing human needs, and some of those needs may necessitate acting as an intermediary between students and the institution. The concept, however, has not been easily applied in the daily routine of the teacher's role.

In an attempt to be advocates for change, far too many teachers have done more harm than good. They have often generated more heat than light, and many schools have responded to the action as a threat and become even more resistant to change. Some teachers have been labeled as "quacks who have found a cause" and their credibility and impact within the school has diminished. This is unfortunate, because the contributions those teachers could have made have been weakened, and in some cases, irrevocably lost.

There are, however, certain principles of advocacy which have surfaced. Teachers who have successfully functioned as student advocates realize that more adequate principles of advocacy must be developed if they are to help the schools become more sensitive to the needs and rights of the individual. Some of these principles have been fully identified; others are in the process of development and emergence. The concept of teacher advocacy is sound, but the methods and objectives have not yet been adequately translated into practice. We offer the suggestions in the following section as guidelines to would-be agents of change.

204

PRINCIPLES OF ADVOCACY

1. *In presenting your case to an institution, base that case upon concrete evidence.*

The teacher who makes a purely emotional attack upon an institution will not be heard. He comes across as a loudmouth reactionary and the institution's response is to harden in its insensitivity to the individual. Too many well-intentioned teachers have defeated themselves and their advocacy by engaging in diatribes against an institution. Their message is not heard because of its blatant delivery. These teachers are most likely to leave the profession out of emotional exhaustion and disgust because the schools have not responded to their efforts.

Evidence moves institutions, not emotionality. The teacher who wants to change school policy must spend many hours developing the concrete evidence to support his demand that the institution alter a part of its behavior. Developing evidence is not an easy task; the teacher must recognize the difference between hearsay and substantial evidence.

2. *Present the evidence in a clear, concise, well-organized manner.*

Some teacher possess the substantive evidence needed to turn an institution around, but their presentation is so poorly organized that they still fail to win their point. Twenty pages of charts and graphs may never be read and absorbed by the busy administrators in charge of school policies and procedures. If the evidence is to be internalized, it must be simplified so that it can be easily read, understood, and absorbed. Presenting complicated evidence will only result in the entire proposal being ignored by those whom it is intended to influence.

3. *Evidence must be documented.*

Evidence cannot be based upon gratuitous assertions, because such assertions can be just as gratuitously denied by an institution.

205

Evidence must be documented and supported by facts, figures, case histories, or a tabulation of events that serve to bolster the credibility of the proposal being presented.

Evidence is not how the teacher feels but rather what he objectively knows as a result of the documentation supporting the presentation of evidence. The teacher who asserts that a drug education program is needed must not only indicate that a certain percentage of the institutional population is using heavy drugs but must also define "heavy drugs" and indicate how and with what measurement the percentage was determined. This may not be an easy task for the teacher who is affective in his life style and professional behavior, but he should look at how effectively Carl R. Rogers has used rigorous research evidence to support his feelings about the needs and nature of the individual.

4. *Devote the largest portion of your working day to teaching in order to develop the evidence.*

Too many teachers are so busy assaulting the institution that they have neglected the learning relationship with their students. Teaching is not just the educator's professional obligation; it can also yield the evidence necessary to affect change within an institution. If the teacher discovers *from his students* that the school's curriculum is unrelated to their human needs, then he has the supporting evidence to back up that belief. Such evidence is highly creditable because it was unsolicited by the teacher. It evolved as a natural outcome of a learning relationship that allowed students the freedom to identify the school's curriculum as a large contributor to their personal and non-academic problems.

Evidence that comes from the source — the students — can only be accumulated by the teacher who spends the largest portion of his working day in actual learning relationships with students. Such evidence, if accurately transmitted from the student to the institution, is far more reliable than a teacher's personal assertion that the institution must change its policies or procedures.

5. *Select the proper audience for the presentation of your evidence.*

   In many cases, teachers with the evidence and documentation necessary for institutional change do not know where to direct their information. They end up presenting the evidence to an audience (individual or group) that has little or no power to effect the desired change. If a teacher merely wants to test the evidence and documentation in order to sharpen its validity and reliability this is fine; but if he really wants to bring about a change, the information must be presented to the individual or group that holds the power within the institution. Teachers who fail to identify the correct audience usually become discouraged because although they possess the evidence and documentation that clearly indicates the necessity for a change in policy or procedure, there is no institutional response to their presentation.

6. *Develop your credibility as a person.*

   Institutions are more likely to make changes in policies and procedures if credibility of the person recommending the changes is good. The institution responds to the credibility of the evidence and documentation; but it also responds to the credibility of the person presenting the evidence. Some teachers possess such a natural and high level of personal credibility that they can move institutional mountains. Others possess such a low level of personal credibility that they cannot overturn an institutional pebble. The teacher with high personal credibility has only to do his job in order to initiate institutional change. Any teacher who wishes to affect policy must cultivate credibility, because any change that occurs within an institutional setting usually emanates from a person who is well received, well liked, and respected.

7. *Study and know your institution and develop a strategy for planned change.*

   In every institution there are forces working for and against change. An analysis of these forces and the institutional context within which they operate is essential if advocacy is to have any payoff for the students or the teacher-advocate. Perhaps the most useful conceptual model for looking at the potential for institutional change and developing strategies for change is the "force field analysis" developed by Kurt Lewin (1936). Lewin postulated that institutional behavior consists of a dynamic balance of situational forces working in opposite directions within the social-psychological space of the institution.

For example, suppose there is a need for a curriculum change in a school. One could see the curriculum as held in a quasi-stationary equilibrium by a balance of existing forces — some pushing towards change and some restraining change (see Figure II). The driving forces for change could be pressures from the community, student dissatisfaction with the curriculum, or organizational rewards for innovation and change. The restraining forces might be basic fear of change on the part of some faculty, faculty satisfaction with the present curriculum, antagonism toward community and student feedback, organizational features creating insecurity, or a lack of supplies, materials, and time to accomplish worthwhile curriculum revisions. Change occurs when an imbalance is created between the sum of the restraining forces and the

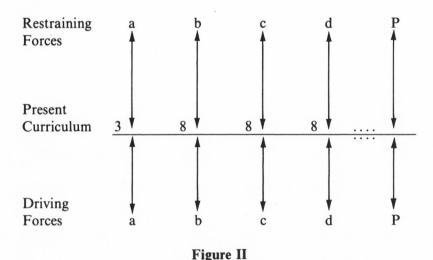

Figure II

sum of the driving forces. The imbalance will unfreeze the old equilibrium and the situation will change until the opposing forces are brought into a new equilibrium.

After identifying the various forces and estimating their significance, the advocate for change can choose from several strategies:

1. Increase old driving forces.
2. Add new driving forces.
3. Reduce the number and strength of old restraining forces.
4. Convert previous restraining forces into driving forces.
5. Employ various combinations of the previous four strategies.

If advocacy is to be effective it must be well conceived and accompanied by a plan based upon careful analysis of the forces impinging on the problem situation. This necessitates careful study of the institution and its conflicting forces.

8. *Identify the problem and decide on the kind of intervention you wish to make.*

As an advocate-change agent the teacher may intervene in an institution in a number of ways, not all of which are appropriate for a specific institutional problem. Blake and Mouton (1969) list nine basic kinds of interventions that can be made at different structural points in an institution to facilitate organizational development.

1. *Discrepancy:* Calling attention to contradictions in or between policy, attitudes, and behavior.
2. *Theory:* Presenting research findings or concepts that enlarge the client's perspective.
3. *Procedure:* Critiquing existing methods.
4. *Relationships:* Focusing attention on tensions between individuals and groups.
5. *Experimentation:* Encouraging comparisons of several alternative approaches before a decision is made.
6. *Dilemmas:* Pointing up significant choice points or dilemmas in problem solving, with attention to testing action-assumptions and seeking alternatives.

7. *Perspective:* Providing situational or historical understanding.
8. *Organization structure:* Identifying problems as inherent in the structure or the organization of work.
9. *Culture:* Focusing on traditions or norms.

Behavioral or institutional change is difficult to bring about in any social system or organization. In order to be successful, an advocate must develop the appropriate conceptual skills for identifying problems and designing interventions that can further student, community, and institutional concerns. Being an advocate-change agent calls for more than "gut-level" thinking and behavior.

9. *Know, understand, and be prepared to work through the informal system of the institution.*

Every institution has informal groups or cliques and informal aspects that can have a great bearing on the way formal processes are carried out. Informal relationships and communications systems should be carefully considered in planning any institutional change. The informal features of an organization, such as the amount of liking members have for one another or their willingness to help and support each other, can be positive and facilitating group processes that can be tapped in planning and implementing change. However, these same processes can also constitute a powerful restraining influence effectively blocking change. Whether in a factory, a school, or a hospital, the informal group relationships may be more important to group members than the approval of their supervisors or the organization they work in. It is essential for advocates to analyze the institution's informal structure and work *with* that structure in planning change. Gaining the support and cooperation of informal groups will require the highest level of human relations skills.

10. *Be aware of your own motivation and needs and place them in proper perspective.*

In every organization and group there are three general elements that should be considered in planning change (Mill and Porter, 1972):

1. *Forces in the change agent:* My motives and needs; my assumptions about people in general and about my colleagues, subordinates, superiors, and peers in particular; my value system; my confidence in the institution; my leadership inclinations; my feelings of security and my tolerance for ambiguity; my own motives as related to the personal needs I am satisfying.
2. *Forces in the group or organization:* The members' needs for independence and dependence; their readiness to assume responsibility; their tolerance for ambiguity; their interest in the problem; their understanding of goals and their role in formulating them; their knowledge, experience, and skill; their expectations; the effect on them of my own assumptions about them, their motives and needs.
3. *Forces in the situation:* The type of organization; pressures of time; consequences of actions; space, material, and supportive resources; restraining and driving forces for change.

In order to deal effectively with these elements the teacher must be honest with himself. To some degree we are all involved in viewing the various aspects of life from our own perceptual plane. We tend to hold to our own nearly conceived concepts of what is acceptable and unacceptable in our own private worlds. We have opinions that are sometimes well-founded and sometimes not; opinions that reflect our own biases as a result of our experience with life. Sometimes we judge without having a valid foundation for judgment beyond our egocentric perceptions. Our feelings about ourselves and others are often based on past interactions that are irrelevant to the current problem situation. We see what we want to see, and hear what we want to hear. Because of these human characteristics advocacy can be an attractive, even seductive, means of fulfilling our personal needs. It is all too easy to see ourselves as white knights sweeping away the forces of evil before us. Advocacy for institutional change requires more than the ability to scream injustice. That kind of behavior may make you feel good and offer a catharsis, but changing institutional policy or procedure requires patience, tenacity, knowledge of the process of change, and competency in effective communications and human relationships. Above all, the advocate must know himself and be skilled in dealing with his own biases. He must try to involve himself through introspection and become more aware of how his personality affects his functioning as an advocate and agent for change.

11. *The most basic principle of institutional change is that the "changee" must be involved in planning and carrying out any change that affects him.*

The effectiveness of the teacher-advocate will be directly related to his ability to involve members of the institution in diagnosing needed change and in formulating the goals and methods of change. Unless the people who will be affected by change participate in the planning and implementation, the prospects for effecting change will be minimized.

There are several phases in the process of change, each requiring different levels of relationship and communications skills from the teacher and varying levels of involvement on the part of the changees (Lippitt, Watson, and Westley, 1958). These phases are:

1. Developing a need for change.
2. Establishing working consulting relationships.
3. Clarifying the problem.
4. Examining alternative solutions and goals.
5. Transforming intentions into actual change efforts.
6. Generalizing and stabilizing a new level of functioning or institutional structure.

In all the phases it is important to give individuals the opportunity to share in the process of change. When people feel they own "a piece of the action" the goals of change are more readily accepted, internalized, and implemented. The broader the base of involvement and support, the better the chances are for successful change.

12. *As a consultant, change-agent, and advocate, use your human relations skills.*

In order to be an effective advocate and consultant, the teacher must function as a vigorous spokesman and ombudsman. He must be a skilled resource person who can help an institution diagnose its problems and formulate a plan of action. He should be a trainer who can help an organization learn the processes and skills necessary to accomplish democratically conceived goals, and he should be a counselor who can listen and communicate with people. Human relations is the heart of advocacy and planned change. Change and growth take place when people are able to perceive, examine, and assimilate experiences and ideas that were formerly disowned or considered inconsistent with the structure of the self and the institution. Change is fostered in a situation marked by acceptance, understanding, empathic listening, constructive feedback, facilitative confrontation, and honesty. In such an interpersonal climate people can explore their own feelings, look at threatening ideas from a secure position, and collaboratively begin to deal with institutional problems in a cognitive problem-solving mode. Human relations are the philosophical, attitudinal, and competency basis for successful advocacy and planned change. People are people and if you cannot get along with people you had better forget about being an effective advocate and change agent. That may sound simplistic, but the art of relating to people and the necessity for commitment, authenticity, and life-long learning about one's self and others may be the most difficult parts of being an advocate for change.

REFERENCES

Aragon, J. A., and Ulibarri, S. R. "Learn, amigo, learn," *The Personnel and Guidance Journal,* 50, (1971) pp. 87-89.

Bennis, W. G.; Benne, K. D.; and Chin, R. (eds.). *The Planning of Change: Readings in the Applied Behavioral Sciences,* (2nd ed.). New York: Holt, Rinehart, and Winston, 1969.

Blake, Robert B., and Mouton, Jane S. *Building a Dynamic Corporation Through Grid Organization Development.* Reading, Massachusetts: Addison Wesley, 1969.

Havelock, R. G. *A Guide to Innovation in Education.* Ann Arbor, Michigan: The University of Michigan, Center for Research on the Utilization of Scientific Knowledge, 1970.

Kincaid, J. "The Challenge of Change and Dissent," *The School Counselor,* 20, (1973) pp. 169-175.

Lewin, Kurt. *Principles of Topological Psychology.* New York: McGraw-Hill, 1936.

Lippitt, R., Watson, J. and Westley, B. *The Dynamics of Planned Change.* New York: Harcourt-Brace, 1958.

Mill, Cyril R., and Porter, Lawrence C. *Reading Book for Laboratories in Human Relations Training.* Washington, D.C.: NTL Institute for Applied Behavioral Science, 1972.

Sarason, S. B. *The Culture of the School and the Problem of Change.* Boston: Allyn and Bacon, Inc., 1971.

Schmuck, R. A.; Runkel, P. J.; and Blondino, C. *Organizational Specialists in a School District.* Eugene, Oregon: University of Oregon, Center for the Advanced Study of Educational Administration, 1970.

Spang, A. T. "Understanding the Indian," *The Personnel and Guidance Journal,* 50 (1971), pp. 97-102.

Sue, D. W. and Sue, D. "The Neglected Minority," *The Personnel and Guidance Journal,* 51 (1973), pp. 387-389.

Szasz, T. S. *The Manufacturing of Madness.* New York: Dell Publishing Co., 1970.

Watson, G. (ed). *Change in School Systems.* Washington, D.C.: National Education Association, Cooperative Project for Educational Development by National Training Laboratories, 1967.

14

Teacher Accountability and Evaluation

The age of accountability is upon us. Federal and state agencies are increasing the pressure on educators to demonstrate concrete and tangible results for the billions of dollars spent in local school systems. Educational engineering, performance contracting, voucher plans, systems analysis, cost effectiveness, behavioral objectives, educational audits, turnkey approaches, and technological support characterize the efforts to establish accountability in education. Accountability has been included in union contracts and has been part of legislation in a number of states. Already the wave of accountability has resulted in some fundamental shifts in the ways that administrators and teachers view their jobs. There is more emphasis on behavioral objectives and the need to define specifically the desired results of instruction.

In the past, failure to learn was seen as a weakness in the student, but the developing view is that if pupils have not learned,

Adapted from Gerald J. Pine, "Teacher Accountability: Myths, Realities, and Recommendations." *Educational Forum,* 51, November 1976, 49-60.

the teacher has not taught. More and more, parents, citizens, community and government agencies, school boards, and educators are holding individuals responsible for specific results in schools. No segment of public education can ignore the growing public insistence upon careful stewardship of human and material resources.

Current criticisms of education and related demands for accountability reflect a variety of societal factors: the escalating cost of education; developments in management techniques that have spurred the sharpening of goals, specificity in planning, and the establishment of cost-effectiveness measures; the Coleman Report, which emphasized educational output rather than input; the politicization of the schools; and rising educational expectations among minority groups without a corresponding rise in educational achievement (Landers, 1973). One can also speculate that the accountability movement is related to the American obsession with rendering every human activity — intellectual, physical, moral, social, and even sexual — accountable in terms of dollar expenditures. Behavioral objectives, systems analysis, and performance contracting fit the American philosophy of things. They are logical, ordered, objective, pragmatic, and precise and they lend themselves to mechanized, computerized, ways of learning and measuring outcomes (Welch, 1974).

The supporters and advocates of accountability are not all of one mind. Some view accountability as a process inspired primarily by a desire to see worthwhile educational goals regularly attained in large measure. For others, accountability may be motivated by the wish to economize on educational costs. And for still others, accountability may reflect a belief that education should control, discipline, and indoctrinate on behalf of a given dogma or the status quo (Romme, 1974). Accountability has so many meanings, and has been used in so many ways for so many different ends that the net result has been professional and public confusion. There is a rush to easy answers, accessible plans of action, and methods of evaluation and there is a developing mythology of accountability. We will be seeing more efforts to establish accountability in the schools and many of these attempts will not be successful. There is an obvious need for careful examination of the mythology, the confusion, and

216

the fundamental questions of accountability in order to develop recommendations for an effective humanistic accountability process.

THE MYTHOLOGY OF ACCOUNTABILITY

Myth 1. *The management and business practices introduced through accountabilty will increase the efficiency and effectiveness of instruction and provide insurance against educational deficiencies.*

Some people feel that schools should incorporate the precise accountability methods that produced "zero fault" aerospace systems. However, the question remains as to whether accountability methods alone produced zero fault systems or whether a *combination* of these methods and national commitment, legislative and executive branch support, and billions of dollars produced such results. Would that we had the same commitment, the same executive and legislative branch support, and billions of dollars for the "Right to Read" program. But what of the accountability methods that led to such fiascoes as the Edsel, and the F-111, or the Lockheed and Grummon aircraft debacles that required government intercession? What about the overruns of 200 percent in the Pentagon industrial complex amounting to millions of dollars each year? Management techniques have been available to business and government for years, but they have not prevented poor performance, inefficiency, costly expenditures, or some colossal failures. Will the techniques do any better in education?

Lake Erie is dying, our rivers are polluted, food companies are selling their cyclamate reserves overseas, the major car companies recall thousands of defective cars each year, aerosol spray products have been removed from the market, dangerous toys and flammable clothing maim and injure children, and obsolescence is part and parcel of consumer products. This is the humanitarian record corporations have compiled in their race to make America productive. Although a wholesale indictment of business and industry would be unfair, it is a fact that the industrial mind-set (profit first, humanity

217

second) has led to some appalling behavior that should be totally unacceptable to educators (Hottleman, 1971).

Indeed, the application of corporate management practices to educational problems could lead to some bizarre results. The following story of a satirical and apocryphal study conducted by a management consultant on the efficiency of a symphony orchestra has been circulating at the University of Wisconsin for some time. If we view the music and musicians as analagous to teachers and learning in education, a telling point can be made about the myth of management techniques. After carefully studying the orchestra, the consultant had several observations and recommendations:

1. *Observation:* For considerable periods, the four oboe players have nothing to do. *Recommendation:* Their numbers should be reduced and the work spread more evenly over the whole of the concert, thus eliminating peaks of activity.
2. *Observation:* All the violins were playing identical notes. This seems unnecessary duplication. *Recommendation:* The staff of this section should be drastically cut. If a large volume of sound is required, it could be obtained by means of electronic amplifier apparatus.
3. *Observation:* There seems to be too much repetition of some musical passages. Scores should be drastically pruned. No useful purpose is served by repeating on the horns a passage which has already been played by the strings. *Recommendation:* It is estimated that if all redundant passages were eliminated, the whole concert time of two hours could be reduced to 20 minutes and there would be no need for an intermission.

   The conductor isn't too happy with these recommendations and expresses the opinion that there might be some falling off in attendance. In that unlikely event, it should be possible to close sections of the auditorium entirely with a consequential saving of overhead expense, lighting, salaries for ushers, etc.

No more needs to be said. This satire speaks for itself and for a substantial number of educators concerned about the complexities of the art of education.

Myth 2. *All professionals are accountable — why shouldn't teachers be?*

We are told society is about to start holding professional educators accountable and that measurable success is the mark of the true professional. If accountability is the mark of the true professional, then as Taylor and Zahn (1972) suggest, we can expect to find that all professionals are accountable in the sense the word has been used. For instance, they speculate on how medicine can be fitted to accountability. A behavioral objective for the recipient of an appendectomy might read something like this:

> At the end of 120 hours following the removal of the appendix, the patient will, without aid, rise from his bed, walk to the window and open the shade without pain. Furthermore, the length of the scar will be within 7 to 11 centimeters long, and the top of which will not be visible with the patient clothed in a bikini covering the anterior of the lower body from the mons pubis to 24-30 centimeters below the umbilical scar.

If the patient performs as outlined in the clearly stated objective, the physician gets his fee. If the patient does better, the surgeon gets his bonus. If the performance does not meet the objectives set up in the contract, the surgeon must forfeit his pay.

Let's turn to another profession, say, law. Imagine that I have been practically wiped out in an auto accident: lost my car, my verve, and time on my job. I attempt to recoup my losses through the courts and my attorney and I set up a clearly stated objective.

> The claimant will, unaided by any springy step, leave the courtroom with a check in his pocket for damages, with said check amounting to no less than $100,000.

Again, being professional, my attorney will accept his fee on the basis of his performance contract.

If we look further in American life, we would have to grant that we have certain expectations in other areas as well. Let's look back at the role of the clergyman. We have long-range expectations that would probably come out something like this if expressed in clearly stated objectives:

> The soul will leave the body within 5 seconds of death and will be welcomed into the Kingdom of God as evidenced by the playing of soft music by Handel and rays of sunshine emanating through the narthex on an overcast day.

Suppose we were to examine one of the oldest professions. What might one reasonably expect here? Consider this clearly stated objective.

> The client will, at the end of 15 minutes, leave the house at an obviously slower rate than when he entered, his footsteps of a slow and shaky nature, the knees slightly bent, with a beatific smile on his face. All previously noticed lines on his forehead will be diminished so as not to be noticeable within five feet, and eyes will have a glazed and disoriented look.

Our lesson need not be limited to pursuits usually regarded as professions. We have been assured that this sort of thing "pervades almost all the rest of American life" (Taylor and Zahn, 1972:357). These examples of clearly stated objectives may be outrageous but they make a salient point.

Myth 3. *There are no existing procedures and practices of accountability.*

There are a variety of procedures and practices currently available for use by supervisors and boards of education to evaluate teachers and hold them accountable. They include such devices and approaches as video taping, interaction analysis, observations, teacher logs, rating scales, probationary periods, in-service training, and written examinations. The relationship between what exists now and what is proposed in the way of new accountability procedures should be spelled out (Landers, 1973). Maybe our efforts should be turned not only toward the design of new accountability systems but also to making what we already have work.

Many teachers have not been inclined to assess themselves and what they are doing because their schools have (1) developed arbitrary evaluative criteria and imposed those criteria on teachers without regard for or recognition of the teacher's involvement in the evaluation process, (2) employed criteria developed in other systems without making adjustments for the essential differences between other school systems and their own, (3) utilized haphazard approaches to evaluation, thus not inviting the confidence or professional respect of teachers, or (4) established adequate criteria but failed to implement the evaluation process in a manner consistent with the principles of democratic and humanistic education.

The procedures available now will work when teachers have a significant voice in designing and carrying out plans of accountability and evaluation. Teachers need the opportunity to work with administrators, community representatives, and others in developing a philosophy of and approach to a humanistic evaluation characterized by an emphasis on positive and constructive feedback promoting teacher growth and enhancing student learning. Without teacher involvement, new approaches will work no better than current methods.

Myth 4. *Accountability and performance contracting are modern phenomena in education.*

We should not be surprised by the failures that have come to light in such highly touted ventures as the Banneker and Texarkansas Projects. The outcomes were no different than that of the thirty-year program of "payment by results" tried by the English back in 1858. Financially, the principle of payment by results was successful in reducing government expenditures in education, but it was a disaster as a means of promoting sound education. It impoverished the curriculum, encouraged monotonous drills and cramming for successful results on tests, and fostered questionable teaching behaviors. The experiment was an attempt to assure a sound minimum of academic attainment for all children, but it was assessed as a national failure (Small, 1972).

There have been other experiments too. The provincial government of Ontario experimented with performance contracting from 1876 to 1882. The experience in Ontario proved that it is possible to raise standards quickly if criteria are defined as mastery of prescribed content. But there was such a storm of protest against the sacrifice of all other educational values for the accomplishment of such a limited end that payment by results was dropped by 1883. A similar experiment was carried out in the state of Georgia in 1819, and was also deemed to be a failure for the same reasons as noted above (Elam, 1970).

This history of accountability in education has practical value. It alerts us to address accountability as a complex issue requiring the careful scrutiny and consideration of fundamental questions that cannot be approached through quick and simplistic planning.

ACCOUNTABILITY FOR WHAT?

It is impossible to discuss the problems of accountability without reference to the goals of education, which in a democracy are too many and too varied to be forced into the procrustean bed of a particular aspect of the total process. The schools are responsible for dispensing a variety of information on cognitive, affective, and psychomotor issues. They are expected to help students develop critical thinking, the ability to solve personal and societal problems, patriotism, good character, cultural appreciation, a strong self-image, empathy, humaneness, vocational skills, driving skills, consumer skills, physical fitness, and much more. With each decade, as other institutions of society abandon more and more of their responsibilities, the list of residual functions of the schools grows longer and longer. Unless specific goals are established that are within the power of the school to accomplish, and unless these goals are considered in some logical order, the discussion of accountability will be without meaning or effect (Landers, 1973).

Can the school, can teachers be held accountable for results? Yes, but only for the results of instruction that are measurable. Instruction in basic skills and knowledge can be tested reasonably well, but this is not true for higher-order cognitive skills, affective and valuing behaviors, and problem-solving skills. As the pressure for accountability mounts, the schools will tend to confine teaching to easily tested material. The more the schools limit teaching, the less responsibility they will assume for affective goals and long-range life values that education should foster.

Most teachers who think about accountability see it as an increased emphasis upon standardized testing practices. And they are probably correct. The chief reason that accountabilty conjures up visions of standardized testing is that written objective tests are the cheapest, most efficient form of mass evaluation of student performance known. Because instruments that measure changes in the attitudes, self-concepts, and values of students are much less reliable than achievement tests, should affective and higher-level cognitive goals go unmeasured? (Esler, 1972)

Accountability Under What Conditions?

Any useful model of accountability must spell out the conditions under which students and teachers will labor to achieve the desired objectives (Esler, 1972). If teachers are to help their students meet specific goals, they must have appropriate manipulative aids, workbooks, media, teaching aids, and the like. This may pose problems for the school districts that have followed the practice of issuing one or two sets of textbooks and expecting the teachers to produce all other necessary materials. Anyone who is forced to operate with less than a full program of teaching materials has genuine cause to question the requirement for accountability. The same is true for those forced to teach in cloakrooms or hallways, or under other substandard conditions. Accountability requires, at the very least, acceptable working conditions, a reasonable amount of time for planning, and a sufficient number of tools and resources for doing the job.

It is imperative that the person held accountable for producing specific results be given significant control over defining the task and the manner in which it will be undertaken, outlining the resources that will be required, and choosing the means and methods of evaluation. As Miller has stated:

> It is unfair and unrealistic to expect a teacher to be accountable for goals which he has had no role in setting, when he cannot choose or control the methods used to accomplish the task, and when the resources necessary to do the job are not available. It is equally inappropriate to expect a student to work resolutely toward reaching objectives which he has had no part in setting. For these reasons, whoever is to be held accountable must participate in goal setting and in selection of methods and materials. Unless these prerogatives are present, it is doubtful that the concept of accountability will ever be successfully implemented. Unless the rules of the game are fair, it will be impossible to find anyone foolish enough to play (1972:615).

THE PHILOSOPHICAL QUESTION

One of the messages coming from performance contractors is that we should only concern ourselves with objectives that can be stated in simple and overt behavioral terms and that are readily measurable at the end of the instruction period (Taylor and Zahn, 1972). But what happens when our goals are complex, extensive, and long-term? The superintendent of schools in Texarkana, Arkansas, states the performance-contracting view in what he must see as clear and simple terms:

> Here are 25 children, and this is where they are in September. Based on what we know about them as students, here's where they ought to be next June. If you get them there this is your salary. If you get them farther, this is your bonus, and so forth (Taylor and Zahn, 1972:357).

"Where they are" and "where they ought to be" are philosophical problems and perhaps the most important questions for educators.

Though educational research has yet to identify any "best" instructional approach for all areas of the curriculum, a model of accountability must define quite specifically, and perhaps arbitrarily, the behaviors to be achieved by the students in a school or school system (Esler, 1972). Defining any discipline with a list of specific behavioral objectives may result in a rather narrow version of that discipline, and may exclude some legitimate goals and objectives that reflect other philosophies. This brings us to the philosophical question of *who* determines toward *where* the schools will move and *what* the schools will teach? The move to accountability must be accompanied by an understanding of the philosophical aspects of education and a fierce determination to see that testers, contractors, and objectives writers are not the sole determiners of the goals of education.

THE MORAL QUESTION

The problem has been nicely delineated by Broudy:

> When accountability is defined as a contract to produce a specified result the contractor may or may not be held accountable for the method he uses. For example, in Texarkana, allegations were made that the contractor had been teaching for the test. Was that cricket? He may use odd methods of motivating the children and the teachers: The contractor may well retort, "You wanted these results, we promised to get them; you get them, what's the beef?" There is something admirably tough minded and sporting about this

no-excuses approach. But suppose the results contracted for are accompanied by other less desirable results? Is it sporting to victimize those who sustain the undesirable results. Even with clear cut contracts bristling with sharp edged objectives and with tests that can be used to find out whether or not the contract has been fulfilled, the moral question is not wholly irrelevant. Too often the pupils are not party to the contract, but they are objects of it, and if they cannot negotiate directly for themselves, somebody — the parents, the school board, the state — is morally and legally bound to do so (1972:126-127).

Let's pursue the moral question further in terms of the more trenchant criticisms of accountability. Does accountability mean that we are no longer interested in *how* children learn, and does it ignore some of the most important research on the cognitive development of children? Is it too goal-oriented, obsessed with fact, and overly attuned to the profit motive? Piaget (1952) has shown that children's thought processes are unlike those of adults; they progress from alogical to logical thinking by accommodating and assimilating new experiences. This important concept underscores the need for learning situations rich with experience. Consider Piaget's concept and Dewey's view of education in relation to performance contracting:

1. *Learning is a direct experience.* How can learning be a direct experience emanating from a child's needs and interests if a performance contractor or a bank of behavioral objectives or criterion-referenced tests determine what the child will study? Instead of subjects that interest him, the child may receive a daily dose of prescribed and predigested lower-level cognitive material served up on a learning package or teaching machine.
2. *Good education is built upon intrinsic motivation — upon its relevance to the child.* In several current experiments with performance contracting, intrinsic motivation is so lacking that children must be motivated to complete their tasks by tokens, candy, and even record players. If tokens are given, what then? Will the child internalize the assumption that reading is worthwhile because you get a reward for it, that it has no implicit value? Is this the value we wish to teach?

225

3. *Learning is a process as well as an end in itself.* Learning can be lost as well as gained, for it is the process of learning and applying basic skills that is valuable. Learning how to learn may be more important than learning a set of facts. Any test score can be increased by high pressure and gimmicks, but will the improvement last?

4. *Learning is random as well as sequential.* Most accountability programs do not seem to reflect this basic principle. The highly structured programmed materials only individualize the rate of instruction — not the material.

One of the educators who protests the systems approach and articulates the moral problem is Herbert Kiiebard of the University of Wisconsin:

> Modern curriculum theory, currently being influenced by systems analysis, tends to regard the child simply as input inserted into one end of a great machine, from which he eventually emerges at the other end as output replete with all the behaviors, the "competencies," and the skills for which he has been programmed. Even when the output is differentiated, such a mechanistic conception of education contributes only to man's regimentation and dehumanization, rather than to his autonomy (Hottleman, 1971:3-4).

Are children and parents in agreement with the contracts that generate these kinds of learning experiences, or are they unseen and unheard victims of an education defined through programs they have had no part in designing?

WHO SHOULD BE HELD ACCOUNTABLE?

Thus far we have discussed the problems of teacher accountability, but there is a broader context. The teacher's accountability is only part of the reciprocal responsibilities of the schools to society, and vice versa. For example, is there any limit to the pupil objectives the schools are to be held accountable for? In the past, the schools had a role in attempting to solve an imposing array of social problems. Are there any "old" responsibilities for which schools are no longer accountable? Or has the list simply kept expanding (Soar, 1973)? Is the family in any way accountable for the readiness or socialization of the child when he begins school? Or is the teacher of kindergarten or first grade accountable for a child who begins with little or no language, no cleanliness habits, or poor toilet training? Is the interest and effort the child brings to his work solely the teacher's responsibility? To what extent is the school or the classroom teacher accountable for the emotionally battered and deprived child who can barely make his way to school each day? To whom are parents, administrators, and citizen groups accountable? Should behavioral objectives and performance contracts be written for parents, administrators, or the community? Is there anyone who can be held accountable for the support schools and teachers need in order to carry out their work? Does the school system and the society it represents have a responsibility to the teacher for financial, moral, and attitudinal support? Is the community accountable for the support of research and planning to improve the quality and efficiency of the educational process in the schools? Questions like these seem to be ignored in discussions of accountability. Are they relevant, or is only the teacher to be held accountable?

How do we deal with accountability as we move toward individualized instruction, alternatives in learning, open education, parental and paraprofessional involvement, community-school partnerships, teacher aides, participatory decision-making, and shared power? Crotty observes:

> Though teachers may be accountable for pupil progress or lack of it, they don't operate in a vacuum. And no amount of exemplary classroom professionalism can offset the failure of others to hold themselves accountable. The student who will not accept a share of responsibility for his own learning, the parent who refuses an active participative role in local schools and who summarily dismisses the annual budget with a *no* vote affect the teacher's success potential. Similarly, administrators, boards of education, and even state legislators must recognize their respective stewardships as they are participants in education. Failure to do so may render the teacher's goals unattainable (1972:149).

Each teacher should only be held accountable for actions that influence, either directly or indirectly, some aspect of the educational system. Many administrators, boards of education, and the general public hold teachers responsible for virtually everything,

227

including their mistakes and failures (Kult, 1972). This is where the moot question is not so moot. Administrators have their jobs, teachers theirs, parents theirs, and school boards theirs, but too frequently the teacher is put in the alarming position of taking the whole weight of accountability on his shoulders. Consider the demand of accountability for teacher performance in educational systems that give teachers zero voice in the system's conception and development (Kult, 1972). Consider, too, the demand of accountability for teacher performance on other externally controlled prerogatives, like pupil-teacher ratios, availability of special services, budgets for textbooks, and so on. It seems logical that the parties calling for teacher accountability are, in fact, calling for their *own* accountability.

In summary, the classroom teacher should not be the scapegoat when the school system fails to produce what the parents, the board, or the administration demands. Although teachers are the likely ones to be held accountable, they often do not have the resources or power to alter policies or practices that must be changed if improvements are to come about. They are not free to buy materials, hire consultants, assign pupils, or initiate new curricula as they see fit, yet these steps are often necessary if a change in the program is to take place (Miller, 1972).

THE QUESTION OF CAUSE AND EFFECT

What is the nature of the cause and effect relationship between teaching and learning? Dyer (1973) takes the position that despite all the theories that have been spun about the teaching-learning process, there can never be an absolute guarantee that any given set of actions by a teacher, or any given set of reactions on the part of students will produce any specific kind or amount of learning. All learning is probabilistic and contingent on variables existing within and outside the school. It is of the utmost importance that this fact be recognized by teachers and everybody else concerned with the education of the young.

If the classroom interaction pattern is to bring about desirable learning, it must be regarded as somewhat of a continuous experiment. In this experiment any number of alternatives are tried by the teacher and students until the desired change in the students' development occurs (Dyer, 1973). The teacher's obligation is to keep the experiment going and to keep it under control. This means first, that the teacher shall use the knowledge he has of his subject and his students to help them select alternatives that seem to have the highest probability of paying off. It means second, that he shall observe what happens as carefully as he can, and alter his strategy as needed. Dyer's model of the teaching process suggests some of the variables that must be considered if we are going to determine the extent to which the teacher can be held accountable and also suggests that the variables are fluid and will change as the teaching-learning situation changes.

The complexity of influences on student learning does not excuse the teacher from his obligation to teach. He is still accountable (1) to his students for creating a classroom environment in which they can learn — and will feel encouraged to learn in — and (2) to the school principal, the other teachers, and the students' parents for contributing to the joint effort to optimize the learning possibilities of each child's total school experience.

The evaluation of teaching and its results is of paramount concern to all teachers, regardless of their theoretical and philosophical biases. The teaching profession cannot move forward on the basis of gratuitous statements about the outcomes and effectiveness of teaching. What can be gratuitously asserted can be gratuitously denied, and incidental or haphazard approaches to evaluation contribute very little to our understanding of teaching or to its improvement.

Evaluating the competencies of the classroom teacher has always been a difficult task. A teacher who has been judged competent often achieves this status as the result of how those who work with him feel about him. This is not unusual, in that the public generally tends to judge the physician and dentist in the same manner. No one outside the field of medicine really knows much about the medical skills of the physician; they tend to judge his competency according to how they feel about him. If their feelings tend toward the positive, the physician achieves a community image of competency. Even in a national presidential election, more often than not the voter casts his vote on the basis of a stronger feeling for one candidate over the other. Very few people vote on the basis of a logical and scientific evaluative procedure.

We need to develop certain criteria and procedures to evaluate teachers with a higher degree of sophistication than at present. Some teachers might prefer to stay with the current nebulous state in which the evaluation of their competency is essentially in the lap of the gods. They feel there is safety in having no criteria, and in working with vaguely-defined procedures, because no one really knows what to expect and they are given more latitude to evade "the moment of truth" about the quality of their teaching.

The ultimate purpose of effective evaluation is the growth and development of the student. Consequently evaluation should revolve around two pivotal concerns. *Are we helping students?* Are we helping them to learn? Are we helping them like themselves and each other? Are we helping them come to grips with the ethical, moral, and social questions that affect the quality of life? *How can we help teachers be more effective and offer more to their students?* In designing an evaluation plan to address these questions, we need to ask who is to evaluate the teacher and what are the minimal principles and conditions for meaningful evaluation.

WHO EVALUATES THE TEACHER?

Who is to judge the competency of the teacher? Those who align themselves with the internal-frame-of-reference concept argue that the teacher is the best source of information regarding his competency. Those who espouse the external-frame-of-reference concept say that the teacher's competency must be evaluated by sources external to the teacher because his self-evaluation may be distorted by egocentrism or defensiveness. A logical compromise is to evaluate the competency of the teacher from both the internal and external frames of reference. That is, the teacher must be a participant in evaluating his competency, but, at the same time, he must allow himself to be evaluated by significant colleagues in the position to adequately judge his competency. The teacher may possess a private perception of competence that enables him to function with apparent clarity and ease. A teacher can see a great deal from his personal viewpoint, but his perceptions will be limited because he has no frame of reference external to himself to challenge an apparently well-structured self. He can learn how others view his competency by participating in a cooperative evaluative process in which his self-image and exterior-to-self image are presented as a composite picture.

Who will evaluate the teacher's competency from an external frame of reference? It appears that the significant others who would be in the best position to render such an external evaluation would be students, other teachers, supervisory staff, and the school principal. Acquiring evaluations beyond these would be left up to the teacher. If he felt that he might profit from the evaluations of others, he might seek more information for a wider external-to-self picture.

The teacher's self-evaluation and external-to-self evaluations would be synthesized in a meeting between the teacher and those performing the external-to-self evaluations. In an open and free discussion, the areas of strength and weakness could be identified and both the teacher and his external evaluators would become involved in firming up the strengths and working on the weaknesses. The teacher could vastly improve his functional role if, when a weakness was identified, discussion centered on whether the weakness was lodged in the person of the teacher or was due to administrative patterns inhibiting the effectiveness of the teacher. For example, if a teacher is externally evaluated to have weak rapport with students, the group should try to discover if the problem was due to the attitudinal makeup of the teacher or to the fact that the teacher was so entwined in extra classroom disciplinary functions that students saw him as more of an authority figure than a teacher. The pursuit of this question would shed much light upon the teacher's proper role and how it affects his functional competency.

Teacher growth is facilitated in an atmosphere in which evaluation is a cooperative process, with emphasis on self-evaluation. Self-evaluation and peer evaluation enable teachers to really judge how much they have grown and what they need to do in order to become more effective. For example, through video-tape recordings, the teacher can determine the quality of the pupils' response to him as a person and can gain valuable insights to help him enhance his teaching. By asking colleagues to listen and critique recordings of his interactions with students, the teacher can learn not only what impact he has on students, but also how he is perceived by peers. This kind of learning fosters self-discovery and personal confrontation, enabling the teacher to become more sensitive and attuned to his students and peers as people.

RECOMMENDATIONS

Accountability is forcing us to ask questions about the goals and values of our educational system. If teachers and schools are to be held accountable, they must know what results are sought. The goals of education will have to be crystal clear. Successful accountability will require improved communication and involvement of pupils and parents (Miller, 1972). This kind of participation should result in better understanding and support of school programs. We cannot be against accountability; we must be able to demonstrate that we are accomplishing something of value in our schools. It is possible, however, that the means we choose may destroy and impede the very goals we seek (Welch, 1974). We need to develop alternative, individualized, and humanistic accountability programs that will accommodate differences in human aspirations, competence, motivation, and performance. Such programs would include behavioral objectives for lower-level cognitive skills as well as subjective, informal, and observational processes for assessing higher-level cognitive, affective, and valuing behaviors.

The following items appear to be the minimal and necessary humanistic conditions for the development of accountability programs that will improve teaching skills and facilitate more meaningful learning for students:

1. A plan of accountability developed by teachers, administrators, parents, and students working together, that has

evolved from a free and open discussion of the philosophical, theoretical, and empirical considerations that influence learning.

2. A clearly stated philosophy and rationale for accountability developed by teachers, administrators, parents, and students.

3. A continuous, on-going process of accountability characterized by continuous feedback and established monitoring points so that the teacher and appropriate supervisory and administrative personnel have specific time referents for gauging and discussing the progress of the teacher and the learning of his students.

4. A clear statement of performance standards and criteria that is understandable and acceptable to teachers, administrators, parents, and students.

5. A plan of accountability that accommodates judgments and observations from both the internal (teacher) and external (supervisor/parent) frames of reference.

6. A plan of accountability that includes an annual review by teachers, administrators, parents, and students of evaluative processes, performance criteria and standards, roles, and responsibilities.

7. A plan of accountability that takes into consideration local conditions, needs, and resources.

8. Clearly defined but flexible methodological procedures for collecting data to test performance criteria used in evaluating and supervising teachers. For instance:

   a. Teacher and supervisor analyze and critique video tapes of the individual teacher's performance in the classroom.

   b. Teachers and colleagues analyze and critique video tapes of the teaching performance.

   c. Teacher conducts personal research into his effectiveness and shares the results for critique with supervisor and colleagues. This might be accomplished through the use of questionnaires or surveys of students, teachers, and parents.

     d. Periodically, the teacher prepares a self-evaluation and the supervisor writes an evaluation of the teacher. Together they share the results and discuss areas of agreement and disagreement.

9. A plan of accountability that can be defined and modified on the basis of periodic feedback from all who are affected.

10. A plan of accountability in which all participants accept some accountability. For each goal the parties involved (students, teaches, parents, and administrators) would decide not only what is to be accomplished but also what they are to be responsible for.

11. A plan of accountability based on needs assessments, philosophical considerations, and goal formulations that is the result of collaborative efforts of teachers, students, parents, and administrators.

A sensible plan of accountability calls for the establishment of new relationships and the reshaping of traditional roles. Many more individuals wil be involved in the governing of education. When the community and the school move into real partnerships the issues of accountability will not be viewed within a framework of superior-subordinate relationships. Shared responsibility and accountability are the keys to successful humanistic accountability.

REFERENCES

Broudy, Harry S. *The Real World of Public Schools.* New York: Harcourt, Brace, and Janovich, 1972.

Crotty, William E. "Accountability and Governance," *The Clearing House,* 47 (November, 1972). p. 149.

Dyer, Henry. *How to Achieve Accountability in the Public Schools.* Bloomington, Indiana: Phi Delta Kappa Educational Foundation, 1973.

Elam, Stanley. "The Chameleon's Dish," *Phi Delta Kappan,* 52 (September 1970), pp. 70-72.

Esler, William K. "Accountability: The Teacher's Perspective," *The Clearing House* (May 1972), pp. 531-534.

Hottleman, Girard D. "Performance Contracting Is A Hoax," *Education Digest,* 37 (September 1971), pp. 1-4.

Kult, Lawrence. "Look Who Is Crying Accountability," *The Clearing House,* 47 (October 1972), p. 82.

Landers, Jacob. "Accountability and Progress by Nomenclature: Old Ideas in New Bottles, *Phi Delta Kappan,* 54 (April 1973), pp. 538-540.

Miller, William C. "Accountability Demands Involvement," *Educational Leadership,* 29 (April 1972), pp. 613-617.

Piaget, J. *The Origins of Intelligence in Children.* New York: International Universities, 1952.

Romme, Stephen. "Accountability Is Here — Let's Improve It," *Journal of Teacher Education,* 25 (Spring 1974), p. 65-67.

Small, Alan A. "Accountability in Victorian England," *Phi Delta Kappan,* 53 (March 1972), pp. 438-439.

Soar, Robert S. "Accountability: Assessment Problems and Possibilities," *Journal of Teacher Education,* 24 (Fall 1973), pp. 204-212.

Taylor, A. J. and Zahn, R. D. "Accountability for the Professional," *The Clearing House,* 46 (February 1972), pp. 356-358.

Welch, I. David. "The Quest for Accountability," *Journal of Teacher Education,* 25 (Spring 1974), pp. 59-64.

15

A Humanistic Atmosphere in Teacher Education

Education becomes a meaningless endeavor unless the education acquired has some impact on the human condition. The pursuit of education solely for self-gratification can result in the learner becoming desensitized to his obligation to use his education for the welfare and improvement of all people. The acquisition of an education is a highly individualized process, but if education remains contained within an individual it becomes defensive and egocentric and insulates the learner from the world instead of putting him in communication with it.

In teacher education, the translation of theory into practice demands a relationship between the functional on-the-job activity of the classroom teacher and his professional program. But teacher education programs must go beyond what is toward a conceptualization of what should be. They have an obligation to do more than produce teachers who accept the status quo and do nothing to advance the humanization of education.

THE TEACHER EDUCATOR

The key to producing a teacher who is skilled enough to develop meaningful education is the teacher educator himself. Course descriptions, physical facilities, and degree-granting powers are not the basic ingredients that provide the student teacher with the qualities necessary for competency in teaching. What makes the difference is the student teacher's association with teacher educators who are authentic persons who have internalized behaviors that facilitate the emergence of others.

We conceive of the student teacher and teacher-educator relationship as vastly different from the traditional superior-subordinate type of association that has typically characterized higher education. The teacher educator must develop a colleague relationship with students; he must perceive himself as a colleague in the learning experience rather than as a traditional lecturer. Being a facilitative educator means creating a learning atmosphere that translates as learner-centered teaching and encourages individuality. If the student teacher is to function as a catalyst for developing individuality among others, he must himself be a free individual. The learner-centered teacher educator respects and encourages the student teacher's right to become, and what emerges from the student teacher is a sensitivity to self. He should not necessarily become a disciple of the teacher educator. The teacher educator's personal freedom allows the student teacher to be free in his own theoretical evolvement. As Arbuckle states:

> In a society of free men, as I would see it, there is no master and there are no disciples. The individual who has moved well along the road of freedom has no need of a master, either to direct him, or to repress him, or to succor him. I would have a hunch there are a goodly number of individuals who have had a relationship with Carl Rogers, either as a student, or a client, or a friend, who don't need him now, because he was part of the human experience through which they came to the point where their level of freedom was such that they had no need to follow him, but they could, rather, follow their self, and trust it. (1964:116)

The learner-centered teacher educator is not doctrinaire in his approach to the various teaching approaches. He realizes that any professional approach to teaching can be effective, provided that the teacher is an authentic individual with sensitivity to the dimensions of the learning atmosphere that encourage the self-emergence of students.

When confronted by a student question like "How do you personally feel about this particular issue in education?" the learner-centered teacher educator responds in a manner that encourages the student to seek out his own personal philosophy on the issue. He does not put his professional stamp of approval on what he might consider the "right" answer. In many ways, the learner-centered teacher educator may be more accurately labeled a "nonprofessor." He deals with questions from his own frame of reference, but he indicates that it is his own opinion and stresses that the only answers that will have meaning for the student teacher are those he internalizes in his own search for the truth of a particular theory or approach.

It would be a contradiction of the essence of humanism to be dogmatic about one's own humanistic viewpoint. Humanistic teaching demands an openness to self and to other viewpoints —the teacher educator's viewpoint never *is;* it is always existentially in the *process* of becoming. This fluidness of self should find its expression in the communicating attitude of the teacher educator toward the learner.

Personal defensiveness, doctrinarism, or dogmatism on the part of the teacher educator will spell the death of inquiry on the part of the student teacher. If the student is to evolve as a person he needs a teacher-education program that encourages both student and teacher to take a view from within as well as from without.

The teacher educator who sees truth in only one theoretical viewpoint will have a hard time tuning in to the student who is searching for meaning from a different theoretical viewpoint. A teacher educator who is blinded by his own biases inhibits his students' search for personal relevance and diminishes their emergence as theoretically sensitive individuals. Every teacher should pause and consider the following warning from Erich Fromm about the psychological undergirding of an autocratic teacher-learner relationship:

> In a psychological sense, the lust for power is not rooted in strength, but in weakness. It is the expression of the inability of the individual self to stand alone and live. It is the desperate attempt to gain secondary strength where genuine strength is lacking (1941).

When a teacher educator charges a student teacher with appreciating his students no matter how different their personal value systems or life styles may be, he is obligated in turn to accept the theoretical differences of his student teachers, especially when their views clash with his own. It is easy for a theoretically encapsulated educator to reinforce students who agree with his personal theories and to subtly block the emergence and expression of viewpoints that differ from his own. Nathaniel Cantor had this to say about accepting differences:

> Democracy, political or personal, thrives on difference. Indeed, the acid test of respect for others is one's ability to abide *difference*. Respect for others means respect for difference, since "others" are not like you. Liking those who are like you requires no effort. To accept genuine difference, that is, to accept others who feel, think or act in ways you do not approve of, and in situations where you are involved, is the test of respect for others (1964:258).

The teacher educator must be a model of permissiveness, acceptance, understanding, empathy, and positive regard if he expects to create a learning atmosphere that fosters these qualities in students. This kind of learning atmosphere is not sterile. It is vibrant with involvement and encounters, and the teacher educator is an active participant in the intellectual and emotional discoveries, rather than a passive observer. It may leave the student teacher with some confused and ambiguous feelings, but as a result the *student teacher learns to move himself* toward his truths instead of sitting and waiting for truth to emanate from the lips of the teacher educator. Snygg and Coombs have explored the personal nature of education and reinforce the concept that it is a process that can only be accomplished by the differentiating self:

> Education, from this point of view, is a process of increasing differentation of the field is something which can be done only by the individual himself. It cannot be done for him (1949:238).

Rogers (1951) states that a learning experience of personal consequence occurs when the learner assumes the responsibility of evaluating the degree to which he is personally moving toward knowledge instead of looking to an external source for such evaluation. The student teacher develops and moves himself when he is involved in a learning relationship that encourages him to identify personal truths and values. He will then be able to create a learning atmosphere that is real rather than mechanical, one in which the dynamics of the student emerge according to the inner, influencing authenticity of the student.

A teacher-education program must create an atmosphere of personal involvement for the student teacher because it is this personal involvement, and the accompanying personal commitment, that results in the translation of theoretical constructs into the actuality of the work setting. The development of this involvement and commitment is what bridges the gap between theory and practice. Bugental sounds a warning note for those who design educational programs that do not result in the involvement and commitment of the learner:

> Too often education becomes a powerful influence toward making persons into objects, toward treating persons as interchangeable units, toward increasing our alienation from ourselves and our estrangement from each other (1965:408).

THE LEARNING ATMOSPHERE
IN TEACHER EDUCATION

If the student teacher is to become involved and committed, he must exist in a learning atmosphere in which the teacher educator is involved and committed. In such an environment, the free exchange of attitudes, ideas, and knowledge becomes the essence of the student teacher's movement toward a personally relevant and applicable viewpoint. A given teaching approach is most often ignored because the particular approach has little personal meaning for the student teacher. Therefore, teacher education must foster personal relevancy; it is only when the student teacher discovers the personal relevancy of an approach or theory that he becomes inclined to apply that theory.

Too many student teachers give lip service to the values of their educational program, but tend to assume self-protective values rather than humanistic ones when they begin teaching. A worthy teacher-education program should help the student teacher find personally meaningful values to carry into his daily functioning. Teacher-education programs that concentrate solely on the techniques of teaching and on "how to" teach will never produce teachers with values that serve as a sustenance for their daily work and enable them to penetrate the core of learner needs. The student teacher's personal development, within the context and atmosphere of a teacher-education program, is the major factor influencing the school teacher's on-the-job competency.

For the teacher educator who feels that the concept of learner-centered teaching has merit theoretically, but is not operative because of the limitations imposed upon him by a particular institution, we offer the following:

> Every group has some limitations, if only the fact that they meet for a limited rather than an unlimited number of hours per week. It is not the fact that there are limitations, but the attitude, the permissiveness, the freedom which exists within those limitations, which is important (Rogers, 1951:396).

The teacher educator who chides a school teacher who is unable to implement a particular teaching theory because of administrative attitudes within his school, and then in turn rejects learner-centered teaching because of limitations he feels are imposed upon him by a university administration exhibits shallowness in his own beliefs. If he rejects the other-directedness of the classroom teacher, but blandly accepts the smothering other-directedness of his own work situation, he cannot rightfully become upset if the classroom teacher uses a similar behavioral model to survive in his own school setting. When an individual finds a personal relevancy for something, he develops a commitment to translate that relevancy into a modus operandi that is functional within the situational limitations. Most limitations are self-conceived and become an easy means of explaining away anything the teacher does not want to become involved with. But even when there are real limitations, the teacher educator can implement what he believes if he allows his inner humanistic and personally relevant attitude to seek its expression. External limitations should not prevent him from creating a learning atmosphere that encourages the emergence of self in the student teacher. If the dimensions of learner-centered teaching are internalized as an approach whereby the student can achieve personal relevancy, the teacher will develop an operational in-class behavior congruent with his inner philosophical rationale:

> He creates a classroom climate which respects the integrity of the student, which accepts all aims, opinions, and attitudes as being legitimate expressions of the student's internal frame of reference at that time. He accepts the feelings and emotionalized attitudes which surround any educational or group experience. He accepts himself as being a member of a learning group, rather than an authority. He makes learning resources available, confident that if they meet the needs of the group they will be used. He relies upon the capacity of the individual to sort out the truth from untruth, upon the basis of continuing experience. He recognizes that his course, if successful, is a beginning in learning, not the end of learning. He relies upon the capacity of the student to assess his progress in terms of the purposes which he has at this time. He has confidence in the fact that, in this atmosphere which he has helped to create, a type of learning takes place which is personally meaningful and which feeds the total self-development of the individual as well as improves his acquaintance with a given field of knowledge (Rogers, 1951:427).

In discussing educational theories, the teacher educator cannot and is not a passive, uninvolved, or neutral person; such an individual brings nothing to a discussion except his physical presence. He becomes totally involved as a catalyst encouraging the participation of student teachers. If he participates from his own personal viewpoint while encouraging the expression of different viewpoints, the issue under discussion will be examined from a variety of perceptions.

THE PERSONAL COMFORT OF THE TEACHER EDUCATOR AND STUDENT TEACHER

As the student teacher grows toward a theoretical viewpoint for teaching, he must not only find personal comfort, but must also find a theory that is comfortable for the student and enables him to emerge as a more adequately functioning person. In an attempt to help student teachers become more effective, some teacher educators have emphasized the importance of developing a responsive naturalness. But some teachers may function in a professionally questionable manner in the name of naturalness or genuineness. Certainly, naturalness or genuineness is a desired goal, but the teacher can develop a biased educational rationale that makes anything he does acceptable in the name of naturalness. The teacher may feel most natural and comfortable when he points out the unreasonableness of a student's negative attitude toward school rules. It may be easier for the teacher to defend institutional values, but it is highly questionable if such defensiveness is going to be of much assistance to the student. A one-sided approach is of no use to the student who may be involved in the process of rebelling against values imposed by authoritative sources.

The teacher must become sensitive to both the positive and negative aspects of his naturalness. He must be willing to examine those aspects of his naturalness that are truly professional in character and should be retained. He should try to distinguish between the aspects of naturalness that are helpful to learners and those that are actually designed to defend his own ego. When the teacher can distinguish between these two types of naturalness, he can contribute significantly to the self-actualization of the learner. He comes to the realization that his comfort as a teacher must be congruent with the comfort of the learner because it is only when both teacher and learner are comfortable that progress is assured regardless of the teaching approach being used. Teacher comfort, without the accompanying and necessary sensitivity to learner comfort, may be beneficial for the teacher, but it is not likely to have much educational value for the learner.

The question is whether the teacher educator's teaching approach is comfortable for students and encourages *their* self-emergence. Some teacher educators may feel that the uninterrupted lecture is the best method for imparting knowledge about teaching. Armed with lecture notes designed to establish a certain distance between self and students, they churn on, comfortable in what they are doing. Meanwhile, the students assume the typical posture — notebooks open and pens in hand — ready to take the copious notes that education has conditioned them to think of as important. They take notes, digest them, regurgitate them on a final exam, forget them, and this is what they know as education. Of course the teacher educator may be comfortable in this structured approach, but what about the student teacher? We would expect him to be highly uncomfortable in such a relationship because he is not involved, challenged, or stimulated. The comfortable teacher educator has structured the relationship so that the student's emergence as a penetrating individual is blocked. Lecturers can save themselves and their students time if they duplicate their lecture notes and distribute them to class members. Then the class discussion can become an exciting encounter in which the student is both cognitively and affectively *involved*. He can become more sensitive to his own personal dimensions and how they affect his positive or negative reaction to a particular topic. This will bring the student teacher to the realization that the most important instrument he brings to a teaching-learning relationship is the perfected self, free from the personal idiosyncracies, hesitancies, nuances, and defenses which inhibit the emergence of the learner.

The teacher educator involved in learner-centered teaching must be more knowledgeable and secure than his lecturing counterpart. He needs to be well-read enough to bring into a dialogue resources ranging from Aristotle to Admiral Rickover. He must be well-integrated enough to be sensitive to the blind spots in his own teaching. He must first *be* before he can create an atmosphere in which the student teacher can *become*.

The technically oriented teacher educator may have some difficulty comprehending the deeper philosophical dimensions of the learning process, but, as Ennis has said: "A few years of communication and understanding on matters of philosophy will be more productive than 50 years of discussion of techniques without philosophy (1961:139)."

Teacher domination of the learning atmosphere by the use of gimmicks, games, canned presentations, "guruism," and monologues will result in the learner absorbing the superficialities of knowledge without ever coming to grips with the deeper issues of himself and how he relates to knowledge — how he discovers personal truths and intellectual relevancies. For the student teacher, learning how to learn should be a process of becoming sensitive to the personal idiosyncracies that move him toward or away from confrontations with the values undergirding certain theoretical constructs. If the learning atmosphere is open and free from personal threat, the student teacher moves toward significant knowledge that has personal meaning. He moves with greater breadth and depth because of the awareness that learning, in the visceral sense, must come about because of the free involvement of the self.

The creation of such an atmosphere demands that the teacher educator possess the same qualities that an effective classroom teacher should possess: personal *authenticity* in the communicating relationship; a *sense of presence,* not only in himself but in the learner; and a sensitivity for the conditions that influence the humanistic *emergence* of the learner. The insightful teacher educator can learn much from Erich Fromm's concept of the effective teacher:

> While we teach knowledge, we are losing that teaching which is the most important one for human development: the teaching which can only be given by the simple presence of a mature, loving person. In previous epochs of our own culture, or in China and India, the man most highly valued was the person with outstanding spiritual qualities. Even the teacher was not only, or even primarily, a source of information, but his function was to convey certain human attitudes (1963:98).

The humanistic teacher-educator must be involved in the process of transmitting attitudes of inquiry, insight, and sensitivity if the student teacher is to become a skillful teacher. Exposure to these attitudes, as embodied in the teacher educator, brings to the student teacher a realization that people learn, and develop, when they are involved in a relationship that stimulates self-emergence. Student teachers absorb the attitudes necessary for effective teaching when they feel the presence of these attitudes in the teacher educator.

In an attempt to identify what happens to the student as a result of his experience with learner-centered teaching, Gordon reviewed eleven studies and found that:

> Students seems to learn as much or more factual information; they participate more; they enjoy the experience; and they acquire certain other important learnings, such as clinical insight, greater personal adjustment,

socially integrative behavior skills of working cooperatively with others, and the freedom to communicate their deeper feelings and attitudes (1955:100).

The personally defensive teacher educator is usually unwilling to risk himself in the human encounter of learner-centered teaching. The greater the number of personal hesitations, the less he is willing to create a learning atmosphere that would expose his private idiosyncrasies. The only recourse he has is to control the learning atmosphere so that his idiosyncratic values are protected — he creates barriers to learning because he draws boundaries around what is to be learned. Gordon has identified certain teacher attitudes that will smother a learning group's thrust toward self-generated and personally relevant knowledge:

> Our own insecurities, our lack of faith in people, our tendencies to use others for our own needs, our needs for prestige and status, our lack of tolerance of ambiguity, our fear of hostility expressed toward us, and the inconsistencies that often appear in our systems of values (1955:154).

If it is to fulfill its obligations to humanity, teacher education must move toward a greater awareness of the process involved in developing a teacher who will make a difference in the lives of those he teaches. The future of education lies in teacher-education programs that move away from outmoded concepts of teaching toward a psychologically knowledgeable concept of the conditions and atmosphere in which a student can become a self-actuated, valuing learner and competent teacher. Long after the student teacher's degree begins to feel the yellowing effects of age, he should still be vitally interested in the processes and conditions that result in effective learning and development. He should be so deeply involved in his professional endeavor that he is constantly shedding more and more light on the intricacies of educational theory and practice and enriching the lives of his students.

REFERENCES

Arbuckle, Dugald S. "The Various Faces of Freedom," *Counselor Education and Supervision,* 3, (Spring 1964), pp. 115-117.
Bugental, J. F. T. *The Search for Authenticity.* New York: Holt, Rinehart, Winston, 1965.

Cantor, Nathaniel. "Maintaining A Creative Difference," *Perspectives on the Group Process,* C. Gratton Kemp (ed.). Boston: Houghton-Mifflin Company, 1964.

Ennis, Mae. "The Need for a Philosophy of Guidance Still Haunts Us," *The Vocational Guidance Quarterly,* 9 (Winter 1960-1961), pp. 137-140.

Fromm, Erich. *Escape From Freedom.* New York: Farrar and Rinehart, 1941.

_____. *The Art of Loving.* New York: Bantam Books, 1963.

Gordon, Thomas. *Group Centered Leadership.* Boston: Houghton Mifflin, 1955.

Rogers, Carl R. *Client Centered Therapy.* Boston: Houghton Mifflin, 1951.

Snygg, Donald and Combs, Arthur W. *Individual Behavior: A New Frame of Reference for Psychology.* New York: Harper, 1949.

Appendix:

Resources for Putting Theory Into Practice

Theories of learner-centered teaching and humanistic education are being applied in a variety of communities and schools. There are many ways of interpreting and translating theory so that it works. We have compiled an annotated list of resources which we think offer concrete suggestions and examples of the ways in which theories of learner-centered teaching have been and can be put into practice. In our judgment these are valuable resources that we hope will be especially useful to all persons committed to implementing the concepts of learner-centered teaching presented in this book.

Readings in
Humanistic Education and
Learner-Centered Teaching

Andrew, Michael A. *Teachers Should Be Human Too.* Washington, D.C.: Association of Teacher Educators, 1972.

A sensible treatment of a topic that often generates rhetoric, this monograph focuses on humanizing teacher education. The author presents the arguments for rethinking teacher skills and processes, the changes this would entail, and some of the results to be expected. It is a thoughtful discussion of the subjective and emotional dimensions of education.

Andrew, Michael D. *Teacher Leadership: A Model for Change.* Washington, D.C.: Association of Teacher Educators, 1974.

An important publication that describes a model for differentiated preparation of teachers in elementary and secondary schools. The model emerges as a framework emphasizing individual autonomy and choice and promotes decision-making and leadership capabilities. The outcome of this multiphased model of career development for teachers is the teacher-leader: a teacher who exerts leadership and opens the way for change in education.

Bash, James H. *Effective Teaching in the Desegregated School.* Bloomington, Indiana: Phi Delta Kappa Educational Foundation, 1973. Part of the Phi Delta Kappa Fastback Series No. 32.

This publication features some very good ideas and practical suggestions on teaching in the desegregated school. Content is arranged around the teacher,

teacher-pupil relationships, teacher-teacher relationships, and teacher-administrator relationships.

Blackburn, Jack E., and Powell, W. Conrad. *One at a Time: All at Once: The Creative Teacher's Guide to Individualized Instruction Without Anarchy.* Pacific Palisades, California: Goodyear Publishing Company, 1976.
    Practical ideas are offered for implementing individualized instruction. A readable, to-the-point treatment of individualization that ought to be of great value to the classroom teacher.

Brown, George I.; Yeomans, Thomas; and Grizzard, Liles (eds.). *The Live Classroom: Innovations Through Confluent Education and Gestalt.* New York: Viking Press, 1975.
    This book is organized for practitioners who want to bring feeling and thinking together in the learning process in order to generate more vitality and better learning in the classroom.

Brown, George I.; Phillips, Mark; and Shapiro, Stewart. *Getting It All Together: Confluent Education.* Bloomington, Indiana: Phi Delta Kappa, 1976.
    By combining thinking and feeling, confluent education makes learning more powerful and valuable.

Combs, Arthur W. (ed.). *Perceiving, Behaving and Becoming.* Yearbook of the Association for Supervision and Curriculum Development, 1701 K Street, N.W., Washington, D.C., 1962.
    This book has become, in our opinion, a classic in existential-humanistic writing dealing with teaching and learning. It contains several chapters written by Carl Rogers, Abraham Maslow, Earl Kelley, and Arthur Combs. The practical implications of their work for classroom teachers are clearly developed.

Corwin, Ronald G., and Edelfelt, Roy A. *Perspectives on Organizations: Viewpoints for Teachers.* Washington, D.C.: American Association of Colleges for Teacher Education and Association of Teacher Educators, 1976.
    Designed to develop among future and practicing teachers an awareness of what organizations are, how organizations affect them, and how they can deal with organizations.

Cottle, Thomas. *The Voices of School-Educational Issues Through Personal Accounts.* Boston: Little, Brown, 1973.
    A personal account of students from different communities and ethnic backgrounds illuminating in a new way issues such as busing, testing, integration, family role, authority, human development.

Dale, Edgar. *The Humane Leader.* Bloomington, Indiana: Phi Delta Kappa Educational Foundation, 1974. Part of the Phi Delta Kappa Fastback Series No. 38.
    A lively, well-written booklet about how one becomes a humane teacher. The author discusses developing a sense of empathy, humaneness through self-discipline, and humaneness in the classroom.

Galloway, Charles. *Silent Language in the Classroom.* Bloomington, Indiana: Phi Delta Kappa, 1976.
  A teacher's face, posture, and intonations may carry more messages than the words used in the classroom.

Glasser, William. *Schools Without Failure.* New York: Harper & Row, 1969.
  This book applies Glasser's theories of Reality Therapy to contemporary education. Glasser details the shortcomings of current education and proposes as an important approach to reduce school failure the use of "class meeting." Glasser's approach is widely known. If you have not read this book we recommend that you do so.

Goodlad, John I. *The Dynamics of Educational Change: Toward Responsive Schools.* New York: McGraw Hill, 1975.
  Criticism of public schools has become more intense in recent years and some observers despair of enduring, constructive change. This book, based on the premise that schools can become more vital, challenges the rhetoric of despair. Goodlad describes recent educational reform in the United States; analyzes the effectiveness of strategies for change in terms of problems, people, and results; and presents a comprehensive, practical strategy for change.

Gordon, Tom. *Teacher Effectiveness Training.* New York: Peter H. Wyden, 1974.
  A detailed description of how the principles of parent effectiveness training can be used in all classrooms, from kindergarten to senior high school. Deals with teacher-student relations, controlling classroom behavior, helping students with problems, and resolving values conflicts.

Greer, Mary, and Rubinstein, Bonnie. *Will the Real Teacher Please Stand Up.* Pacific Palisades, California: Goodyear Publishing Company, 1972.
  A book full of personal accounts of teaching children with sections on the community of the classroom, the group as a way of exploring ideas, and "let yourself be seen."

Gross, Beatrice, and Gross, Ronald. *Will It Grow in a Classroom?* New York: Delacorte, 1974.
  The best kind of shop talk with teachers discussing their roles, the curriculum, and old and new ways of touching young minds.

Hahn, Robert. *Creative Teachers: Who Wants Them.* New York: John Wiley & Sons, 1973.
  A study of the creative process in secondary school teaching: how it has been stifled and how it might be nurtured.

Hopkins, Lee Bennett, and Arenstein, Misha. *Partners in Learning.* New York: Citation, 1971.
  The authors, both experienced teachers, recommend dozens of practical ideas for achieving child-centered classrooms, including ways of grouping children for units of study, handling current and special events, and utilizing audiovisuals, poetry, fiction, art and music.

Jones, Tudor Powell. *Creative Learning in Perspective.* New York: Halsted, 1972.

The emphasis in this book is on clarifying the term "creativity" and placing it in perspective with the outline of the difficulties involved and the atmosphere necessary to make creative teaching and creative learning possible.

Lederman, Janet. *Anger and the Rocking Chair: Gestalt Awareness with Children.* New York: Viking Press, 1969.

A vivid, clear, and honest account of what can be done to provide real education for students in the classroom by getting in touch with their feelings.

Lippitt, Peggy. *Students Teach Students.* Bloomington, Indiana: Phi Delta Kappa, 1974.

Older children helping younger ones learn is not a new idea, but Lippitt gives practical advice on how to use the cross-age helping program in any classroom.

Otty, Nicholas. *Learner Teachers.* New York: Penguin, 1972.

A highly personal diary, both intimate and humorous, of the first probationary year. A provocative case study for those who hope to reform teacher training.

Postman, Neil, and Weingartner, Charles. *Teaching as a Subversive Activity.* New York: Delta, 1969.

A challenging book that goes beyond the familiar criticisms and indictments of American eduction to propose basic ways of liberating both teachers and students for humanistic learning.

Purkey, William W. *Self Concept and School Achievement.* Englewood Cliffs, New Jersey: Prentice-Hall, 1970.

This book focuses on how the self-concept develops in social interaction and what happens to it in school. It suggests ways for teachers to reinforce positive and realistic self-concepts in students.

Robert, Marc. *Loneliness in the Schools (What to Do About It).* Niles, Illinois: Argus Communications, 1974.

We have discussed how lonely teaching and learning can be. This book addresses the issue of loneliness in a forthright and helpful way. Many valuable suggestions are presented.

Rogers, Carl R. *Freedom to Learn.* Columbus, Ohio: Charles E. Merrill, 1969.

We believe that this is one of the most important books written on humanistic education and learner-centered teaching. The theme of the book is that students can be trusted to learn and enjoy learning when a facilitative person can set up an attitudinal and concrete environment that encourages responsible participation in selection of goals and ways of reaching them.

Ruchlis, Cy, and Sharefkin, Belle. *Reality-Centered Learning.* New York: Citation Press, 1975.

Reality-centered education focuses on subjects students consider real. This book discusses how the environment of the school and community can be brought into the school curriculum.

Schmuck, Richard A., and Schmuck, Patricia A. *A Humanistic Psychology of Education — Making the School Everybody's House.* Palo Alto, California: National Press Books, 1974..
  This book deals with various strategies for humanizing our schools.

Silberman, Melvin L.; Allender, Jerome S.; and Yanoff, Jay M. *The Psychology of Open Teaching and Learning: An Inquiry Approach.* Boston: Little, Brown Company, 1972.
  A problem-oriented investigation of teaching and learning to aid teachers in making personal decisions about their classrooms, with suggested materials and activities.

The Teacher in 1984. Futurist Working Papers. Gresham Teacher Challenge Conference. Durham, New Hampshire: New England Program in Teacher Education, 1972.
  A collection of papers written by such educational leaders as Dwight Allen, John Bremer, Francis Keppel, Stephen Bailey, and John Brademas, focusing on future directions and changes in teaching and teacher education required for creating a more humane world.

Torrance, E. Paul, and Pansy, J. *Is Creativity Teachable?* Bloomington, Indiana: Phi Delta Kappa Educational Foundation, 1973. Part of the Phi Delta Kappa Fastback Series No. 20.
  The booklet summarizes the results of a survey of 142 experiments designed to provide information about the teachability of creativity in elementary and secondary schools. It describes in some detail several teaching procedures used to help students think creatively.

Vallett, Robert E. *Humanistic Education.* St. Louis: C. V. Mosby Company, 1977.
  Vallett's book describes public and private school humanistic-affective education programs, examines commercial materials, and includes curriculum guides and activities. The focus is on five levels of affective education for elementary and secondary students: understanding human needs; expressing human feelings; self-awareness and control; becoming aware of human values; and developing social and personal maturity.

2

Books on Alternatives in Education

Berger, Evelyn, and Winters, Bonnie A. *Social Studies in the Open Classroom: A Practical Guide.* New York: Teachers College Press, 1973.

Specific and practical suggestions on how social studies can be an integral part of the open classroom. The focus is on intermediate and elementary grades.

Chernow, Fred B., and Genkin, Harold. *Teaching and Administering the High School Alternative Education Program.* New York: Parker Publishing Company, 1975.

A practical book that discusses nitty-gritty topics relating to initiating and organizing an alternative educational program.

Cornett, Joe D., and Askins, Billy E. *Open School Evaluation System.* Austin, Texas: Learning Concepts, 1976.

The *Open School Evaluation System* contains a manual and three inventories: *Inventory of School Openness* (ISO), *Open School Teacher Attitude Scale* (OSTAS), and *Open School Parental Attitude Scale* (OSPAS). The manual contains instructions for administering and scoring the inventories, as well as suggestions for reporting results. Developed for administrators, program staff, and internal or external evaluators, the system serves three major functions: a guide or model for curriculum development, a basis for continual program monitoring, and a comprehensive means of evaluation.

DeTurk, Philip H. *P.S. 2001: The Story of the Pasadena Alternative School.* Bloomington, Indiana: Phi Delta Kappa Educational Foundation, 1974. Part of the Phi Delta Kappa Fastback Series.

257

A clearly written personal account of the birth and life of a free school.

Fantini, Mario D. *Public Schools of Choice: A Plan for the Reform of American Education.* New York: Simon and Schuster, 1973.
An excellent introduction to and exposition of alternatives in public education by a man who is generally recognized as one of the most effective and knowledgeable leaders in alternative schooling.

Fantini, Mario D. *Alternative Education: A Sourcebook for Parents, Teachers, Students, and Administrators.* New York: Doubleday, Anchor Press, 1976.
A valuable guide for anyone interested in options for public schools.

Glatthorn, Allan A. *Alternatives in Education: Schools and Programs.* New York: Dodd, Mead, and Company, 1975.
This book is very practical in its approach, providing suggestions and ideas for planning curriculum, staffing, facilities, and evaluations for all kinds of alternative schools and programs.

Goodlad, John I., et al. *The Conventional and the Alternative in Education.* Berkeley, California: McCutchan, 1975.
Six contributing authors develop a scholarly perspective toward and prospects for alternative educational programs.

Hertzberg, Alvin, and Stone, Edward. *Schools are for Children: An American Approach to American Education.* New York: Schocken Books, 1971.
A comprehensive account of how the open classroom works, and the theory behind it, written by two American elementary-school principals.

Matters of Choice: A Ford Foundation Report on Alternative Schools. New York: Ford Foundation, 1974.
This report reviews what the Ford Foundation has learned in funding alternatives in education.

Morton, Richard J., and Morton, Jane. *Innovation Without Renovation in the Elementary School.* New York: Citation Press, 1974.
The authors give numerous practical suggestions for opening up a school building built for teacher-centered instruction in self-contained classrooms. They assert that innovative programs can be put into effect in most schools with walls.

National School Boards Association. *Alternative Schools.* NSBA Research Report 1976-3. Evanston, Illinois: National School Boards Association, 1976.
A clearly written report of practical value to school administrators, teachers, school board members, and people in the community. It covers such topics as: What good to alternatives do? What problems do alternatives create? How much do alternative schools cost? How are students matched with options? How are alternatives evaluated? How are staff selected and trained? How can planning processes be initiated?

258

Parker, John L. *The Liveliest Seminar in Town.* Bloomington, Indiana: Phi Delta Kappa Educational Foundation, 1972. Part of the Phi Delta Kappa Fastback Series, No. 27.

A personal account of how the author and several friends, while in Harvard Graduate School, moved from talk about planning an innovative high-school program to actually implementing plans and launching an exciting new high school — John Adams High School in Portland, Oregon.

Perrone, Vito. *Open Education: Promise and Problems.* Bloomington, Indiana: Phi Delta Kappa Educational Foundation, 1972. Part of the Phi Delta Kappa Fastback Series, No. 3.

This booklet, written by a well-known leader in open education, focuses on open education in the elementary school. The author discusses what open education is, materials and equipment, use of human resources, reading, and evaluation.

Pflum, John. *Open Education: For Me?* Washington, D.C.: Acropolis, 1974.

A practical down-to-earth guide for teachers, demonstrating that freedom with responsibility can make open education work. It discusses how to organize and schedule programs, how to integrate teachers with special skills, and includes lists of kits and materials.

Postman, Neil, and Weingartner, Charles. *How to Recognize a Good School.* Bloomington, Indiana: Phi Delta Kappa, 1973.

What is school? What is a good school? The authors distinguish between functions and conventions of school, pinpointing conventions that best promote educationally valuable experiences.

Riordan, Robert C. *Alternative Schools in Action.* Bloomington, Indiana: Phi Delta Kappa Educational Foundation, 1972. Part of the Phi Delta Kappa Fastback Series No. 11.

The author describes what goes on inside two public alternative high schools; indicates some of the successes, problems, and patterns of development that recur in many alternative schools, and suggests some of the tasks that must be accomplished if alternative schools are to have a deeper and more lasting impact than previous educational fads.

Roberts, Arthur D. (ed.). *Educational Innovation: Alternatives in Curriculum and Instruction.* Boston: Allyn and Bacon, 1975.

This book is divided into three parts. Part one looks at some major reforms in education such as Montessori and "schools without walls" and includes suggestions for implementing these changes. Part two talks about specific curriculum alternatives in English, social studies, science, reading, etc. Part three focuses on materials and staff development — simulation games, instructional uses of junk, and differentiated staffing.

Rounds, Susan. *Teaching the Young Child: A Handbook of Open Classroom Practice.* New York: Agathon Press, 1975.

A practical, detailed guide to organizing a stimulating and workable open classroom for kindergartens and first grades. Topics covered include reading readiness, "You and Your Body", cooking in the classroom, and things to make for your room.

Smith, Vernon. *Alternative Schools: The Development of Options in Public Education*. Lincoln, Nebraska: Professional Educators Publications, 1975.
An accurate portrayal of the why and how of alternatives in education. This book relates the alternative schools movement to the issues of the more conventional educational program. It provides busy people with understandings on which to base decisions concerning the development of alternative schools.

Smith, Vernon; Barr, Robert; and Burke, Daniel. *Alternatives in Education: Freedom to Choose*. Bloomington, Indiana: Phi Delta Kappa, 1976.
This book explores links between the development of options in education and the future of education and society. It traces the options available in the past 200 years and specifically examines the development of alternatives from 1965 to 1975. After comprehensively viewing the options available and emerging, the authors give perspectives on choice in public education.

Smith, Vernon; Burke, Daniel, & Barr, Robert. *Optional Alternative Schools*. Bloomington, Indiana: Phi Delta Kappa Educational Foundation, 1974. Part of the Phi Delta Kappa Fastback Series No. 42.
This booklet describes types of alternative public schools, their impacts, and problems.

Terrence, E. D. *An Organizational Explanation of the Failure of Alternative Schools*. Palo Alto: Stanford Center for Research and Development in Teaching, 1975.
Explores a three-stage developmental sequence for alternative schools.

Weinstock, Ruth. *The Greening of the High School*. New York: Educational Facilities Laboratory, 1973.
A sparkling and provocative report on changes and alternatives in high school education. It discusses the need for change in high schools and presents nonconforming models of school programs and settings and how they came to be.

3

Classroom Exercises and Activities

Baughman, Dale. *Baughman's Handbook of Humor in Education.* Englewood Cliffs, New Jersey: Prentice-Hall, 1974.

We all need to laugh; indeed, laughter may be one of the best means to humanize schools. Read Baughm's book on how, when, and where to use humor in education. His selection of educational humor is a gold mine of material.

Brown, George. *Human Teaching for Human Learning: An Introduction to Confluent Education.* New York: The Viking Press, 1971.

This book describes a Ford Foundation project on affective education. Many examples of affective techniques that have been used in the classroom that are given. A series of personal commentaries by teachers involved in the project is included. There are numerous practical ideas for teachers who wish to implement confluent education.

Canfield, Jack, and Wells, Harold C. *100 Ways to Enhance Self Concept in the Classroom.* Englewood Cliffs, New Jersey: Prentice-Hall, 1976.

An excellent resource of one hundred practical and concrete ways to enhance students' self-concepts, this book offers a variety of exercises and approaches that can be adapted to unique classroom situations and needs.

Casteel, J. Doyle, and Stahl, Robert J. *Value Clarification in the Classroom: A Primer.* Pacific Palisades, California: Goodyear, 1975.

A comprehensive study of values in the secondary classroom that encourages the development of values education as an integral part of academic study. Thirty-nine specific values lessons are included.

Curwin, Richard. *Discovering Your Teaching Self: Humanistic Approaches to Effective Teaching.* New York: Prentice-Hall, 1976.
This text can be used by individuals, pairs, or small or large groups. The activities are designed to develop self-awareness and consciousness toward students in the classroom.

Flynn, Elizabeth W., and LaFaso, John F. *Designs in Affective Education.* New York: Paulist, 1974.
This book contains 126 teaching strategies on themes of communication, freedom, happiness, life, peace, and love. Each strategy is categorized by traditional high school courses, is flexible as to time and content, and may be used in a variety of settings.

Fromkin, Howard L., and Sherwood, John J. (eds.). *Intergroup and Minority Relations: An Experiential Handbook.* La Jolla, California: University Associates, 1975.
An important collection of activities and exercises that facilitate understanding and communication in race relations, community relations, and groups in conflict.

Galbraith, Ronald E., and Jones, Thomas M. *Moral Reasoning: A Teaching Handbook for Adopting Kohlberg to the Classroom.* Anoka, Minnesota: Greenhaven, 1976.
The authors present a teaching process for stimulating elementary and secondary classroom discussion on social and moral problems. The book is based on Lawrence Kohlberg's theory of moral reasoning and development.

Hall, Robert T., and Davis, John U. *Moral Education in Theory and Practice.* Buffalo, New York: Prometheus, 1975.
This book suggests ways the theories of moral education and values clarification can be translated into practical classroom activities, and shows the use of case studies and simulation games.

Hawley, Robert C. *Value Exploration Through Role Playing.* New York: Hart, 1974.
A description of specific role-play techniques applicable in junior and senior high schools. The book gives 18 formats for role-playing and discusses how this technique can be applied in the teaching of subject matter, the development of moral judgment, and decision making.

Hawley, R. C., and Hawley, I. L. *A Handbook of Personal Growth Activities for Classroom Use.* Amherst, Massachusetts: Educational Research Associates, 1972.
The authors describe personal growth as "striving towards maturation" characterized by self-reliance and self-actualization. They offer a variety of activities that can be used in the classroom to promote personal growth.

Hawley, R. C.; Simon, Sidney B.; and Britton, D. D. *Composition for Personal Growth: Values Clarification Through Writing.* New York: Hart, 1973.

A practical handbook on the teaching of values through student writing. Focuses on self-awareness, interpersonal relations, personal growth, and the formation of identity.

Hendricks, Gay. *The Centering Book*. Englewood Cliffs, New Jersey: Prentice-Hall, 1976.
  A collection of awareness activities for children, parents, and teachers.

Hopson, Barrie, and Hough, Patricia. *Exercises in Personal and Career Development*. New York: APS Publications, Inc., 1973.
  This book provides secondary teachers with a group of practical exercises in personal and career development. Exercises are presented in a concise format. Each exercise has an outline that includes an objective, suitability group, time needed, size of group, recommended help or helpers required, materials needed, and a description of the exercise.

Howe, Leland W., and Howe, Mary Martha. *Personalizing Education: Values Clarification and Beyond*. New York: Hart, 1975.
  This book contains hundreds of specific suggestions for classroom activities touching upon all subject fields, plus projects and activities in goal development, values awareness, personal relationships, and the solving of personal problems.

Hunter, Elizabeth. *Encounter in the Classroom*. New York: Holt, Rinehart, and Winston, 1972.
  A lucid presentation of how group process and encounter-type activities have been and can be used in the classroom. It reflects National Training Laboratories concepts of group interaction. A readable, practical, and provocative book with concrete examples of facilitative activities and exercises that can be used to enhance self-concept.

Mattox, Beverly A. *Getting It Together*. San Diego, California: Pennant, 1975.
  The author describes 45 specific classroom exercises in moral education, applicable from first grade through high school and discusses ways of using moral education in the classroom.

Morris, Kenneth T., & Cinnamon, Kenneth M. *A Handbook of Nonverbal Group Exercises*. Springfield, Illinois: Charles C. Thomas, 1975.
  This book includes 160 exercises and 85 exercise variations.

Poppen, William A. "Games for Guidance," *Guidance Strategies and Techniques*. Denver, Colorado: Love Publishing Company, 1975.

  An article presenting games that can be used in the classroom to humanize education.

Reiehert, Richard. *Self Awareness Through Group Dynamics*. Dayton, Ohio: Pflaum, 1970.
  The author describes twelve group experiences for classroom investigation of values, attitudes, freedom and responsibility, respect, trust, prejudice, and

male-female conflict. Each lesson plan includes definitions, the problems involved, exercises for group experience, and discussion subjects.

Schrank, Jeffrey. *Teaching Human Beings: 101 Subversive Activities for the Classroom.* Boston: Beacon Press, 1973.
Designed to make the best possible use of lively materials to get students to think about themselves and their society. Activities include simulation games, group encounters, and the use of books and films.

Simon, Sidney B.; Howe, Leland H.; and Kirschenbaum, H. *Values Clarification: A Handbook of Practical Strategies for Teachers and Students.* New York: Hart Publishing Company, 1972.
This clearly written book describes seventy-nine classroom exercises designed to help students clarify their values. Several examples of how each exercise can be used are given.

Stanford, Gene, and Roark, Albert E. *Human Interaction in Education.* Boston: Allyn and Bacon, 1974.
A valuable book for the classroom teacher. The authors provide a good collection of process-oriented interaction activities that are based on experiential learning principles.

Swift, Marshall S., and Spivack, George. *Alternative Teaching Strategies: Helping Behaviorally Troubled Children Achieve.* Champaign, Illinois: Research Press, 1975.
This book covers such topics as the inattentive child, intellectual dependency, the impatient child, and other children with learning problems. Suggested activities encourage promoting relevant talk, increasing initiative, coping with negative feelings and actions, and fostering self-esteem.

Thayer, Louis (ed.). *Affective Education: Strategies for Experiential Learning.* La Jolla, California: University Associates, Inc., 1976.
This handbook describes fifty structural experiences designed to strengthen the affective components of learning. Each activity has a standard format that includes the goals, group size, time required, physical setting, materials, step by step process, variations, and notes. All the activities were designed by teachers who were involved in humanizing their teaching-learning approaches.

Thompson, Charles L., and Poppen, William A. *For Those Who Care: Ways of Relating to Youth.* Columbus, Ohio: Charles E. Merrill, 1972.
This book focuses on how to use games to humanize education. An excellent source of practical group games.

Weber, Kenneth J. *Yes, They Can! A Practical Guide for Teaching the Adolescent Slower Learner.* London: Methuen, 1974.
A collection of practical, creative activities that can bring the slow learner into full participation in the learning process.

264

Windley, Charles. *Teaching and Learning with Magic.* Washington, D.C.: Acropolis, 1976.

Written by a magician, this book explains how to set up a Magic Learning Center and discusses sixty-five tricks and projects to facilitate the learning of science, math perception, and creativity.

4

Curricula and Training Programs in Affective and Humanistic Education

ACHIEVEMENT MOTIVATION PROGRAM

Alschuler, A.; Tabor, D.; and McIntyre, J. *Teaching Achievement Motivation.* Middletown, Connecticut: Education Ventures, Inc., 1970.

This curriculum focuses on an individual's strengths and helps to develop higher levels of motivation to achieve, personal resources, and success experiences through individual discovery and group reinforcement. Personal goals, values, and conflict of values are studied in the context of the individual's strengths.

BECOMING: A COURSE IN HUMAN RELATIONS

Cromwell, C. R.; Ohs, W.; Roark, A. E.; and Stanford, G. *Becoming: A Course in Human Relations.* New York: J. B. Lippincott, 1975.

An activity-centered course for high-school students consisting of three modules. Module 1, Relating, is addressed to a group building, distinguishing between thoughts and feelings, and teaching listening skills. Module 2, Interaction, focuses on developing skills in understanding and working with others. Module 3, Individuality, emphasizes the stereotyping process, values clarification, and the role of sexuality in interpersonal relations.

C-GROUPS

Dinkmeyer, D. C., and Carlson, J. *Consulting: Facilitating Human Potential and Change Processes.* Columbus, Ohio: Charles E. Merrill, 1972.

This approach offers a concrete model for training teachers in humanistic approaches through group process. It is labeled C-Group because so many of its components begin with the letter C — Collaboration, Consultation, Clarification, Confidential, Confrontation, Communication, Concern, and Commitment.

CLASSROOM MEETINGS

Glasser, William. *Schools Without Failure.* New York: Harper and Row, 1969.

Glasser sees the major problem of the schools as the problem of failure. He proposes the use of the class, led by the teacher, as a counseling group, that daily spends time developing the social responsibility necessary to solve behavioral and educational problems within the class, so that outside help is rarely needed. His concept of "the classroom meeting" has been implemented in classrooms all over the country and is one of the most prominent and well-known approaches to psychological education.

CURRICULUM OF CONCERNS

Borton, Terry. *Reach, Touch, and Teach.* New York: McGraw-Hill, 1970.

Terry Borton has designed and implemented in the Philadelphia public schools the *What-So What-Now What* system of learning. *What* connotes sensing a new stimulus or experience. *So What* is the transforming of the stimulus into some kind of meaning for the individual. *Now What* is the acting function that rehearses possible actions and picks one to put into the world as an overt response. The program focuses on teaching students how to handle their concerns and feelings, how to understand and be responsive to others around them, and provides a means for them to act in constructive and effective ways in their interpersonal relationships.

CURRICULUM OF INTENTIONALITY AND HUMAN RELATIONS

Ivey, A., and Alschuler, A. (eds.). *Psychological Education.* A Special Issue of the Personnel and Guidance Journal, 51 (May 1973).

The central objective of this curriculum is the development of the intentional individual — a person who has a sense of capability, who can generate behaviors in a given situation, and who can respond to changing life situations so he looks forward to longer-term goals. Students are taught varieties of selective attending to human relations and are encouraged to develop units in human relations. Teachers learn a number of ways to teach important concepts of human relations in conjunction with regular academic work. Micro teaching provides a framework where complex human-relations behaviors are considered and taught. This curriculum was developed by Al Ivey at the University of Massachusetts.

DECIDING

Gelatt, H. B.; Varenhorst, Barbara; and Carey, Richard. *Deciding.* Princeton, New Jersey: College Entrance Examination Board, 1972.

This is a three-part course of study on decision-making, showing how values, information, and strategy all play a part in making decisions about life and personal problems. It includes thirty-two exercises.

DELIBERATE PSYCHOLOGICAL EDUCATION

Mosher, R., and Sprinthall, N. "Psychological Education: A Means to Promote Personal Development Through Adolescence," *The Counseling Psychologist,* 2 (1971), pp. 3-82.

Mosher and Sprinthall have developed a curriculum consisting of systematic educational experiences designed to directly affect the personal development of adolescents. The curriculum draws on developmental, counseling, and educational psychology and the humanities. It is conceptualized as a series of coordinated courses focusing on various stages of the human life cycle. Adolescents study the principles of early childhood development, child development and care, middle childhood, adolescence, interpersonal relations and marriage, and vocational and occupational decision making. A significant part of the curriculum is experiential.

DIMENSIONS OF PERSONALITY

Linbacher, W. *Dimensions of Personality.* Dayton, Ohio: George Pflaum, 1969.

This graded program in affective education makes it possible for teachers to give systematic attention to the life of the child. The program is group-centered, activity-oriented, and seeks to involve parents in considering the affective education of the child. This is a commercially developed program for all six grades at the elementary level and is available from Pflaum/Standard, Dayton, Ohio.

DUSO

Dinkmeyer, Don. *DUSO* (Developing Understanding of Self and Others) *Manual.* Circle Pines, Minnesota: American Guidance Services, 1970.

Developing Understanding of Self and Others consists of kits of activities and materials designed by Don Dinkmeyer to facilitate the social and emotional development of children (K-4). The DUSO activities make extensive use of listening, inquiry, and discussion approaches to learning. The programs are based on the premise that every child, in the process of growing up, is confronted with normal developmental problems and that the classroom teacher can help children with these problems. Kits are available from the American Guidance Services, Minneapolis, Minnesota.

EMOTIONAL EDUCATION

Ellis, Albert. *Emotional Education.* New York: Julian Press, 1972.

Derived from rational-emotive therapy, the Emotional Education program teaches children concepts of how people think, feel, and behave. This is accomplished with regular "lessons" in emotional education, through role playing demonstrations, and in the course of actual problems that may arise in the classroom during the day. The Emotional Education program is designed for normal children and is implemented in *The Living School* in New York City.

HUMAN DEVELOPMENT PROGRAM

Bessell, H., and Palomares, U. *Methods in Human Development.* La Mesa, California: Human Development Training Institute, 1973.

The Human Development Program is designed to promote healthy emotional growth in children and facilitate learning in the affective domain especially in three areas of emotional development: self-understanding (awareness), self-confidence (mastery), and human relations (social interaction). The major strategy is to employ cumulative, sequential activities on a regular basis. The vehicle is the Magic Circle (8-12 members) which meets for 25-50 minutes each session. The program is available for preschool and K-6 levels with general materials available and adaptable for secondary school levels.

HUMAN RESOURCE DEVELOPMENT

Carkhuff, Robert R. *The Development of Human Resources.* New York: Holt, Rinehart, and Winston, 1971.
Carkhuff, Robert R. *Helping and Human Relations,* Vols. I and II. New York: Holt, Rinehart, and Winston, 1969.

This program is built on a skills model and emphasizes skills acquisition. Behavioral skills are defined as behaviors that are operational, repeatable, trainable, and predictable. Helping, interpersonal problem solving, program development, behavior modification, training, physical research and evaluation, and management skills are taught in this program.

HUMANISTIC EDUCATION

Weinstein, G., and Fantini, M. *Toward Humanistic Education.* New York: Praeger, 1970.

This is a curriculum approach that focuses on three important concerns of students: self-image, disconnectedness (how one fits or does not fit into his world or the whole scheme of things), and control over one's life. Teachers learn how to functionally relate and integrate these intrinsic concerns and feelings to the curriculum and to their teaching styles.

INFLUENCING HUMAN INTERACTION

Kagan, Norman. *Influencing Human Interaction.* Washington, D.C.: American Personnel and Guidance Association, 1976.

This curriculum is designed to help counselors, teachers, and administrators develop effective communication skills. It focuses on skill in the facilitation of interpersonal "straight" communication and an increased awareness of one's own interpersonal style.

THE INTERACTIVE PROCESS OF EDUCATION

Gorman, A. H. *Teachers and Learners: The Interactive Process in Education.* Boston: Allyn and Bacon, 1974.

Gorman offers an approach in which the emphasis is on developing group-process skills. In the group-process approach, strong multi-way conversation about content and personal concerns is encouraged with the teacher acting as moderator, guide, and observer. Students not only learn subject matter, but also learn about themselves; how they react to each other, to subject matter, and to the world as a whole. Activities and exercises used in this approach are primarily derived from the National Training Laboratories. Value clarification and Gordon's communication-effectiveness training are also used.

TOWARD AFFECTIVE DEVELOPMENT

Dupont, H.; Gardner, O. S.; and Brody, D. S. *TAD (Toward Affective Development).* Circle Pines, Minnesota: American Guidance Services, 1972.

This program is activity-centered and consists of lessons, activities, and materials designed to stimulate psychological and affective development. Students are encouraged to develop realistic self-images, to consider their unique characteristics and aspirations, and to use imagination and think creatively. A major emphasis is placed on peer-group interaction. For grades 3 through 6, the program is available from American Guidance Services, Minneapolis, Minnesota.

MY FRIENDS AND ME

Davis, Duane E. *My Friends and Me.* Circle Pines, Minnesota: American Guidance Services, 1977.

A program of group activities and materials designed to help teachers and parents assist the healthy personal and social development of young children. The FRIENDS program includes 190 activities for groups of children in preschool and day care settings and 38 related family activities that invite the children's parents or caretakers to extend insights gained at school. Activities are sequenced in spiral order around the themes of personal identity, social skills, and understanding.

TEACHER EFFECTIVENESS TRAINING

Gordon, Thomas. *Teacher Effectiveness Training.* New York: Wyden, 1974.

This program incorporates the principle of Parent Effectiveness Training and specifically teaches classroom teachers: 1) non-evaluative skills for helping students solve their own problems, 2) a method for involving a teacher and a student in the process of resolving their own conflicts, 3) a method for getting a class to work out a contract with the teacher that defines rules of classroom behavior, and 4) methods for conducting effective group counseling with troubled or underachieving students.

5

Organizations Concerned With Humanistic Education, Alternative Schools and Change Process

Alternatives Foundation
1526 Gravenstein Highway
North Sebastopol, California 97452
An excellent resource for directories of free schools and personal growth/social-change workshops.

Associates for Human Resources
P. O. Box 727
Concord, Massachusetts 01742
AHR offers a variety of workshops for counselors, classroom teachers, and school administrators. Personal growth, organizational development, change processes, humanistic education, Gestalt approaches, and other human-development skills workshops are available. AHR offers consulting services to schools that wish to humanize the classroom.

Association for Humanistic Education
West Georgia State College
Carrollton, Georgia 30117
This group offers workshops, conferences, and publications for teachers, administrators, counselors, and psychologists interested in humanistic education.

Association for Humanistic Education and Development
1607 New Hampshire Avenue, N.W.
Washington, D.C. 20009
A division of the American Personnel and Guidance Association, this organization publishes *The Humanist Educator,* a quarterly journal of articles

dealing with both the philosophical and practical aspects of humanistic education. AHEAD is committed to the encouragement and furtherance of humanistic ideas and practices in education and in all helping services concerned with human development.

Association for Humanistic Psychology
416 Hoffman Street
San Francisco, California 94114
This association publishes the *Journal of Humanistic Psychology,* an important periodical that contains articles by the leading humanistic psychologists. The annual conference of the Association is a "must" experience.

The Center for Humanistic Education
University of Massachusetts
Amherst, Massachusetts 01002
(Gerald Weinstein, Director)
The Center offers graduate and undergraduate courses in Education of the Self, Value Clarification, Humanistic Curriculum Development, Theory of Psychological Education, Race Relations, and Strength Training.

Center for New Schools
59 East Van Buren
Chicago, Illinois 60605
CNS assists parents, students, and educators interested in setting up alternative schools. One of the resources they offer is the CBL Box, full of information on community-based learning. Their publications include titles such as *Decision-Making in Alternative Secondary Schools, Planning for Change,* and *Strengthening Alternative Schools.*

Development and Research in Confluent Education
Department of Education
University of California
Santa Barbara, California 93106
(George I. Brown, Director)
These people are interested in developing curriculum and training teachers in the area of confluent education. Their aim is to integrate the knowledge and activities of the human-potential movement with the traditional classroom curriculum.

Educational Development Center
55 Chapel Street
Newton, Massachusetts 02158
EDC is a non-profit organization specializing in development of curriculum materials and teacher training programs. They are involved in many humanistic projects.

Educator Training Center
2140 West Olympic Boulevard
Los Angeles, California 90006

Founded by William Glasser, the Center conducts in-service training programs all over the country, helping to create "schools without failure." The principles of reality therapy are translated into practical staff development workshops aimed at building the self-worth of students through effective communication and motivation.

Effectiveness Training Associates
110 East Euclid
Pasadena, California 91101
Under the direction of Thomas Gordon, ETA is an organization whose object is to help people develop effective human relationships in order to fulfill their own potentials, help others fulfill their potentials, and resolve conflicts in a spirit of mutual respect. It prepares people to lead Parent Effectiveness Training, Teacher Effectiveness Training, and Leader Effectiveness Training groups.

Esalen Institute
1776 Union Street
San Francisco, California 94123
EI is the first Growth Center established in America. It always has several top-flight workshops for educators in humanistic and confluent education.

Human Development Training Institute
7574 University Avenue
La Mesa, California 92041
The Institute trains teachers in the theory and practice of the Magic Circle approach. Teachers learn to use cumulative, sequential activities on a daily basis to facilitate learning in the affective domain, especially in three areas of emotional development: awareness, self confidence, and human relations.

International Consortium for Options in Public Education
Center for Options in Education
School of Education
Indiana University
Bloomington, Indiana 47401
A graduate program training teachers for work in alternative schools.

The National Alternative Schools Project
School of Education
University of Massachusetts
Amherst, Massachusetts 01002
The Project offers assistance to those interested in or involved with alternatives.

New England Center for Personal and Organizational Development
Box 575
Amherst, Massachusetts 01002
The Center's main emphasis is on providing workshops in humanistic education.

275

New England Program in Teacher Education
Pettee Brook Offices
Durham, New Hampshire 03824

A New England alternative to existing Research and Development Centers and Training Institutions. It develops projects and offers services in identified needs areas and helps to build expertise among teachers at the local level. It sponsors the New England Information Center which provides access to existing files of resource persons, programs, products, information packets, and computerized information systems.

NTL Institute of Applied Behavioral Science
1201 - 16th Street, N.W.
Washington, D.C. 20036

Conducts seminars for educators at its many centers around the country. Seminars include those in Student Involvement in Learning, Change Accents in Education and Educational Leadership, as well as the Basic and Advanced Labs in Personal Growth.

Racism and Sexism Resource Center for Educators
1841 Broadway
Room 300
New York, New York 10023

Council on Interracial Books for Children and the Foundation for Change.

Resource Center on Sex Roles in Education
1201 - 16th Street, N.W.
Washington, D.C. 20036

The purpose of this organization is to help eliminate sexism in education through consultation, workshops, training programs, research, and publications.

6

Tapes on Humanistic Education and Psychology

The following tapes are available from:

Audio-Seminars in Education
Sigma Information, Inc.
545 Cedar Lane
Teaneck, New Jersey 07666

Accountability From a Humanistic Perspective
by I. David Welch
A broadly ranging commentary that offers invaluable observations and solid practicality in dealing with the issue of accountability in education. An informative and thought-provoking seminar on tape.
3 one-hour tapes:
1. Humanistic accountability.
2. Side 1: The teacher as a professional.
   Side 2: How important is the concept of intelligence to teachers?
3. Side 1: Apollo, Dionysus, and the cult of efficiency.
   Side 2: Accountability and the effective helper.

The Affective Development of Children and Teachers in School
by Edward W. Schultz
An exploration of the affective facets of the school situation, and their potential for both children and teachers. The author provides guidelines for affective communication, and for the development and evaluation of affective curricula. This series of talks is of unusual interest to those working with children.

3 one-hour tapes:
1. Guidelines for affective communication.
2. A matrix for developing affective curriculum.
3. Program development and evaluation considerations for affective education.

Affective Learning in Elementary and Early Childhood Education
by Kevin J. Swick

These tapes present an exhaustive exploration of a crucial aspect of elementary and early childhood education. The series is superbly organized and provides the teacher with viable methods and means of relating to pupils, parents, and staff in the context of affective learning.

3 one-hour tapes:
1. Rationale and meanings.
2. Teacher behaviors for meeting needs of children.
3. Relating and responding to staff, parents, and children.

Environmental Forces Affecting the Quality of Education of Black Children
by George Henderson

This series offers an intensive examination of environmental forces affecting the education of black children. Historical insights are combined with thorough analyses of the evolution and implications of the current situation.

12 one-hour tapes:
1. The urban plantation: A discussion of historical conditions that still plague blacks.
2. Health: A look at health conditions that affect education.
3. Employment: A look at unemployment and underemployment in black communities.
4. Housing: A discussion of housing segregation, welfare, and the black matriarchy.
5. Crime: Development and effect of juvenile delinquency and adult crimes.
6. The importance of color: The importance of "Negro" and "Black"; and a discussion of Black Nationalism.
7. From slum to slum: Effects of environmental forces on slum children.
8. From slum to suburb: A discussion of factors that resulted in one black escaping poverty.
9. When schools fail: Analysis of lower-class children in middle-class schools.
10. Preparing the community-at-large for desegregation: Strategies and techniques for designing and implementing school desegregation.
11. From desegregation to integration: Ways administrators and teachers can make desegregation succeed.
12. Beyond integration: Human relations concerns for educators.

Humanistic Teaching
by I. David Welch

A carefully constructed analysis and complimentary methodology are presented here. The personal factors that constitute and characterize the teacher's composite functioning are discussed in depth. Welch also offers a philosophical approach to the process of education and applies this logically developed philosophy to everyday classroom interaction. An exciting, utilitarian series.

6 one-hour tapes:
1. Becoming an effective teacher.
2. Teaching as fostering healthy personality development.
3. Side 1: The person of the teacher.
   Side 2: Encounter with a master teacher.
4. Teaching as fostering personal exploration and discovering of meaning.
5. Side 1: The problems approach to teaching.
   Side 2: A humanistic approach to discipline.
6. Side 1: The goals of education.
   Side 2: Some laws of change.

Human Relations in Education
by George Henderson

An in-depth series on the meaning and modes of human relations in education. An incisive analysis of the gamut of influences affecting the development and implementation of a theory of human relations.

6 one-hour tapes:
1. Introduction — values clarification.
2. The helping relationship.
3. Group dynamics in the classroom.
4. Workshops.
5. Human relations and educational technology.
6. Evaluation and research.

Self-Actualization
by Robert E. Valett

A practical and in-depth guide to the challenging process of self-actualization, presented in a lucid manner. This series is designed to be used as a professional tool by the listener and provides thoroughly detailed techniques to implement in a self-actualization process.

6 one-hour tapes:
1. The process of self-actualization.
2. Models of self-actualizing persons.
3. Self and social actualization.
4. Self-relaxation.
5. Active meditation.
6. Psycho-social synthesis.

Sexism in Education
by Myra and David Sadker

This discussion explores the sex biases in education that limit the options of children of both sexes. The authors explore the negative impact of a male-oriented society on females (leading to a loss of academic ability and self-esteem as they progress through school), and the consequences of sexism in higher education.

279

3 one-hour tapes:
1. Sexism in the elementary schools.
2. Sexism in the high schools.
3. Sexism in higher education.

The Use and Preparation of Classroom Scenarios Emphasizing the Use of Action, Feeling, and Emotion in the Teaching-Learning Process
by Robert William McColl

A "grassroots" approach is taken in this practical series. Procedures are presented in a lucid manner that makes them easy to adapt for classroom use. This is a good tool for the classroom teacher who has had little experience with creative role-playing, as well as for the experienced teacher interested in understanding and achieving the subtler points of scenario use and preparation in the classroom.

3 one-hour tapes:
1. Side 1: Introduction to scenarios and role-playing "games", their use, and problems to be aware of.
   Side 2: Preparation of a scenario.
2. Examples of two scenarios (proxemics and diffusion) with an emphasis on conflict.

7

Films on Humanistic
Education and Psychology

From MEDIA FIVE
110 North Cole Avenue, Hollywood, California 90038

Reality Therapy — Dealing with Discipline Problems
   Dr. William Glasser's Reality Therapy is shown in live-action sequences applied to familar elementary school discipline problems.

Transactional Analysis — The Okay Classroom
   Dr. Thomas Harris' *I'm Okay, You're Okay* concepts of Ego States, Transactions, and Strokes are applied to the elementary classroom setting.

Using Values Clarification
   Dr. Sidney Simon demonstrates several Values Clarification strategies and explains his approach to the valuing process (Secondary).

Games We Play in High School
   Roles, games, and T.A. are applied to the high-school setting. Psychological games of *both* teachers and students are demonstrated with commentary by Dorothy Jongwald, author of "Born to Win."

T.E.T. (Teacher Effectiveness Training) in High School
   Documentary footage shows how Dr. Thomas Gordon's no-lose method can effectively be used in secondary classes.

From PERENNIAL EDUCATION, INC.
1825 Willow Road, Northfield, Illinois 60093

Teen Sexuality: What's Right for You?
This film portrays a health class and their teacher sight-seeing in New York City. Moral values, male-female differences, pornography, homosexuality, and venereal disease are some of the issues covered. (Secondary level).

Human Growth — III
This newly revised film presents adolescent sexual development as a part of an overall normal physical, emotional, and social process. The film is designed to establish an atmosphere in which sex can be discussed without embarrassment or tension.

From PSYCHOLOGICAL FILMS, INC.
110 North Wheeler Street, Orange, California 92669

Touching
This film features Dr. Ashley Montagu discussing the key concepts of his recent book, *Touching*. Utilizing research and medical opinion, Dr. Montagu develops the case that touching is necessary for human life.

Reflections
Dr. Carl Rogers talks extensively about his life and his work. Dr. Warren Bennis is the interviewer in this sensitive and revealing film.

A Time for Every Season
Dr. Everett Shostram describes the natural flow of emotional energy along the continuums of weakness-strength and anger-love. Like the seasons, these emotions are a normal condition of life, to be realized and experienced. Dr. Shostram demonstrates this tenet of Actualizing Psychology in a group setting.

From AMERICAN PERSONNEL AND GUIDANCE ASSOCIATION
1607 New Hampshire Avenue, N.W., Washington, D.C. 20009

All Kinds of Weather Friend
This award-winning film tells the story of the Portsmouth, New Hampshire, project, which brought parents and grandparents into the classroom as para-professional counselors to work with children in a counseling and human-development curriculum. Dr. Dwight Webb describes this revolutionary new model for Elementary School Counseling. (Winner, 1975 APGA Best Film Award.)

Carl Rogers on Education (Part I)
Carl Rogers on Education (Part II)
Two thirty-minute films in which Rogers describes how people acquire significant learnings and indicates the directions in which education must change to have real impact on students.

8

Directories, Guides, and
Bibliographies of Resources

The Affective Domain: A Resource Book for Media Specialists
Communications Services Corporation
1333 Connecticut Avenue, N.W.
Washington, D.C. 20036
A catalog of films, filmstrips, cassettes, and other media relating to affective education.

Barth, Roland S., and Rathbone, Charles H. *A Bibliography of Open Education: Advisory for Open Education.* Newton, Massachusetts: Educational Development Center, 1971.
This booklet aims to provide a starting place for parents, teachers, and administrators interested in open education, and is also designed to assist further exploration for those already familiar with open education ideas. It includes three bibliographies on books and articles, films, and periodicals.

Catalog of NIE Education Products, Volumes 1 and 2, 1975
U.S. Government Printing Office
Washington, D.C. 20402
Provides descriptive information on 660 products and programs funded, in whole or in part, by the National Institute of Education. The purposes of the catalog are to inform educational practitioners, developers, policymakers, and publishers about a wide range of school-oriented products developed with research and development funds, and to provide information to help potential consumers make decisions about the most appropriate educational products and programs for their needs. The thirteen subject-area categories of the products range from aesthetic education for elementary school students to post-secondary education.

Educational Programs That Work, 1975
Far West Laboratory for Educational Research and Development
1855 Folsom Street
San Francisco, California 94103

A combination sourcebook and reference guide to innovative demonstrator projects carried on under the auspices of the U.S. Office of Education during 1975-76. These programs were selected because of their unique successes in academic/experiential areas where more traditional approaches to schooling have failed. The programs fall into categories like secondary alternatives, early childhood and parent readiness, environmental studies, reading/language/math, and special education.

Canfield, Jack. *A Guide to Resources in Humanistic and Transpersonal Education.* Amherst, Massachusetts: Mandals, 1976.

Contains annotated references to over 500 resources including books, curricula, classroom exercises, tapes, films, curriculum development projects, newsletters, journals, growth centers, and consulting organizations.

Hough, J., and Duncan, J. *A Living-Learning Catalog: Somewhere Else.* Chicago, Illinois: Swallow, 1973.

A directory to non-school learning with 400 annotated entries informing the reader of people, places, networks, centers, books, and groups that he or she might not otherwise know about.

Howard Suzanne. *Liberating Our Children, Ourselves.* Washington, D.C.: American Association of University Women, 1975.

This is a handbook of women's-studies course materials for teacher educators and classroom teachers. There are nearly 300 articles, books, papers, organizations, and other resources listed. This is an important resource for anyone interested in eliminating sexism in the schools.

Human Values in Children's Books. New York: Council on Interracial Books for Children, 1976.

This volume reviews 238 books, identifying the values they transmit to children. The books are examined for sexism, racism, materialism, elitism, individualism, and ageism.

Johnson, Laurie Olsen (ed.). *Nonsexist Curricular Materials for Elementary Schools.* Old Westbury, New York: Feminist Press.

A compilation of specific materials and techniques to help dispel traditional sex-role stereotyping that limits children's potential.

Learning Directory: A Comprehensive Guide to Teaching Materials
Westinghouse Learning Corporation
100 Park Avenue
New York, New York 10017

Lists over 200,000 items that can be used in the classroom.

Racism in Career Education Materials. New York: Council on Interracial Books.

Presents the findings of a major study of 100 career education materials by a six-person team of the Council on Interracial Books. The materials from all grade levels — printed and AV — were examined for evidence of racism. The booklet includes a description of their criteria, the results and findings, suggestions to teachers, lesson plans, and a bibliography on racism.

Schrank, Jeffry. *Media in Value Education: A Critical Guide.* Chicago: Argus Communications, 1970.

A comprehensive summary of nearly 100 films that can be used in value education, along with suggested questions for discussion.

Sexism and Racism in Popular Basal Readers: 1964-1976. New York: Council on Interracial Books, 1976.

A detailed analysis of the Baltimore Feminist Project, a group of concerned educators, parents, and students. The best study we have seen, it comprehensively explores both racism and sexism, going beyond a mere counting of the numbers of minorities and women to discuss connections between the books' subtle messages and the effect of the racism and sexism on all students.

Social Studies School Service Catalog
10000 Culver Boulevard
P.O. Box 802
Culver City, California 90230

A rich compilation of simulations, paperbacks, teacher resource materials, games, exercises, and activities that deal with such topics as values, racism, sexism, psychology, sociology, human rights, native American studies, and other important issues in humanistic education.

Spredemann Dreyer, Sharon. *The Bookfinder: A Guide to Children's Literature About the Needs and Problems of Youth.* Circle Pines, Minnesota: American Guidance Services, 1977.

This reference work describes and categorizes 1,031 current children's books according to more than 450 psychological, behavioral, and developmental topics of concern to children and young adolescents. The design of *The Bookfinder* makes it possible to identify books according to their themes and to read synopses of their contents before deciding to obtain or recommend particular books. An excellent source of ideas for bibliotherapy.

White, Marian E. *High Interest/Easy Reading: For Junior and Senior High School Students.* New York: Citation Press, 1972.

Here is an annotated list of hundreds of easy-to-read books abut many subjects, geared to students who do not usually enjoy reading.

Zuckerman, David W., and Horn, Robert W. *The Guide to Simulations/Games for Education and Training.* New York: Information Resources, Inc., 1976.

A comprehensive 500-page annotated review of simulation games in all fields, for all ages. The guide includes articles about simulations and their uses.

INDEX

Accountability
  procedures for, 220-221
  historical background, 221-222
  mythology of, 217-221
  procedures for, 220-221, 231,
    232-234
  students cooperating with, 233
  teacher, 215-234
Activity-centered classroom, 156-160
  and reading achievement, 158-159,
    161
  and writing, 172-173, 182
Adjustment, concept of, 107, 111-113
Administrators, school, 26, 108, 221,
  227, 228, 229
Adolescence
  and nonconforming behavior,
    70-71
  and vocational objectives, 65-66
  awareness during, 100-101
  humanistic view of, 55-73
  independence during, 59-60
  physical and sexual development
    during, 58-59, 62-63
  responsibility for education during,
    108-109
  self-definition during, 56
  social relationships during, 63-64
  values during, 60-62

Behavior
  changing, 115-116
  evaluation of, 125
  humanistic view of, 85-106
  patterns of, 144
British Infant Schools, 158, 159

Change, teacher as agent of, 205-213
Coleman Report, 216
Communication
  in the classroom, 10-12
  of learners with teachers, 15
Cultural differences
  and educational expectations, 216
  and students, 203-204

Defense mechanisms, 71, 137

Emotions
  effect of on behavior, 92-93
  effect of on learning, 45-46
Empathy
  and teaching, 101
  development of, 11-12, 42
Equalization of the learning relationship, 129-139
Existentialism
  and concepts of motivation, 75
  and learning, 120-121
  and societal concerns, 43
  in teaching, 111
Evaluation. See Accountability,
  teacher.

"Force Field Analysis," 208-209
Freedom, with responsibility as
  as synergistic concept, 198-200
  and values, 195, 196

"Gospel of Relaxation," 27-28
Growth, process of, 14

Illiteracy, increase in, 197.
  See also Reading, Writing
Informal classroom. See Activity-
  centered classroom
IQ
  and reading, 150-151
  teacher response to, 153-154

Learner-centered teaching.
  See Teaching, learner-centered
Learners
  and sense of competence, 41, 44,
    48, 50-53, 66
  and values development, 36-37
  defensiveness of, 100-102
  growth and development of, 20
  insight, achievement of in, 15
  interaction with teacher, 17, 81
  self-concept of, 41, 44, 48, 64, 66,
    93-94

286